Why My Guardian Angel Wanted to Quit

An autobiography by
John P. Cressman

Paperback - 978-1-7351302-5-5
Hardbound - 978-1-7351302-4-8

Cover Photography By Jacqueline A Platts, owner of JA Photography
Book editing and design by Rebecka Yaeger of Becka's Best Author Services.

Printed by Maverick-Gage Publishing in conjunction with
IngramSpark, in the United States of America.

First printing edition 2020.

Maverick-Gage Publishing
Allentown, PA
info@maverick-gage.com
www.maverick-gage.com

I was a Spoiled Brat, a Holy Terror, and a Little Devil

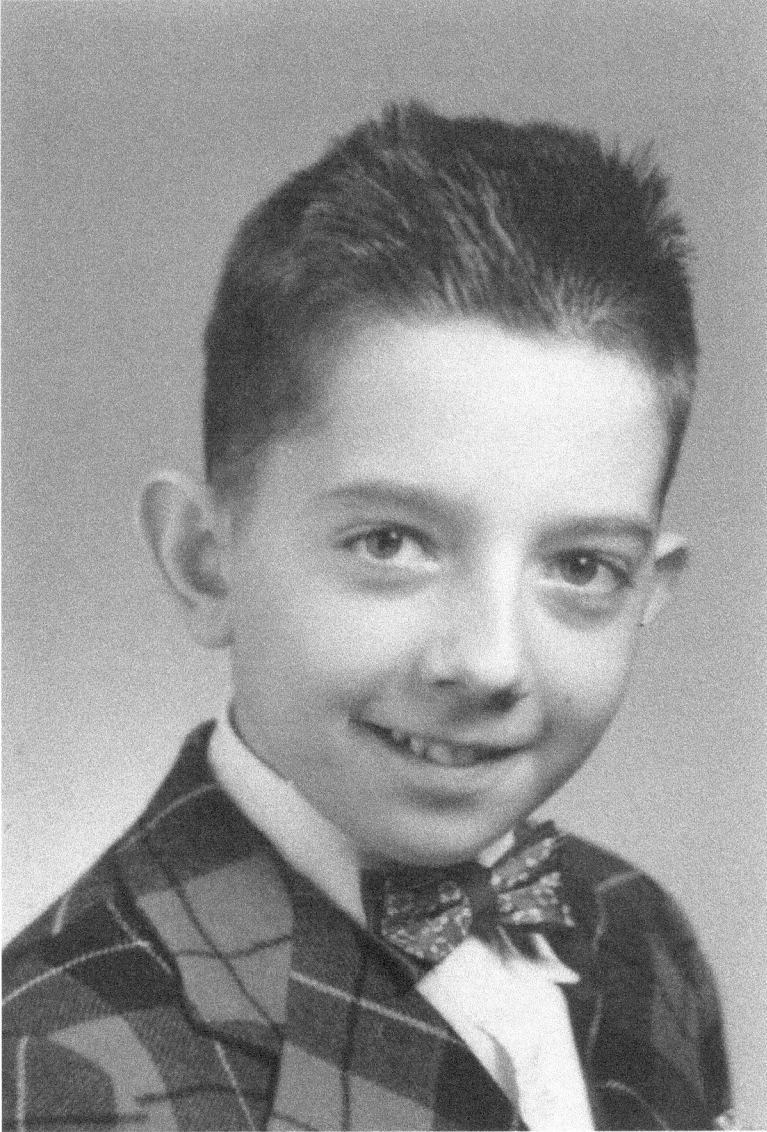

This kid even into adulthood gets into so many crazy and near-death shenanigans that he develops a relationship with his Creator and humorously causes his guardian angel a heart attack with his antics.

PURPOSE OF THIS BOOK

The purpose of this book is to allow my kids, grandkids, and others to know what it was like growing up in a different generation before TV, cell phones. Electronic games, and when TV did come along, it was three stations that were black and white. I have heard I am a lot like my grandfather, but I hardly knew him. He liked hunting, fishing, the outdoors, animals, canoeing and swimming but I did not do much with him. I would have loved to hear the stories of how it was when he grew up during the depression and World War I, hunting and fishing stories but I never did, and that experience is gone now. I remember my grandparents, aunt, uncle, cousins, my parents, and myself going to one church at one time. I know nothing of his beliefs in God just that he went to church.

I would like to challenge all the readers of this book to ask questions about what they believe about God and where those beliefs came from. I will be asking questions in this book about things I have wondered about and hope you will think about those questions. My whole life I have wondered about what I see and experience and if there is a God. After 74 plus years of life, 52 plus years of being a Christian, I had many unanswered questions about what in the world is God doing. I spent at least 25 plus years of intense Bible study and questioning my purpose in life, God's plan for mankind and asking if my beliefs are from the Bible or from religious tradition, I finally found an answer that satisfies me.

I pray that you will also ask why you believe what you believe.

TABLE OF CONTENTS

GOD IS LOVE

GOD IS A SHEPHERD

GOD HAS SECRETS AND MYSTERIES

ON TOP OF A MOUNTAIN-I SEE THE ANSWER IN THE DISTANCE

THREE WEEKS IN THE TAR HEEL STATE

MY "PERSONAL" CONCLUSION AND SPECULATION

INTRODUCTION

This is the story of a young boy who was loved by his mother so much that she called him Johnny Angel. He was an angel around her, but when he was free of her watchful eye; he went through a metamorphosis into a little devil (as his grandmother called him) and did many stupid and dangerous things probably because he wouldn't listen and insisted on doing things his way (His sister called him a spoiled brat and his aunt called him a holy terror).

At an early age, he fell in love with the outdoors and wanted to explore the entire world. In kindergarten he found a lifetime friend and together they thought they were a reincarnated Daniel Boone and Davy Crockett. They wanted to leave civilization behind to follow mighty rivers, cross amber waves of grain, explore unchartered wooded wilderness timbers, scale the purple mountain majesty, see the fruited plains just like the early explorers and pioneers did. They wanted to chart unknown territory, fight, or befriend wild Indians just like Lewis and Clark. They wanted to live off the land, eating roots, bark, wild fruit, native trout and be wilderness survivors.

But because John's mother wanted to be sure Johnny Angel had his favorites, like watermelon, pancake mix, syrup, butter, milk, peanut butter jelly sandwiches, just in case of emergency. John would also come to appreciate nature as a creation that required a Creator. He would call out for help to this Creator, the God of the universe, as he got into many dangerous, life threatening, wild and crazy adventure situations. He found that when he prayed for help, this God did not turn his back on him because of the way he acted, but He showed love and compassion toward him by protecting him and answering his prayers. Because of his mother's prayers, would a guardian angel be provided, and would it survive all his antics? John hoped so.

John would desire to learn more about God's love as his life of adventures progressed. It seemed to John that this loving God did not see his misbehavior as a Little Devil but as Johnny Angel and saved him from sure disasters and at least one near death circumstances.

As a child he got lost in a dark cave, had a panic attack while climbing on a cliff, hung on for dear life on the side of a speeding locomotive, he got trapped in an elevator, found himself between an angry mama bear and her cubs as she tore the bark off a tree instead of John's flesh, and found himself face to face with a poisonous snake with huge fangs ready to sink into this foolish kid as he cried out terrified to this God.

Later in life, John found himself in similar circumstances as he got lost in the darkness of sin, filled with panic as he felt like he was ready to fall off the cliff of this world into a bottomless pit. He found himself speeding along Satan's train, wishing he could jump off but unable to, because Satan, the mighty serpent, had his fangs deeply embedded into John's heart, injecting his poison. John once again cried out to God for help and He answered, saving John from death and gave him a new life.

Once God changed John's life, He would give John a beautiful creation of God to marry and together they would continue having unbelievable, inspiring adventures with each other, and with their 6 children and their 16 grandchildren. Together they would teach others God's way and to have faith and trust in Him. They would also teach how to enjoy life and enjoy all the adventures this planet offers. They would share their story of love for the God that first loved them and brought them together and helped them through many anxious situations.

They would also continue to have adventures together and as they search to learn more about God, they would not only feel like they were experiencing the frontier but also feel like they were experiencing what it was like to be an early Christian searching for God's plan.

As John talks about his adventures in this book, he adds humor by asking what people may have said or thought as they saw his mischievous behavior. He also adds more humor as he imagines how his guardian angel (if he had one) may be reacting to his troublesome behavior, giving his angel some human characteristics like having an anxiety attack or wanting to change assignments or call in sick.

Chapter 1: A CLAUSTROPHOBIC TODDLER WANTS FREEDOM

I remember the day all my kids were born. Each day was an important day for both our families. It was also an important day when my grandkids were born. My wife was at the birth for many of them and as soon as possible, their aunts, uncles and I went to see them and greet them into this world.

When I was born, I do not think hospitals were a visitor-friendly place, so no one could be with my mother when I was born. For the longest time, I heard and believed storks brought babies to mothers, so I figured no one was allowed in to see it. I am not sure if anyone was there to see me at the hospital, but I know my mother's family was happy that I was a boy since I had one sister and my mother's sister had two girls. Being the first boy in quite a while meant that they would give me everything I wanted, plus I could do anything I wanted, and I could do no wrong and did I ever take advantage of that.

I was born September 29th, 1946 in center city Allentown, PA. My parents were Carl and Miriam Cressman. My mom's parents were still living, and their names were Ormonde and Hazel (Raber) Bartholomew. My dad's parents were Abraham and Sally Cressman. I never knew my dad's parents very well, but I understand that my grandfather was a schoolteacher. There were quite a few teachers and preachers in the Cressman family. I spent more time with my mom's parents. We lived on the second and third floors of a house they rented.

It seems I had an exploring, adventurous spirit, and a feeling of claustrophobia at a young age. I am not sure how old I was, but from what I understand, I was jumping in my crib, trying to see out the window, and jumped so high that I flew over the side, hitting the floor and breaking my nose. I am sure that in my mind; I did not want to be confined in a small, boring crib looking at wallpaper. It was time to explore this great planet of ours and see what was out there, so I started jumping and getting higher each time just to see out a window. Eventually, I jumped over the railing on my way to freedom. I now had the freedom to see the world from a doctor's office and the inside of a hospital to deal with a broken nose.

I am sure my mother told all the nurses that her precious little, sweet, innocent Johnny Angel had an Ouchy and needed to be tenderly taken care of, but the hospital personnel wandered why she would say that after hearing I tried skydiving out of my crib.

Somewhat later, I saw the great outdoors from my stroller and wanted out of that stroller to be free to run and see the world. I squirmed and wiggled trying to get out of that stroller, but as my sister tried to restrain me, I ended up with a hernia and the opportunity to see my friends at the hospital again for my first surgery. I, the little devil, was welcomed back again and am sure my chart listed the diagnosis as *Little Devil*.

As a child, I remember my dad playing a lot with me outside and taking me places to play, which led to a love of the outdoors. We played hide and seek at West End Park in Allentown, Nazareth Park and Catasauqua Park. I remember rolling down a grassy hill and walking along a stream with my dad and remembering him helping me learn how to ride a bicycle. He laughed, kidded around and joked a lot, especially when his three brothers came over for a picnic. We all enjoyed playing badminton, croquet, and everyone acted so crazy that I thought they were so funny. (Sounds like a Cressman get together today.) My dad's brother had two kids, my cousins, but I only ever saw them a few times in my life and have no idea where they are now.

I remember seeing movies of me, as a child, running around West End Park with my family. I had a strange hat on my head with a propeller on top as I was sticking my finger in water fountains to squirt everyone around. An early sign of my mischievousness and devilish nature. To be sure, I would need a guardian angel someday.

I also remember Sunday being a church day going to a morning Sunday and Church and then eating a delicious home cooked meal. They filled the afternoon with fun, relaxing picnics and just a restful, fun day. Then it was back to church for an evening service. There were laws in Allentown, and I think elsewhere, in the '50s that prevented stores from being open so there was not much to do other than go to church, rest and play.

Those were some wonderful memories. In my lifetime, I have rested on both the Saturday Sabbath and Sunday and keeping no assigned day of rest, but never seemed to achieve the same restful day as I recalled as a child. We are way too busy these days.

My family did not fish, but when I wanted to learn how to fish, my mom and dad took me out, anyway. Everything went fine until my line got all tangled on the reel, so we went home. Eventually, my friend, Sam and I learned to fish on our own. We rode our bikes to every stream and lake in the area. I will have to give my parents credit for giving it a try and allowing me to do something I wanted to do, even though they did not understand how to do it. My grandfather took me deep sea fishing one time and I enjoyed that time with him.

Chapter 2: KINDERGARTEN EXPLORER

I was finally old enough to go to school and see more of the world. We walked several blocks to half a day of kindergarten, playing on monkey bars, eating cookies, drinking chocolate milk and a nap. I do not remember all the details about how I met Sam Wilcox, who loved the same things I did and would be a great lifelong friend even to this day. It seemed like we both enjoyed the challenges of the monkey bars more than anything else. This training would come in handy as we got older, and they invented television with Sam and I watching Tarzan movies. Eventually we went looking for our own trees to climb and vines to swing on. We would climb a lot of trees and various obstacles in our lives, so it probably helped that the two of us had learned to hang on for dear life. Climbing and falling off the monkey bars helped us to learn to watch where we put our hands and feet. When my dad took me out to the playgrounds to play, he always told me to be sure I had a solid grip with my hand or a solid footing before letting go to move on. That is an excellent lesson in life. If you are going to try something risky, be sure you have something solid to hold on to.

In 2009, I went to my 45th class reunion, which was my first time attending a class reunion. While there, I was reunited with a girl from my neighborhood, named Phyllis. I knew her from third grade all the way to twelfth grade and had not seen her in about 45 years. In those early years, I thought she was a sweet, young, beautiful girl and I remember having a crush on her. I did not remember too many of my fellow classmates, but I was looking forward to seeing her again.

I was expecting her to remember me in high school, how good looking I was in my '50s style crew cut hair with a little curl in front, like Elvis. I also hoped she would remember how muscular I was from working out and being on the wrestling and gymnastics teams. Perhaps she would even remember my superior intellect, which was clear from earning the highest grade in auto mechanics and was awarded a complete toolbox in front of the entire school. When we finally met, the first and only thing she could remember about me was how I got everyone in the neighborhood to climb trees. What a legacy?? Climb trees? What a hurt to my ego. Was that who I am? We were just eight to ten years old and real good friends. I was always looking for someone to climb trees with whether it was a boy or girl; it did not matter. Those trees were a lot of fun and kept us out of other types of trouble, you could say. It just helped me understand that I have always had an adventurous spirit. That was a different time after we moved out of Allentown city, I will talk about later.

I believe my parents both worked, so after a half day of kindergarten, I walked home with a group of other kids and parents. I would stop at my dad's parents' house around 11th and Turner St., which was on the way home, and then I would spend the afternoon there. They were rather elderly, and I remember little about them or what I did when I stayed there. When I started going to first grade at McKinley Elementary School, it was right across from their house, so I went there after school until my parents came home from work.

My dad was a mail carrier, and my mother worked as a medical secretary. During the summer, my dad would hide me on his mail truck and take me along while he delivered mail. It seemed like he knew everyone, and everyone talked to him as he delivered mail. He had a good sense of humor and did many wild and crazy things as he delivered mail. Maybe that is where I learned my crazy behavior. People seemed to be glad to see him, and he appeared to brighten their day. They also seemed to be glad to see me along with him, they thought I was such a cute little boy, such a well-behaved angel. (I am such a deceiver). This also gave me a chance to see more of Allentown and what I could explore.

I was recently in a building overlooking the old post office at 5th and Hamilton Street in Allentown, and it brought memories of hiding in the truck while my dad loaded up the truck with more mail. It was against the rules to have me in there, that is why I hid. He wanted to have me along, even if it meant breaking the rules. It looks like that is his legacy to me.

I remember the stories of how he wanted to learn how to play the piano and organ, but during the depression, his parents could not afford lessons, so he volunteered to clean up the church and taught himself how to play on the church piano and organ by sneaking into the church later. He would leave a window unlocked, so he could go back and practice organ and piano.

Looks like I was not the first Cressman to be sneaky and do some devilish things. Later in life, as a shop teacher, I would sneak my kids into my auto mechanic shop and later my auto body repair shop during my in-service days and teach them the names of tools or later when videos came into being, they would watch auto repair videos.

A DENTIST CAUSES NIGHTMARES FOR 60 YEARS

It was always a bad sign when my mother would ask, "Oh my cute little Johnny Angel, how would you like to have the tooth fairy pay you a visit?" That meant, would you like to have some money left under your pillow? That was a secret code that meant I had to go to be tortured, Oops I mean go to the dentist. To me it was like I would be tied up, duct taped to a chair, ugly, horrible, mean people glaring at me with bright lights in my eyes. Jacks then opened my mouth and held open with vice grips. I was then gassed as I choked and gagged, unable to breathe until I went unconscious. Although it did not happen that way, it sure seemed that way to me. Basically, it meant sitting in the dentist's office scared to death, sometimes crying, sometimes begging not to go in there and sometimes being carried or forcibly dragged in there screaming, kicking and fighting. Today, if you had that much fear of another person, it may cause an investigation of the dentist to see what was going on back there. But back then, it was just let us "get 'r done".

I am not sure of the exact age or why I was having some teeth pulled, but I remember having it done. I am not sure if it started with my first tooth being pulled or after that, I just have memories of the chair, the lights, the room, and the equipment and being there several times. It was a unique room than where the dentist repaired cavities. The worse memory is being held down by the male dentist and then his female assistant placing a piece of gauze over my mouth while pinching my nose shut so they would force me to breathe through my mouth. Then a liquid would be dripped unto the gauze from a small tube about three inches long and maybe a half inch round. I fought as hard as a young boy could and held my breath as long as I could, which probably was not long. Eventually I would have to gasp and breathe in that awful stuff, and then that's the last I would remember until I woke up.

I believe back then they used medical ether to put me to sleep. When I woke up the dentist would hand me the ether tube with my tooth in it. I never could figure out how the tooth got into that tube. I figured somehow, he placed the tube over my tooth and the tooth just popped out right into the tube. Later I would find out about the pliers, the twisting, and the pulling. No wonder I was put to sleep. I mainly remember waking up and feeling sick, groggy, and having some remembrance of real bad dreams. It was something I did not enjoy and was not pleasant. I became terrified of the dentist. I am sure it did not help matters when I moved my tongue the wrong place one time and hit a circular drill, he was using causing blood to gush out of my mouth. I also became terrified anytime I saw gauze, a mask, or any thought about being restrained. I am not sure if this terror was the beginning signs of extreme anxiety or one of the causes of it.

The photo below is my daughter Melody, her husband Greg and their son Ethan showing how it looked to me.

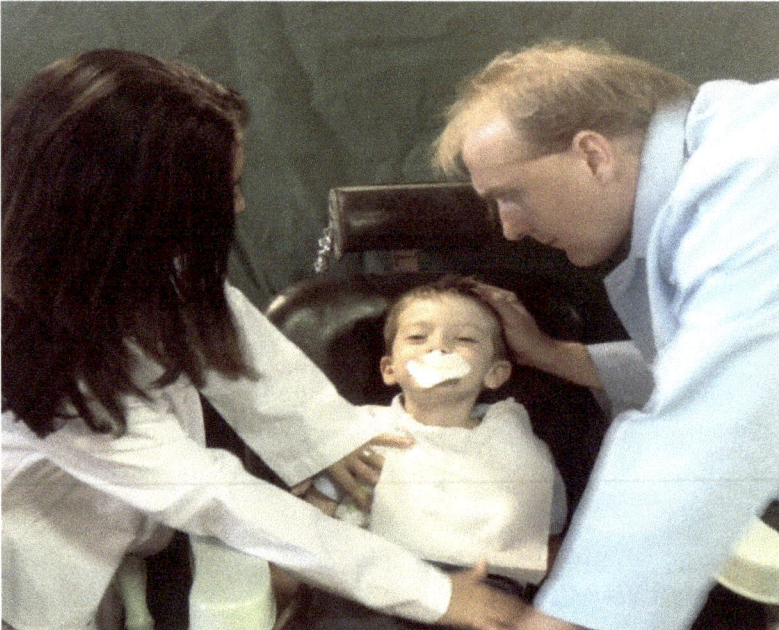

I would take the tooth in the tube back home and place it under my pillow at bedtime. I would wake up the next morning with money under my pillow. Unfortunately, I only got paid once for each tooth. If I tried placing the same tooth under the pillow several nights later, the tooth fairy seemed to be all knowing and always watching me, so I learned you just cannot fool the tooth fairy. (By comparison, I could go fool Santa by being bad during the year and still get gifts. I could also fool Santa by going to different stores with my mother, dressed differently and tell Santa, as I sat on his lap, different toys that I wanted, and I would get them all.) The same thing was true at Easter when there was an Easter Bunny in stores and like Santa, I could ask for gifts. After it was all over, at least I had some extra spending money, from the tooth fairy, to buy some candy which possibly seemed worth it. Probably, the buying of candy led to more tooth extractions. Being Johnny Angel, my mother kept a lazy Susan filled with various candies to reward me with. However, the sugar made my skin turn red, little horns pop out my head metamorphosing into a little devil. I think it was the rise in blood sugar.

We moved when I was about eight years old and we changed dentists as well. After that, I do not remember being put to sleep to have teeth pulled. They were taken out while awake with a local anesthetic. I did not care for the twisting and pulling but at least I was not held down nor forced to breathe anything plus afterward; I had no terrible memories. I had another incident of terror when in Vietnam, that reinforced my fear of anesthesia. I needed some surgery, and they tried local anesthetics, but it did not work so they put a mask over my face and said take a deep breath, but I smelled the ether and I freaked out and started fighting it. Several big Marines came over, held me down and forced me to breathe it in until I passed out. From that point I was terrified of masks and refused any anesthesia except for local anesthesia, even for surgeries until age 60.

A VIEW OF THE WORLD FROM THE TOP OF THE ROOF

I am so happy that all our married life we had a house with a yard, and some trees around. Now all my grandkids also have a house with a yard. I hope they realize how blessed they are. None of them had to live in a row home with no yard like I did the first 7 or 8 years of my life. All our married life we had a big yard and access to the country or mountains. Our kids experienced plenty of room to play in, trees to climb, ropes to swing on, tree houses to build, ground to grow a garden in, fresh air to breathe, streams close by to swim, fish and play in and in many a case even some good well water or mountain spring water to drink. I am not sure if we bought houses with all those things for the kids or for me. Ha ha. The locations were well worth the extra drive to work.

The house they raised me in had no yard, but our back porch had access to the flat rooftops of several garages to hang clothes out to dry and walk around seeing the neighborhood. All my kids and grandkids have a washer and dryer aside of each other and washes and dries all the clothes automatically right there. My mother would carry the dirty clothes down two flights of steps and wash clothes in the basement. It was just an open tub type washer that she moved around and plugged in. When the clothes were clean, she ran them through rollers to get the water out. She then would carry them back up two floors to hang them outside on a clothing line on the flat garage roof. Once dried, she carried them into the house to iron them. "Those were the good old days"? Ha. Maybe it was not the good old days for my mother. No need of jogging or finding time to go to a gym back then, life produced a good workout including strength training. She lived to be eighty-three, so I guess all that hard work did not hurt her. She also worked a full-time job, so she was quite a woman.

My mother would let me go out on the roof with her to help hang up clothing as it seemed my parents were always involving me in their work, so I would someday know how to do it myself and know what work was involved in just living a normal life. As I got older, I helped my mother dry dishes and vacuum the carpets and helped my dad empty the ashes from our coal furnace. On a Saturday morning, I had to do the vacuuming before being able to go out and play, which meant exploring this magnificent creation of God. When we moved to a house with a yard, my sister and I had to mow an enormous lawn with a push type reel mower. As we pushed it, the wheels turned the blades and cut the grass. If there were gas engine mowers, we did not have one. If we got lazy and did not cut the grass regularly, it was so physically draining to push that mower through high grass. The lesson was to not be lazy and do our work when we were supposed to.

Like my father, who was rather sneaky, I became rather sneaky. I may have been mischievous back then, or maybe I still am, but probably was like other young boys my age. When my mother was not home, I would sneak out on the rooftop, which had neither railings nor any protective devices around the edges just for the challenge to see how close I could come to the edge without falling off. (It is a good thing there were not any child protective agencies around back then-I would be in a foster home). That was another step of my desire for adventure and danger, to see how close I could get to the edge without falling off. First, I crawled to the edge and slowly looked over. Gradually I would just walk up to the edge and looked down with no fear.

Talking about the roof, one of my scariest moments in my life came when I was older. I had a sister seven years older than me, named Carol. One day I heard my mother talking on the phone and to my shock, I heard her say that Carol had "fallen off the roof" and something about a lot of blood. Oh no, I thought, and I realized I had not seen Carol all day. I ran to the living room and cried and cried. I could not believe my sister had fallen off the roof, probably breaking every bone in her body and laid there in a puddle of blood until someone found her. I felt bad because I did not see her or say goodbye.

When my mother asked me what was wrong, I said, "I heard you say Carol fell off the roof and there was a lot of blood" and I think she is probably dead. She looked perplexed as she heard my words, but finally explained she meant she was sick and not feeling well. My mother took me to Carol's room, and I saw she was in bed. Later, I found out that "falling off the roof" was secret code used, at least in my family, for a girl's time of the month or maybe when they became that age to start, I am still not sure. How silly people were in the 1950s, ashamed and wanting to hide something natural. Later, as I got older, I would hear more secret code that adults did not talk to their kids about. Many topics were taboo. No wander they were taboo because when I learned about them, it turned me into a real little devil. When I heard words or expressions, I did not know or understand, I asked other people, but they said, "don't ask",

It is time to get back to the story. From the rooftop, I could see what was happening around the neighborhood and what there was to explore. Across the street there was a building with metal milk containers that made a lot of noise and milk trucks driving around. It was a milk bottling plant where milk came from the farms in metal containers and was put in glass bottles and shipped to homes, like ours, and stores. If I remember right, we had milk delivered to the door fresh every morning in glass bottles that we put back out when they were empty. There were no plastic or paper milk containers to fill up landfills. My wife and I have tried as much as possible to get raw milk fresh from a dairy, in glass bottles, our whole married life. It was also cost a lot less getting it from a dairy to cut the middleman. Now they call it organic raw milk and charge twice as much as regular milk. We learned to drink raw milk shortly after getting married from some farmers in our church.

There were also enormous trucks coming down the alley next to our house. I wondered where they came from and what was in them. As I looked from the roof, I also saw smaller trucks coming down the alley loaded with tires and I wondered where they came from. Another day, there came trucks pulling trailers with a tank all covered with black stuff that had a strange smell. Where did they come from and what was that strange smell? I could not wait to get old enough to get off the roof and satisfy my curiosity.

Here is one last story about our porch. One Sunday, after Church, I was in an inflatable swimming pool on the porch close to the edge. I heard someone talking below me as they came from the garage to the first-floor apartment. I wanted to see who it was but could not see over the solid railing since I was too short. To get high enough to see over, I stood on the side of the pool. Here is a test question like you get in school.

What do you think happened when I stood on the side of the pool?

A. It provided a good high place to see who was there

B. I slipped off and fell in the pool

C. The side collapsed, and water poured out of the pool, flowed over the porch like a waterfall and totally soaked the people coming home from church underneath.

Unfortunately, it was C. It took a long time to convince everyone that I did not do it on purpose. How could my parents and the other people even think something could possess me as to do it on purpose? The people below probably wanted to have an exorcism to get rid of the Little Devil that did that. That was not a Johnny Angel day. My guardian angel probably thought I was a barrel of laughs.

Chapter 3: 6 YEARS OLD AND BECOMING A LITTLE DEVIL

Sam and I had continued to become better friends as we entered elementary school together. On Saturdays, Sam would come to my house to play. Our parents seem to approve of the friendship. Sam's father was a minister, and my parents were both organists in 2 different churches, so our families had religion in common and it was easy for us to bond. Finally, it was time to explore the neighborhood. Finally, we walked up the alley to see where the trucks came from. Back in the good old days, in the early 1950s, there were still a lot of factories that made clothing in our area. That is what we found, a large, tall building with lots of open windows. (That was before there was air conditioning.) There were also lots of noises coming from machines (That was before occupational safety and noise laws). We noticed outside the building a big pile of gigantic boxes and piles of empty spools that at one time had thread on them. It was perfect material to build a fort or hut to hide in, like in western movies on TV. We had just got a TV that was gigantic and had an oval screen. It was black and white. Western movies like Hopalong Cassidy, Lone Ranger, Gene Autry and The Cisco Kid were just starting to be shown. Sam and I especially enjoyed the cowboy movies. We spent many a Saturday playing and hiding in the multi-room cardboard forts we had made. It turns out the trucks we saw were loaded with clothing that was made there. When we peeked in the windows, we saw a lot of people sitting and working machines with a lot of thread flying around off spools and out came clothing. We did not understand what was going on.

One day, we found a spool with thread still on it and we took it back to my house. We wondered what we could do with it. Maybe we could make a snare and catch wild animals like the Lone Ranger. However, there were no wild animals in center city Allentown, so what else could we catch? We decided that it would be fun to make a gigantic spider web and see if we could catch a truck coming down the alley with the thread. We wound the thread, many times, across the alley using the two corner posts, one on our porch and one on our neighbor's porch across the alley. We hid and waited for a truck to come. Our waiting paid off, there was a huge truck roaring down the alley heading right for our trap. We watched with anticipation as the truck approached.

Guess what happened when the truck hit the thread.

A. The thread broke. The truck driver smiled and kept going.

B. The truck was stopped like Spiderman's web and had it in its grip.

C. The posts and porches came crashing down as the truck hit it and like a domino effect caused every porch on the block to collapse.

It was A, but what if the thread had been stronger? Would the truck have caused the pillars to break and thus the porches would crumble? I would have blamed it on Sam, perhaps saying he turned into "Sam-son" like I heard in Sunday school. I remembered the story of Samson pulling the posts of a temple down, causing it to collapse and the entire building to crumble, because the people were a Little Devilish and did not listen to God. I bet the truck driver turned and looked like what kind of juvenile delinquents live there? I am sure my guardian angel had another pleasant laugh at the things we did and posted a video on a heavenly Facebook page to share with other angels. But maybe he protected our porches. In the photo, our three-story house was the one with white posts to the right of the alley. The other photo shows our back porch and garage roof where my mother hung clothes.

One day we also explored the milk bottling plant across the street, but nothing exciting happened there. There was nothing to play with and besides, we kept getting chased away by the workers.

Then we found the tire company up the alley. There were stacks of tires six to eight feet tall in this huge area aside of the company. It was a perfect place to use the tires for building tunnels, huts, forts and climbing areas and play cowboys and Indians. Sometimes trucks would bring more tires or pick tires up, so we would sink to the bottom of a stack of tires and wait until they were gone. Fortunately, our hiding stack was never picked up. Gene Autry would have been proud of us, the way we were hiding quietly, unseen as the Indians passed by, I mean the workers passed by.

Today, my kids as well as other parents spend a lot of money on tubes and tunnels for kids to go through and climb on. My parents did not have to buy them. I wonder if they appreciated all the money; we saved them. They never knew what we were doing and how dangerous it was. Remind me to tell my parents how sorry I am. They thought I was such a good boy and could be trusted to roam the streets of Allentown safely. It was just one of those innovative thing's kids did in the '50s making their own entertainment. My dad told me stories about his childhood during the depression and having no rubber tires for his bicycle, so he wrapped anything he could find around the wheel to grip the road. I know parents buy many things for their kids to keep them home and safe, but I just must wander if any creativity, inventiveness or imagination is stifled these days.

Sam and I also found a roofing company where the trucks and trailers came from. The ones I had seen that were covered with black stuff. It turned out to be tar. We did not play much there because when we got tar on us, our parents started asking questions and got angry.

Sometimes I wonder how we or other children ever survived our younger years. I like to use my imagination to think about guardian angels and do they respond to stress the same way we do. Just think, our guardian Angels must have had to work overtime to unseeingly get us out of trouble. In today's terms, I am sure there was no unemployment among our guardian angels. We were good job creators.

THE LITTLE DEVIL STRIKES AT HESS BROTHER'S DEPARTMENT STORE

We lived only several blocks from the Allentown's downtown stores including Hess Brothers Department Store, Sears, and many 5&10 cent stores. There were still some trolley cars on Hamilton Street but being replaced by buses. As my mother walked me up to the stores, I learned the way to get there on my own. We did a lot of walking back then. We walked to school, church, and shopping and even to the grocery store. Everything was within four blocks of our house.

Once I knew the way to Hess's, I showed Sam. We spent some Saturdays going to the different stores. Easter time was interesting because the 5&10 cent stores had baby chicks, ducks and rabbits for sale which were dyed various colors.

We moved from Allentown when I was eight, so we did all these things when we were between six and eight years old. This adds new meaning to the TV advertisement "Parents, do you know where your children are"?

Unfortunately, it is not as safe these days for a young child to walk the streets without an adult. That is one of the unfortunate changes that have occurred through the years.

One day, Sam and I were in the store and doing our exploring of the es-calators, different floors, toy department and the elevators. We were riding the elevator up and down and up again until we got bored. Then it happened, we were in an elevator all alone and we thought how cool it would be to watch as the floors went by with the doors open so we, or maybe just me, stuck my fingers in the gap between the doors and pulled them open.

What do you think happened next?

A. The doors opened, and we watched in awe as the floors went by.

B. The elevator stopped in between floors and the alarms went off.

C. We fell down the elevator shaft and died

B is correct- and boy, were we in big trouble now. However, after about 45 minutes of maintenance men working to save us, we were free, and they told us to never come back without our parents. We did go back but had the feeling we were being followed by men in black suits and sunglasses, so we behaved. We did a lot of wild and crazy things and may not have listened to what adults said, but we were always humbly, respectful when in the presence of adults. I think I heard the maintenance man say as I left. What kind of idiot would open an elevator door while moving? What a Little Devil he is. There went my chances of receiving "Child of the year" award from Hess's. It could have been worse, so I am sure my guardian angel protected us.

Our summer vacations included renting a cottage at Waldheim Park on the south side of Allentown. It was on the side of a mountain in a mostly wooded mountainous area. Sam often went with us and we found fresh adventures and places to explore there. These included lots of wooded areas, two quarries where everyone went swimming at and lots of rocks. We would eventually go hiking and find our way back to Waldheim Park on our own.

That is the end of our adventures in center city. We would soon move to an area away from town. Most likely the same story could be told by many children living in center cities. We all made use of what is available to us to. Although we were mischievous, we never damaged property or hurt other people. Back then it was safe for six to eight-year-old children to wander the streets alone. There were not the dangers that plaque our children in inner cities today.

I believe in a time after Jesus returns and makes city streets safe for children and the elderly. Zechariah 8:4-5 NIV It says; This is what the Lord Almighty says: "Once again men and women of ripe old age will sit in the streets of Jerusalem, each with cane in hand because of his age. The city streets will be filled with boys and girls playing there. That sounds like me now, a ripe old age person sitting down with a cane in hand, watching and enjoying my kids play with their kids. I fulfilled prophecy. What I am experiencing is just a taste of what is coming to the entire world when Jesus returns.

WHO KILLED THE CHURCH PIPE ORGAN? NOT JOHNNY ANGEL?

Both my parents were church organists in different churches. I went to church with my mother and my sister went to church with my father.

Both my parents played at older churches that were made of rock and appeared to be more like a castle with a basement that looked like a dungeon to a young boy like me. I was told that church was God's house and like any curious kid wanted to explore this castle and look for God. My grandfather was a taxidermist, and I enjoyed looking through his shop for souvenirs like deer's legs, rabbit's feet, antlers and many other parts of animals.

What would I find in God's house? When I was at church with my mother for choir practice and Wednesday night Bible study, I would explore since most of the church was empty. I only explored lit areas of the dungeon, I mean the basement, since it was very scary there alone and dark.

I saw a room that I always wanted to explore, but it was dark when I peeked in. One Sunday morning during church, I went into the basement and opened the door just to see a gloomy room. I felt around for a light switch and found one, but it did nothing as I switched it back and forth. I figured the light was broke, so I went back to church services and had a seat.

During the last song, my mother was playing a hymn when the organ sounded very strange and then it sounded draggy like it was dying, then gradually slowed down to a dead stop. My mother jumped up with a strange look on her face and walked over to the piano to finish the hymn.

At dinner after church, my mother said to my father about how embarrassed she was when the organ died, and she had to play the piano. Then she said the deacons said someone had turned off the pipe organ air pump in the basement. When I heard that, I knew it was me and I started choking and had to get up and leave the room. I eventually came back and acted dumb, which was not too hard to do.

After a few weeks of thinking how cool the organ sounded as it died, I had to do it again and again. Eventually, it seemed men started following me every time I left church services; I think they suspected that it was the sweet, innocent organist kid that was doing it. Eventually, they put a lock on the door. The pipe organ must not have had a flaming type guardian angel at the door.

I never found God in that church. I looked in all the rooms and secret hiding places but saw nothing. I was not sure what to look for; would I find a regular person, a Casper the Ghost type being or an invisible something.

Me and others have looked for God in a building but did not find Him there. I wondered, where is he? That would be one of many things they taught me I found not to be true. Why did people think God lived in a building? It would take quite a few years of searching to find out where he lives now. Wait until the conclusion to find out, though.

NO TV OR VIDEO, JUST AN AM RADIO

I know my grandkids were born into a world that has cell phones, video games, I-pod, I pad, laptop computers and amusement parks to experience any thrills you want, but it was not always that way. I am not sure when TV came into homes, but at our house in Allentown, I mostly remember gathering around the radio. The radio had western plays on, but I remember seeing western movies on our TV, maybe when I was 5 or 6. I remember the radio being on during the day and my mother listening to Arthur Godfrey and him always saying something like "How wa ya, how wa ya, how wa ya or it could have been Hawaii-Hawaii-Hawaii since he played a ukulele and lived in Hawaii. I also remember gathering around the radio to listen to scary stories.

Another commercial I remember on the radio was "More Park sausages mom, more park sausages please" You can type in those words in goggle and hear the commercial on YouTube. I did not know the meaning of the ad, so I figured it was a kid asking his mom to take him to a park called Park Sausage since I loved going to the different parks.

WHAT IS A PUTZ?

My dad had put up a train set, which was popular in the '50s. Many people had the 3 track Lionel train sets and later came the 2 track American Flyer trains and even later the HO train sets. We had them all. My dad made a putz which comprised trains, mountains, tunnels, villages and all the things actual trains would go through. The most exciting thing was when he would allow me to operate the trains. When he was not there, I would sneak into the basement and try to figure them out and then repair the damage before he came home. It was most popular around Christmas time, but he kept ours up all year around. My two grandkids enjoying a Putz.

Chapter 4: THIRD GRADER DAVEY CROCKET HEADS WEST

When I was in third grade and about eight years old, we moved to the south side of Allentown. This was only a few miles from the birthplace of Daniel Boone, who was born in Birdsboro, PA. Maybe we are related. We moved into a single house of our own with a big yard and several trees and lots of wide-open country around us to explore. There were some TV shows starting to make an appearance for children, but I mostly remember having to make our own entertainment. The shows I loved on TV were western movies or cowboy and Indian movies.

One of my first memories of our new house was the vacant lot across the street where a gigantic pile of dirt had been bulldozed for a house foundation on the next lot over. I had never played in dirt before, so it was a fresh experience.

On Saturdays, Sam's parents would drive him over and pick him up, or as he got older, he would ride his bike to our house. We both had bikes so anywhere we wanted to go, we rode our single speed heavy balloon tire bikes. We would often go hiking and exploring around the neighborhood to see what was out there.

As we got older, there was competition for our exploring in the form of TV shows like the Our Gang, The Little Rascals, Sky King, Roy Rogers, Gene Autry, Davey Crocket, Daniel Boone, Tarzan, Ramar of the Jungle, Howdy Doody, Popeye the sailor man and many cowboy Indian movies. It seemed there were a lot of good, clean adventure shows about the early west and the pioneer days. These adventurous shows would have an influence on what we did and what we thought much like GI Joe, Ninja Turtles, Woody, and Buzz Light Year had on my kids. We found more wooded areas where we would build tree houses and forts to play cowboys and Indians.

In the winter, we would make trails to go sledding on, usually down steep and winding trails with cliffs off to the side to make it more challenging. It was stay on the trail or die trying. One time a girl came to try our hill and wanted to go down the hill sitting up. We told her it was too dangerous and too hard to control, but the rebellious thing did it, anyway. She hit a tree going too fast and broke a leg. There was no 911 to call or rescue squad, just a parent who came and drove her to a doctor.

BECOMING BLOOD BROTHERS

One of the first things that happened was that we found an old junk car in the lot across the street. We were playing on and around the car having a good time, but we both ended up bleeding from broken glass. Just like Daniel Boone and the Indians did, we touched our fingers together and became blood brothers just like in the movies. We did not understand that that bond would last a lifetime.

Sam moved to Lancaster PA after the eighth grade so basically, we explored the south side of Allentown from the third to the eighth grade.

Exploring a little further away from home, we found a small river called Trout Creek. Finding water was a whole new experience and offered lots of opportunities to play there for hours. It seemed to us like the Colorado River. We built dams, went swimming and searched the woods around the Creek. Along the Creek there were two huge drainpipes about three feet high, which were probably our height. It was like finding our own gold mine or Indian cave, so we had to go in and find out where they went. There was a small amount of water flowing through the pipe, so we had to straddle the water and walk on the sides. We walked so far that the opening appeared as a little light speck far away. We had to test the echo with Tarzan yells and attempts at yodeling. It was very dark, and it smelled like an old outhouse, so we turned around and never went in again. I do not know what was coming out of the pipes, but it turned the creek a slightly bluish color and there were no fish below that point. We went swimming above that point. It may have been coming from a sewage treatment plant or a factory. I am glad there was no big release of water while we were in there.

One day while exploring the woods, we found a piece of wood covering a hole in the ground. It turned out to be a tunnel entrance. We did not know what to make of it, so we crawled in to learn what it was being careful. We had seen on TV how miners in the old west-built tunnels to look for gold. Could this be an old mine shaft with genuine gold in it that would make us rich? Maybe it would lead to Blackbeard's treasure. We had to find out. The tunnel was probably twenty feet long and went into a larger opening like a room. Someone had dug it and covered it with wood, branches and leaves to hide it. We wondered who had built this way out here in the woods. Were they wild Indians, buffalo hunters, escaped convicts, hobos, gangsters planning a burial for someone like Jimmy Hoffa in a few years? We never knew, and we never went in there again. However, it gave us an idea to build one of our own; it was so cool or whatever terms we used then.

Eventually, with my parents' permission we dug up our yard and made a tunnel, a large room and then covered it with boards, dirt, and the grass we had removed. (Can you imagine parents today allowing their yard to be dug up to build an underground tunnel and hut?) That became our secret club house like Our Gang. I allowed no one in but Sam, the earth worms, and centipedes. Eventually, we opened it up to others in the neighborhood, even the girls, but very few girls went in. What respectable girl would go in a tunnel with a kid that appeared to be wearing a red suit, had horns and a pitchfork? That was me when I turned into a Little Devil. Sam and I even slept in there several nights.

During my life, I found that whenever I found a fresh experience, I had to sleep there to prove myself a real Daniel Boone. After a heavy rain, it became more like a muddy swimming pool. Years later, the wood rotted, and the roof caved in. We filled it in with dirt, but as the wood rotted, the earth sank, and you could always see an indentation where the tunnel and room were. There was always a memory of what once was there. That was my legacy to the new owners to let them know that a true cave man kid lived there. The owners of Zandy's Steak Sandwich Shop, my favorite place to eat, bought the house from when my parents moved. Every time I go to Zandy's, I have a story to tell.

The photo shows the drainpipes we went into, Trout creek and railroad tracks where we played.

HERE KITTY-LET'S CUDDLE

As I watched more western movies with the cowboys sleeping outside, I wanted to try it. One night I put some blankets down on the ground in our back yard. I covered up with some more blankets and went to sleep under the stars just like a real cowboy. During the night I woke up and saw our black and white and white cat aside of me, so I went to pick it up to put it under the blankets with me. Here is a question for you.

What happened when I went to pick up my cat?

A. I put it under the covers, and we cuddled all night.

B. It did not recognize me and attacked me.

C. It had a mouse in its mouth and got loose under the covers.

D. It was not my cat; it was a skunk and it sprayed me good.

Unfortunately, it was D and did I ever stink. We threw the blankets away and my mother made me wash and wash. I never saw that happen on western movies. After that, my parents bought me a tent and a cot.

COWBOYS- TRAINS -VILLAINS AND DAMSELS IN DISTRESS

Today kids want all the items to pretend to be a Buzz Lightyear, the Hulk or Darth Vader. We watched TV shows with cowboys, explorers, and frontiersmen so Sam and I pretended to be cowboys, early settlers and conquering the Wild West. Going deeper into the wilderness, we next found a bridge over Trout Creek with train tracks. We followed the tracks and found an area with a lot of sidetracks where railroad cars were ready to connect to other trains. There were boxcars, tank cars and old wooden passenger cars. This was the most outstanding find ever. Now we could be like Roy Rogers, Gene Autry, Lone Ranger and all the other cowboys that climbed all over trains to save the pretty women and to prevent the robbers from getting the gold. We could also pretend to save the damsels after the villains tied them to the railroad tracks.

Maybe we could get the girls in the neighborhood to let us tie them to the railroad tracks so we could rescue real damsels in distress as a train came. We got no volunteers, even though I promised to play house with them. We climbed all over the cars using the steel ladders on the outside. We ran along the roof jumping from one car to another and then all around the insides and even jumping out the doors to roll on the ground. We eventually took our cap pistols, cowboy hats and vests along to make it more realistic. What is a cowboy without a real cap gun and cowboy clothes?

Finally, I got some real cowboy clothes and saw a real damsel in distress on the railroad tracks. Sam and I rescued her from certain death. She looked a lot alike my future granddaughter. The photo below is my granddaughter Amy who sure looks like a damsel in distress needing rescue and me and my grandson, Parker, in our cowboy outfits.

After several weeks of playing cowboys, we got bored. Cowboys jumped on moving trains. You guessed it correctly, that would be our next adventure. Since this area was where trains changed cars around and added to a train. Once a train was ready, they moved it to the main track. We watched as they started off slowly and sped up out of sight.

Cowboys always jumped from their horses to a moving train, but we had no horses, so we tried running a long side the box car or tanker, grabbing the ladder, and jumping on. We would ride for a while, maybe several hundred yards, and then jump off into a grassy area with no rocks and roll down a hill like the cowboys did after a fight with the bad guys. Sometimes there were still steam locomotives that came through, and we especially loved to ride them. Life just kept getting better and better. The challenge was to see how long we could stay on the train as it sped up and then jump off without getting hurt.

Then we would walk back and wait for another train. Then one day, a terrible thing happened. We stayed on too long and now the train was speeding up too fast to jump off. We looked for our cell phones to call for help. (OOPS, not invented yet) We were scared to death not knowing where we would end up, since we used to watch as the trains went out of sight. I remembered my aunt getting on a train and going to Philadelphia. Were we headed there? Sam was on another car and it was too loud to communicate by voice, but we sure did with our eyes and body movements. His eyes were as big as golf balls and my mouth opened so wide that I felt my tongue dragging on the railroad bed. We wrapped our arms and legs around the ladder hanging on for dear life as the ground flew by faster and faster. I am sure people saw us hanging on the ladders as we sailed through the intersections, but what could they do, there were no cell phones to notify the authorities. They saw the look of terror on our faces with our mouth open and eyes bulging. We saw their surprised looks as we went by and their gasping for air. We hoped that perhaps someone in the engine or caboose would see us and slow down the train.

That is the first time in my life I remember really wanting to pray sincerely to God for help. I frequently said the "Lay me down to sleep" prayer at night and the God bless the grub prayer at meals, but I had never talked to God any other time. I heard about a God in church and as I prayed, I was hoping there was a God because we needed help and there was no one to rescue us. We needed this train to slow down or stop. I knew our arms could not hang on the ladder forever. We were just helpless, hanging on as if our life depended on it and it really did. Looking down, we saw the railroad ties go by at an ever-growing speed. I do not know how long or how far we went, but at that age, it seemed like forever and seemed like jet speed.

Later in life, I would recognize the area as just before Emmaus which was about 10 miles from where we started. I did not know why, but finally, we felt the train not accelerating and coasting along. Then we realized the train was slowing down. A new hope raced through our bodies as we heard that wonderful sound of the squealing of the brakes as they were being applied. An awesome feeling of peace and thankfulness to God came over us as we slowed down enough to make a jump for it.

We started to watch for a safe area to jump to. The ladders were at least two feet off the ground, and we were still moving along too fast. We realized we would have to jump and roll in preferably grass or soft dirt so to not get hurt and we did. We were in the grass as the caboose went by and the conductor was outside and yelled "you boys stay away; you could get hurt".

If he only knew we had just jumped off his death trap. It seemed like once we were off, the train picked up speed and went on. We could not help but wonder if there was a God that caused that train to slow down and how did He do it? Like, what happens when you pray? Are there angels that hear our prayer first like a guardian angel and then does he call God on His spiritual cell phone hotline. Does he ask for a message to be sent to the engineer to slow the train or what? I know we have direct access to God because of what Jesus did but I also know that angel in Hebrew means a messenger. I wondered if angels have the power to change circumstances.

I always have fun imaging what they can do and what we will be able to do as spirit beings someday. Angels appeared to some in the early church to show them which way to go. Just wondering. There would be more times we would get ourselves in a dangerous situation and ask God for help. We were now safe, but boy did we have a long walk back home which took us most of the day to get back to an area that we recognized. We went home exhausted and dead tired, never telling our parents what had happened. If we were exhausted, did our guardian angel need a nap or ask for a day off? I am not sure if we ever went back to the railroad again. Maybe it was time to explore more of what was out there. There was a big mountain out there calling us.

Around this time, I had joined the Boy Scouts and was looking to use some of my skills. I wanted to build fires, camp out, and live off the land.

AUDITIONING FOR TARZAN STUNT DOUBLES

Before moving to the mountain adventures, I better mention about the tree climbing legacy Phyllis remembered me for. Sam and I loved to climb all kinds of trees. We found a real exciting experience to do with a certain type of tree. I am not sure what kind of tree they were, but they grew straight up, were very flexible and with just enough branches to climb on. We would climb toward the top of this tree and cause it to sway back and forth. We could touch the ground and kick up and sway around in circles or side to side or just slowly sink to the ground and then get off. It took skill to climb slowly enough to allow the tree to bend slowly or sway the direction you wanted. It was like the early bungee cord rides of today. It turned out to be a terrible experience if the tree broke or bent too fast and we hit the ground too hard or worse yet if we landed in stickers. All were painful. Too bad there was no video camera available to send a copy to Home Funniest Videos. This is the part that many of the neighborhood kids, including the girls, got involved in.

I was just watching a competitive event on TV lately and saw where they stuck a flexible pole in the ground and people would shimmy up the pole and then cause it to bend after which they tried to get some momentum to jump off and see how far they could go. I wonder if someone in the neighborhood made that popular.

At Waldheim Park there were no swimming pools yet, so everyone went to a quarry in the mountains to swim. At a deep end there was a rope attached to a branch, so people could swing out and jump in the water. It was a genuine thrill to do that. I watched as some kids swung out, got too scared to jump off at the prime point and fell off on to the shore or rocks in the shallow water. OUCH.

While at Waldheim Park one summer, my parents said to not go to the quarry to swim or swing on the rope unless an adult was with me, but I often did anyway. I liked to do what I wanted to do and when I wanted to do it. There is a price to pay for that attitude. Were my parents trying to say that I, Johnny Angel, did not know what was safe for me? One day I was riding my bike up the rocky trail to the quarry when I hit a big rock and started going back down the hill backwards. I eventually went off the trail and fell onto some broken glass on the ground. I got up to continue but felt something wet on my lower back. It was blood and a lot. I took my shirt off and held it against where I thought the blood was coming from. I got scared but continued up to the quarry, anyway. I went swimming and tried to wash the blood out of my shirt and off my body.

It seemed to stop once I was in the water. Maybe the quarry water had some healing power, like a secret ingredient to heal. Maybe it was like the healing Pool of Bethesda in Jesus' time mentioned in John 5:1-15. If I could only find the ingredient, I could be rich. I could not tell my parents I disobeyed and break their trust, so I went back to our cottage and hid the bloody shirt and towel. Several days later, my parents found the bloody shirt and towel and asked about it. When they saw the cut, it was already starting to heal but should have had stitches. My mother said, my poor little Johnny, I bet it hurt so much but my father looked at me like you little devil, I should spank you. They said I would have a nasty scar and I do. It seemed my parents always found my hiding places. I wonder how much they really knew about what I was doing.

One time while exploring the woods near our house, we found an enormous tree where other kids had tied a rope. They would climb the tree, sit on a big knot and swing from one of the higher branches. It was an awfully long rope and really swung a great distance. It was a lot of fun, but we were out of our neighborhood and the other kids did not want us there, so we built our own.

We found a rope and tied it on our apple tree in our yard. It was not as high as the other one and soon became boring. To make it more exciting, we moved the rope to a higher branch, but then the rope was too short to hold from the swing off point. Our rope became more challenging because the rope was too short, and you had to dive for the rope as someone threw you the rope. However, you had to dive at the right time to grab it and then hang on for dear life or down you went, face first. All the neighborhood children had fun doing it, including the girls. Fortunately, no one ever broke a bone, but there were many bruises from missing the rope. I would say the generation that grew up in the '50s grew tough.

My neighbor was an industrial plumber and knew how much I loved to swing, jump and climb. We had no large trees in the yard, so he built a pipe structure, probably twenty feet high. He bought a good rope and positioned it exactly right so the rope would reach our apple tree at two places. It reached to a lower branch, maybe five feet high, for the sane, sweet, innocent girly types and a higher branch, maybe ten feet high, for us real Tarzan types.

We used to also swing on vines like Tarzan. We could find vines near my house or up on the mountains. It was fun to swing across rocks or swing in a circle, but the best excitement came from swinging across a small valley or ditch. One time the vine broke and I fell on a rock on my back. I could not move and thought I broke my back but soon felt better to continue swinging. While hiking with my family, I would show them how to swing on a vine and have some free fun.

Below are my grand kids Zack and Dakota swinging on a vine out over a river while bike riding. The best swing was at our house.

I do not understand how we ever survived all those years or why we did not get serious injuries. Maybe our guardian angels were really working overtime. I wonder if they get overtime pay. To continue a rather unfortunate legacy, my son Sam Adam, named after Sam, dove for a tree branch like we used to do and missed. He fell from a second-story porch to the ground face first. He broke his two wrists and jaw and knocked out a few teeth. My other son David fell off a castle and broke his clavicle bone. My daughter Melody fell out a tree and broke her wrist. That reminds me of a verse in the Bible Numbers 14:18 The LORD is slow to anger and filled with unfailing love, forgiving every kind of sin and rebellion. But he does not excuse the guilty. He lays the sins of the parents upon their children; it affects the entire family, even children in the third and fourth generations. That is terrible, are my grandkids and great grandkids in trouble for my shenanigans. I will pray not. All those injuries should have been me.

That swing got a lot of use for years by Sam and I and other neighborhood kids. Sam still lived in center city Allentown and all most every Saturday would ride his bike over to my house. In those days, we rode our bikes wherever we wanted to go. I remember riding to the other side of town to cut my grandmother's grass or riding across town to go swimming at the city pool. There were no school buses then. We had a choice to ride a city bus, walk, ride a bike, or have our parents drive us to school. I usually rode my bike. All that bike riding helped Sam to develop big muscles and endurance since he won the 880 track events in junior high school and cross-country events in high school. I ran the 880 on the South Mountain Jr. High track team and Sam ran it for the Central Jr. High track team. The girls would cheer, scream, and yell for Sam but appeared not to see me. Fortunately, my friend named Phyllis was a cheerleader and she would be the only one yelling "run Johnny run" so I just kept on running and running. I just kept running until one day I stopped.

One time the coach made sugar tablets available and said to only take one to give us more energy to run faster so we could beat Central. If one makes you run faster, I figured I would be like lightning if I took a handful. Instead of faster, I could hardly move, I became very sluggish as I struggled to run. Phyllis saw the entire group was behind me as we went by the cheer leading area, and she just kept screaming for me. She did not know the entire group had passed me once and was now on their second lap while I was still on my first. I was so embarrassed, I just quit at the finish line without running the second lap. Sam was a fast runner, and the girls loved him. He was becoming a real chick magnet. He also was an excellent football player. He continued to do well in sports in school while I played trumpet in the marching band.

There was one another boy who lived two blocks away named Jed and then there were about six girls. Phyllis was my age and in most of my classes in elementary school. She would hang out with us more than others and mostly would try the crazy stuff we did. She is the one I met at the class reunion that remembered me as the tree climber.

As a Boy Scout, I learned how to shoot a bow and arrow. I was trying to imitate an Indian and would climb the apple tree in our yard and shoot arrows at a target, then swing from the tree and shoot some more. One day after school, I was shooting arrows from the tree and I lost my balance and fell out of the tree. I had the arrows stuck in my belt and they all broke but fortunately did not puncture me. That could have really hurt. (I owe my guardian angel a dinner for possibly turning the arrows to not stick in me) I gathered up the good arrows I had shot and went to climb up the tree again. When I grabbed the branch and tried to pull myself up, I felt an excruciating pain in my wrist. At the time I did not know it, but I had broken my wrist and probably had just set it because the x-ray showed a break but perfectly lined up.

I knew I, Johnny Angel, could not tell my parents the truth about falling out of a tree, so I made up a story and said I fell at school before coming home. Eventually my mother went to the school and demanded to know how her son got hurt. One lie led to another to cover my behind. I owe the school an apology as well. My mother called our family doctor, and he came out to the house that evening. You know, that was a long time ago when the doctor made house calls. It is a different time now. Maybe there were no emergency rooms in the 1950s. We went somewhere to get an x-ray and were told it was broken. Then I remember a doctor putting a cast on it. That slowed my adventures down for a couple months. My guardian angel was probably stressed out by the whole thing and needed a break.

Chapter 5: 6TH GRADE AND GREAT EXPLORERS LIKE LEWIS AND CLARK

My wife and I did more camping with our kids, so once married, our kids also took their kids camping. Many a time my wife and I have been camping with the grandkids to introduce them to it.

My mom and dad were not interested in camping, but I had an adventurous spirit and a love of the outdoors, so I was exposed a little differently. I learned about camping by being a Boy Scout and going to the Boy Scout summer camp.

Experiencing camping made my love of the outdoors grow which made me want to camp out at any exciting place I saw. I would camp out at many exciting places in my life.

Just like Lewis and Clark who followed rivers exploring the west, Sam and I moved beyond the railroad, following Trout Creek to see where it went.

OUR WILDERNESS BECOMES MAC TRUCK HEADQUARTERS

We used to play in the wooded area along the creek, which we thought was real wilderness. Eventually it was cleared, a road put in and became the Mac Truck World Headquarters Building (which now moved to SC), a housing development and eventually a city swimming pool. I used to ride my bike to South Mountain Junior High School along a beat-up country road to a dirt road, then a trail through the woods riding over a narrow wood bridge crossing Trout Creek to the school. By the time I graduated Junior High school, it was a paved road all the way with a regular bridge over the creek through what would become a housing development.

As we kept exploring, we eventually found Waldheim Park, where my parents had rented a cottage a few years earlier. It was on the South

Mountain. I remembered one quarry where everyone went swimming and another one that was very deep, steep, and dangerous. I am not sure if there were any public swimming pools at the time because we always went swimming in a creek, lake, or quarry.

ROCKS-CANYONS AND CAVES, OH BOY

I also heard tales of huge rocks, canyons and caves up in those mountains from others who lived at Waldheim. It was the perfect place to explore as we were getting older. Since we would leave my house early and spend all day Saturday hiking and exploring. We no longer could go home for lunch, so my mother would pack us a lunch with some peanut butter jelly sandwiches, an apple, some celery and carrot sticks plus a bunch of candy bars. Later, as we learned how to build a fire, we took a few hot dogs to cook. My Boy Scout training was paying off. I had a canteen for water, a backpack for our lunch and other items needed, plus we eventually learned how to build a safe fire to cook on or warm us up if it got cold.

As we went up into the mountain, we found enormous boulders maybe thirty to forty feet high. There were cliffs, canyons, small caves, and lots of vines to swing on. Just like Kit Carson, Wild Bill Hickok and Jim Bowie surveying the west, we were amazed and thrilled at the find in this "uncharted wilderness" country.

We often would cut a vine and swing rock to rock or across small valleys or ditches. One day the vine broke, and I fell flat on my back on some rocks. The pain was intense, and I could not move. I was sure I had broken my back and was paralyzed, but eventually Sam helped me up and I was OK to go on. I often wonder if that is why I have so much back trouble today.

I was really impressed by what we saw. I wondered how the rocks got there, what made the canyons and why were there mountains at some areas and valleys at other places. I wondered what caused water to bubble out of the ground on the side of the mountain. How did spring water flow uphill underground to the top of a mountain and then flow out and downhill to the ocean? What made the spring water so cold and taste so good to drink after drinking chlorinated water from the city? What made the sound of water flowing over rocks so alluring that I wanted to sit there or camp there, and what made it so easy to think about things as I sat alongside of a spring or little stream? I wondered why I got such a good feeling as I stood on top of a mountain with a breath-taking view of Allentown and the entire Lehigh Valley. I could even see the roof of my house from the top of the mountain. While at my house, I felt so big and so important, but from up on the top of the mountain everything looked so small with so many people and houses out there. In Mk. 6:31, Jesus took his disciples to a secluded, desolate spot to rest, relax and be refreshed. I know that feeling. It seems to help increase the opportunity for God to communicate with us.

CREATION VS EVOLUTION

To this day, I still ask the same questions as I have seen more of the wonders of this planet. I have developed a love of reading what the geologist's theory about an area that I am in. I am not sure about all the details of how these wonders happened, but I believe in a Creator God and give thanks for the inspiring views, the relaxation got while being outdoors and the enjoyment we can get from them. I love the mountains, streams, the oceans, and everything in between. I would really come to appreciate all the wonders of earth and how it seemed to be created for our benefit. If there were mountains to hike, climb or snow ski or sled down, whitewater to raft or kayak on or just sit there in awe of what you see. Then there is the ocean to enjoy fishing, boating, cruises, surfing, swimming or again just sitting on the beach in awe of the beauty and yet power of the seas. And there is everything in between. Because there are about 6000 years of recorded history since Adam and Eve in the Bible, some people think the earth is 6000 years old. Scientists and geologists say the earth is millions of years old and accredits the theory of evolution as the source. Is one right and the other wrong?

In Job 38:1-7, God asked Job where he was when He formed the earth and made it. I think the earth was created beautiful since God also said the angels rejoiced and sang at the creation of the earth. In Gen 1:1 it says in the beginning God created the heaven and the earth, period, end of the sentence and I believe it. Next verse says, Now the earth was formless and empty, darkness was over the surface of the deep, and the Spirit of God was hovering over the waters. I ask myself if God created something without form and empty, wasted and full of darkness, was that something to rejoice about. Is that the way you create something?

I once heard a sermon that the Hebrew word for "was" has several meanings and one is "to become". I must wonder if the earth was created beautiful at one point possibly millions of years ago, and then when Satan rebelled against God with the battle that occurred made the earth a waste. Possibly, Satan was first given the job to take care of the earth and animals but did not do it, so it was given to Adam. In Gen 1:2- was God restoring the earth to its beauty for man to be created and to enjoy.

This is my belief and I have no argument if geologists claim the earth is millions or billions of years old. Lots of debate still going on. I would argue with anyone claiming a big bang theory with evolution. There are so many holes in the theory of evolution that. I wonder how it could be taught. When I think about the laws that make this earth and how we depend on them, it is amazing that anyone could believe all this just happened.

As I give thanks for the beauty of the earth, I also must wonder what made the deep valleys and the high mountains. Some valleys just look like the earth was torn apart and where mountains are; I can see where hundreds of feet of layered rock strata were just snapped and came through the earth pointing upward like a compound bone fracture. Also, I see the violent side of nature through hurricanes, tornadoes, floods and wind and the damage they can do. Did God cause the various violent actions to this earth, or did they happen through natural circumstances, or was it just part of a terrible war between spirit beings. Is it part of Adam's sin?

If the earth is millions of years old, can you imagine the patience of God to wait all those years to create man and to wait another 4000 years for Jesus Christ to come to his world to die for our sins and then wait another 2000 years to end the rule of Satan on this earth and make this once again a beautiful, peaceful planet? The Bible says in Romans 8:23-24 NIV, the whole earth groans, like a woman in labor, for the day of Christ's return. That sure makes me feel small when I question why God did not act as fast as I thought He should have when I prayed for Him to correct things in my life.

PANIC ON A CLIFF-I WANT MY MOMMY

To enjoy this beautiful creation of God, Sam and I spent a lot of Saturdays climbing rocks, cliffs and exploring caves. One of my favorite spots was this area of enormous boulders, maybe 30 to 40 feet high, sitting on the edge of a canyon looking like it could fall into the canyon at any time. This huge boulder had the back side tapered and easy to walk up to the top. The front side was basically straight up and at the edge of the canyon.

Along Trout Creek, there were some cliffs we used to climb all the way to the top of, so we were "experienced, seasoned cliff climbers" and decided to someday climb this enormous boulder. There were no TV shows to show us how to climb a cliff safely. We only saw cowboys and Indians scaling boulders and cliffs with no problem unless there was a fight and one fell down.

One day we were climbing around the base of this enormous boulder and decided it was time to take the challenge, try our rock-climbing skills and climb up to the top from the front. We started up by using the little cracks and rough surfaces of the rock to put our hands in to pull us up. At the same time our feet felt for other holes, so our legs could push us up. We were doing so well but were terrified when we looked down to the canyon and rocks below us, waiting to break every bone in our youthful bodies if we fell.

I was in the lead and then it happened, I looked down and saw how far it was to those terrible rocks below and how close to death we were. I searched for a place to grab onto and another place to put my foot but could not find any. After a while, panic struck, and I froze. I was afraid to slide my foot down to try to find a slot for my foot to go down and afraid to go up without a solid footing. Sam could not move at all until I moved. He was rather reluctant to go back down also, so we just stayed there about ready to cry. Once again, we were hanging on for dear life.

Here is one of those questions again. What happened next?

A. We cried and screamed until our mommies came

B. We used our Tony The Tiger instant parachute and floated to safety.

C. Sam fell down and broke his crown.

D. None of the above

It was D. Fear does strange things to us. There we were, terrified to move up or down for what seemed to be an eternity. We both just silently prayed again for some help from the God that saved us from the speeding train. It then appeared as though the fear seemed to leave, and a new hope emerged.

After a while, my brave buddy Sam said he saw a ledge above my foot, so I moved my foot there and could push myself up to grab another spot with my hand. I found a solid spot for my hand and then could continue to the top. What a relief to be finally away from the chance of falling into that abyss. Once again, we both thanked God and felt He protected us from a stunt that could have produced terrible injuries or even death. (I wonder if our guardian angels ever go to God and say I quit, these kids are just too much trouble.) I am sure they do not, just a thought. I am sure my guardian angel felt sick when he saw his duty assignment for the week was Sam and I. After that adventure, we never climbed another cliff. Later in the Marine Corps, I would repel down cliffs with all the proper safety gear and what a better feeling that was. It is so much better to do things correctly in a safe and intelligent way. Like I said before, nature can provide much enjoyment, but there are rules to follow to assure a safe adventure.

As I went through Marine Corps boot camp and infantry training, it was a lot like things I had done with Sam. There was climbing, swinging on ropes, jumping, crawling, digging holes in the ground to hide in, and being stealth to avoid being seen by others. We were good at that.

The photos below show my kids must have a dare devil in them. My girls Tammy and Melody like to sit on the edge of an overhang rock. My son David likes to imitate my stories of hanging off cliffs. Some of my kids seem to enjoy climbing cliffs the safe way on a man-made cliff with safety harnesses.

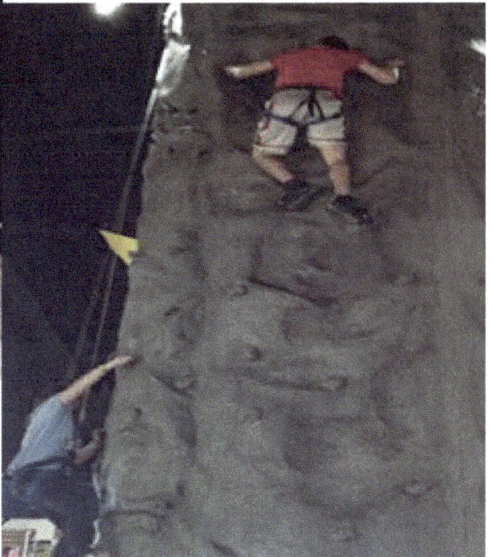

HOT WHEELS

As a young boy, I often roller skated with the neighborhood kids on the sidewalk with steel-wheeled roller skates. It was a rough ride hitting the gaps and stones on the sidewalk. I got many cuts, scrapes and bruises from falling on the sidewalk, usually from going too fast or trying to make a turn too fast. At some point my dad started taking my cousin, Norine, and I roller skating at Dorney Park. I believe it was on Sunday afternoons, or possibly Saturday afternoons. It was much easier and safer to roller skate on a hardwood floor with fiber wheels. I loved to roller skate and would continue to do so much of my life. I always hoped to be a boogie-woogie organ player at a roller-skating rink but they switch to records and later digital music.

THE BIRDS AND THE BEES VISIT

As I got older, maybe 12 or 13, girls started coming up to me and asking me to skate couple skates with them. Probably since my father saw me skating with girls, he must have told my mother because one day my mother came up to me and wanted to talk about girls. I did not need that talk since being the only boy in the neighborhood I knew all about girls. In my mind in, I knew girls cried easily when playing tackle football, some could not hit a baseball as far me, they cried and screamed hysterically when a cat came up and ate the baby rabbits out of a nest in our baseball field; they were not as daring when sleigh riding down the steeper hills as me and would not climb trees as high as me, and some were afraid to crawl through the long skinny tunnel leading to my underground hut.

When I played hide and go seek with the girls, they would give themselves away by giggling or talking. Girls also hid at least with one other girl and I hid by myself. If I wanted to go hiking, the girls would go in the local woods around our houses but not into the deeper wilderness. I also knew girls were excellent negotiators since to get them to play baseball and football with me, I had to play "house" with them. I knew also that if I did not do what the girls wanted, they would be mad for a few days and not talk to me no matter what I said. I also noticed that the girls were always dressed neat and clean and nice compared to me, who wore the same dirty clothes day after day. (My wife says I still do) But there was something different about girls, but I was not sure what, other than they were pretty to look at. There also seemed to be something in me that seemed to make me want to protect them, treat them nicer and look forward to their compliments. Today, if I voiced those observations, I would be called a sexist. There seemed to be changes taking place as we got older and finally, we quit football and just played baseball.

A legacy I prefer to not pass down is a weakness inside of me around girls, and they could make me do things I did not want to do. If I said no, they would smile, turn their head a little to the side and giggle and with a soft sweet voice say "come on Johnny, do it for us, we need a handsome, big robust boy like you. If you will do this for us, we'll do whatever you want later". I was such a sucker, I just caved right in.

Strange as it may sound, many years later while in Japan I went to different clubs. In the clubs, there were Japanese girls hired to talk to and be friendly to us young Marines if we bought the girls drinks. They would say to me "You are number one Marine and you are so handsome, so big and strong and so smart, you buy me a drink and I'll talk to you as long as you want". I would spend my whole paycheck in just a few days. The girls called me Oki-Sakana 大きな魚 which in English means "BIG SUCKER". They showed me how to write it in Japanese so I would remember.

I also knew girls were "scaredy cats" (forgive me) since they frightened easier than me. I had a crush on this one girl I went to school with named Phyllis, and I thought she was so pretty and such a nice girl. We were both in the same class since I had moved there in third grade. I also went to a local Bible study once a week in which she would stop by my house which was on the way and we walked there together.

Coming home it was dark, and we had to walk about four blocks through dark lonely streets. When the wind blew on a moon-lit night, the branches moved and cast moving shadows all around us. It was very eerie and spooky, causing Phyllis to get scared and grab my arm for security. There was a chicken butcher shop along the way which all of us kids at one time or another had peeked through the fence and saw chickens running around without their heads. Everyone avoided that area at night. When the wind caused the tree branches to squeal as they rubbed each other, and the shadows were moving; it made us think the dead chicken ghosts were after us. As we walked home together, I felt like such a hero to be so brave and not be scared (or pretend to not be scared).

On the real dark, scary nights, I would walk an additional block with her to her house and then back home. (It seems like God put something in a man to want to protect a woman.) When we played house, I dreamed of playing the part of the husband to her, protecting her and holding her hand, but every time it came up the other girls said I had to sit close together like their mommies and daddies did. I wanted to do that but that seemed rather sissy like to me and what if someone would see me playing house with girls, so I came up with an excuse to go home?

These were the same girls that in third and fourth grade played a game like today's show and tell. We played this game with one boy and one girl that the winner and loser had to go in between two row homes and the winner had to tell the looser what to show. I will leave that up to you and your imagination to figure out what we showed. I was one of two boys among about 5 girls, so I had to go often to either see it or show it. The other boy seemed to enjoy playing that game, but I thought climbing trees was more fun. I was not sure where this playing house stuff would lead, so when I felt uncomfortable with the situation, I went home. Little did I know, this going home stuff when I felt uncomfortable would be repeated many times in my life when girls wanted to "play house".

When my mother wanted to talk to me about girls, I told her I already knew about girls. She told me as I got older, how I looked girls would change but warned me to never kiss a girl. She said kissing a girl was a sin and would make her pregnant and she would have a baby for me to take care of and there would be no more adventures, simply hard work. I did not understand what she was talking about since girls were the last thing on my mind and especially kissing a girl, which seemed to make me nauseous. When I thought about what she said, I wondered how the body knew the difference between kissing your mother, grandmother or sister compared to kissing a girl and how that kiss would end up making her pregnant. I figured kissing a girl on the lips made her pregnant, and that was why my family did not kiss on the lips. There was nothing to worry about as far as girls go since I was more interested in bike riding, hiking, and rock climbing, swinging on vines, sledding and other outdoor activities and figured who would want to kiss a girl, anyway.

LOST IN A DEEP, DEEP CAVE

There were quite a few holes and small cave openings along the South Mountain, but most of them were only a few yards long. I wondered how they got there. There were a lot of signs of earlier mining. I wondered if these holes were man made or created by nature. From what I have read, the crashing together of plates beneath the earth, earthquakes, glaziers and floods created a lot of what we see on this planet.

One day we were walking along the bottom of a canyon when we saw a hole in the rocks along the side of the valley. It was not a large hole, just big enough to crawl through. I had a small flashlight with me, so we peeked inside. It appeared to open into a large room, so we could not resist the temptation. We slowly drug our small bodies inside and found a larger cavern inside large enough to stand up and walk around. We saw there was an area between rocks that made a tunnel going deeper into the mountain that we could explore even more. We decided to come back next week with better flashlights and some food in case it was a very deep cave.

The photo below shows the cave entrance 50 years later. It looks like some tried to cover up the entrance with rocks. Maybe someone got lost or hurt and needed to be rescued.

The following week, we came back with several flashlights to explore what was in there. We left one flashlight on in the main cavern to hopefully wc could see our way back if we needed. We went through the entrance to the tunnel and walked and sometimes squeezed in between the rocks following the passage. Then it dropped to another level beneath us. We climbed through this very dark narrow passage as we used the flashlights to search for the way to go. It was not like a gold mine we had seen on TV.

Instead of being a straight tunnel, there were just openings between rocks to climb through. Instead of going straight, it kept going down deeper and deeper, so we were basically climbing down rocks. We would have continued, but I dropped my flashlight and stood there horrified as we heard it hitting rocks as it fell.

Once again Sam's eyes looked like golf balls and my mouth dropped open so much, I felt my tongue on the limestone rocks as we heard my flashlight continue on bouncing off rocks as it fell what seemed like forever finally hearing a splash when it hit water. Our flashlights did not penetrate the darkness very well, so it was rather scary when we realized it was so deep. We headed back before we lost our last light.

Sam turned off his flashlight to see if we could see the light in the main cavern. When he turned the light off, we did not see a thing including our own noses. I had never seen such darkness in my entire life, not even a light in the distance from the cavern where we left the light on, nor any light from the crack or any other source. For the first time we realized how it would be to be lost in here. Horrified as we wondered, is this going to be another life-threatening experience? Maybe we should have brought some rope, breadcrumbs (like the cartoons) or something to mark our path. Maybe we should have told someone where we were going, or maybe we should have brought another person to stand outside in case we got lost. However, we never considered it was too dangerous and to not go in there at all. As we looked around in the pitch-dark crevices, everything looked the same.

What would happen if our flashlight quit working or we dropped the last one into what seemed to be a bottomless pit? No one knew where we were. If we were lost, would anyone ever find us alive or would they even ever find our bodies. We felt our stomachs drop as we realized how deep it was and what would happen if we fell in there. Realizing we only had Sam's flashlight remaining, I remembered a little pen light in my pocket that I brought along in case of emergency. I had borrowed it from a box of penlights my mother had for Christmas Eve Candlelight services. Once again, we wondered if this was going to be one of those praying moments. You better believe it was, as we silently prayed to a God that appeared to be able to rescue us from anything. I wondered if praying was like Aladdin's lamp and only get so many wishes or prayers answered. Hopefully, we had not used all our requests yet. As our hearts raced and pounded on our chests, we searched for openings back out.

What happened next?

A. We never found our way out and died a slow, painful death and were never found.

B. A prehistoric monster appeared out of the depths and chased us out

C. We searched and finally found a way out. Thank you, Jesus.

D. Sam put a message in a bottle and dropped it in the water. Phyllis found it in a creek and saved us

It was "C". Feeling a new spirit, we searched and finally found what appeared to be the way up and out. We climbed our way back out and fortunately for us, there appeared to be only one way. After what seemed like an eternity, we were very relieved to eventually see the light shining in the main cavern and just knowing we were safe. Did our guardian angel lead us out like angels lead Peter out of prison in Acts 5:19. One more time we were thankful to be alive as I thought about screaming out "thank you God" but silently thanked this God that just seemed to be full of love and concern. We would continue to stop at the cave occasionally and go in the cavern part, but never again went any further since we already knew what was there. This time, only my guardian angel would think this kid is not as innocent as some believe, and I am sure he asked for a week's vacation after that scare.

Looking back now, it was probably at one time an underground river or spring that came up from the depths of the earth and flowed out into the canyon. Maybe even during Noah's flood, which the Bible says in Gen. 7:11. The springs of the great depth were opened. At one time there must have been a lot of water flowing through there. I would hate to be in there during a flash flood.

Many years later, I would be taken on a tour of Crystal Cave, Lost Cave and Penn's Cave and a few coal mines. Penn's Cave was a tour by boat which was interesting. A guided safe tour is the best way to see a cave or cavern. All the caves were like ours, weaving around rocks and formations, and during the tour, they would turn off the lights to show the complete darkness. The kind of thick darkness is an unforgettable experience.

When Sam and I were in that cave, it was a terrible feeling being in that cave with the lights off and being in a situation absent of light. So dark, we could not see our noses or anything. It was like being blind. It gave us such a feeling of hopelessness, confusion, so lost, such despair as we were touching and feeling for hope and finding a way out. There would come another time in my life when I would explore the cave of sin and the adventures of the world, getting lost in the darkness, feeling the same hopelessness and blindness as I did in that cave with the lights out.

Crying out to be rescued, Jesus Christ turned that light on for me to follow him out of sin. I hope and pray that my grandkids will see and follow the same light. Jesus in Jn. 8:12 says he is the light of the world. Also, in Matthew 5: 14 Jesus said Christians are also the light of the world. Would not that be outstanding to have the entire family be a light to help people out of darkness. Like the song, I would let my Little Light shine rather than hiding that light under a bushel.

Chapter 6: MOMMY'S LITTLE MISCHIEVOUS HELPER

At a young age, I would help my mother dry dishes and help with cooking. One day after school, before my parents came home, I made some Jell-O from gelatin like my mother did. I read the directions and boiled the water, went to the unmarked canister set and added sugar plus all the other ingredients and let it cool for a while. My dad used to add ice cream after cooling for a while and then whip it into a fluffy, delicious dessert. I did that and let it cool to surprise my parents with a special dessert. I did everything right; I thought. After supper, I pulled out my surprise and served it up.

My mother said, oh Johnny, you are such a good boy, a little angel. I am so glad you use your free time, productively. It looked beautiful, but after the first bite we all ran for the bathroom about the same time to get rid of it. It turns out for my mother kept sugar and salt in an unmarked canister. I grabbed a canister with white granules in it thinking it was sugar but unfortunately it was salt. It looked the same to me. I innocently used the salt instead of sugar.

I learned to always taste it first, if in doubt. (I guess you say that my heart was right, but the end was wrong because of not following the rules. Are good intentions enough?) I eventually would try various recipes like cakes, burgers, pancakes, waffles, etc. My dad was always one to add or combine various foods to see how it tasted. His specialty was adding various things to pancakes and waffles. I would eventually try the same things when married, but no one liked it but me.

My son, David, is also following in that legacy because he added pickles to pancakes one day. (Who would know that this experience of drying dishes and baking cakes would help win the girl of my dreams someday?)

In those days, there was no air conditioning, so my dad put awnings up in the spring and took them down in the fall. They helped keep the sun from shining in the house and heating it. I went out on the roof with him to put up the awnings and he taught me how to use tools and climb on a roof safely. Eventually, I would explore the whole shingled roof and layout to get a suntan.

When I saw Army movies and paratroopers, I wanted to do it. I started sliding off the edge, holding on to the edge and then dropping to the ground. Later I could stand up and jump off the roof to see what it would be like. In gym class, we learned that if you jump off something to roll as you hit the ground, so I did that. I started at a low level and worked my way up to a higher level. As I jumped from higher levels, it really hurt when I landed so I did not go higher. I wonder if my guardian angel laid on the ground as I jumped to prevent an injury. Did other angels come give him CPR? Once again in Marine Corps boot camp, we did a similar thing, so I was ready for it. I wonder if my guardian angel laid on the ground to cushion my landings or had a leg splint handy.

Helping my dad to fix things helped me to learn to use carpenter tools to figure out how to fix something. My grandfather was a machinist, so I inherited some mechanical ability from them.

USS LITTLE DEBBIE

When my niece Debbie was born, I was so excited I built a wood boat and called it "Old Debbie". I took a motor off a plastic boat I had and made a battery holder, so it turned out to be a motorboat. We tried it in a nearby lake and it worked good except I forgot to angle the motor to go in a circle and it took off straight and kept going across the lake. Fortunately, it was not an enormous lake, so when it ran aground on the other side, I went and got it. People on the lake probably said what the devil is going on with this chaos. From then on, I liked to build, repair things and work with hand tools. It seems like the teens of the '50s and '60s learned to be good at switching, replacing or repairing parts on their cars like carburetors, cylinder heads, transmissions, and differentials to see if that would make their cars faster. Many items were not easily replaced and had to be repaired at a machine shop.

This would be my lifetime profession. I would become an auto repair technician and later a collision repair technician. I would learn diesel engine and heavy equipment repair in the Marine Corps. Later in life, I would become one of only a few in the USA to be ASE certified as a Master Auto Technician, Master Collision Repair Technician and Master Truck Equipment Technician.

One of my passions would be to wonder and question how something works, but my greater passion was to wonder how this great earth came about. I wondered what was around the next curve, what was under the water, what was in that cave, how did those rocks get there, what made that valley and did all this happen intentionally or accidentally?

BUILDING A SOAP BOX DERBY RACER

Sam and I saw on the Little Rascals, Our Gang TV show that they built derbies out of old wood crates and put wheels on them and had races. Several blocks away, there were older boys that had built derbies and raced them down nearby hills and streets.

This was something that enticed our adventurous spirits, so we had to make one to experience what they experienced. We got a wood crate from a nearby grocery store and took the wheels off my Radio Flyer wood wagon. Sam and I did some hammering and some bolting and WA-LA, we were ready to roll. I lived at the top of a hill that was 3 blocks long and that hill made a great downhill ride on the derby. We did not know how to make brakes that worked well, so if a car came, we would either steer around it or turn into someone's yard. There were times we would turn down another road and continue downhill at another block.

One time, a car came that appeared to be a collision but I bet my guardian angel turned my wheel to miss the car, but I hit the curb, went air born and I am sure my guardian angel quickly flew under me as I rolled over several times. I still got bruised up, and it was so horrible it caused the neighborhood girls to scream and cry. I wonder if other angels thought my angel should ask for a reassignment. What sweet little boys will do for fun. I soon abandoned the idea and went back to hiking.

Sometimes I wonder how our generation survived with some stunts we did. We were a do-it-yourself group that built and repaired whatever we needed. We repaired and modified our bicycles, and then in high school we took old slow cars and made them lean, mean racing machines with a lot of horsepower. Even today, you see the baby boomers driving these old cars that they have fixed up themselves. I often see a beautiful restored old car coming and hear that purring sound of glass-packed mufflers expecting to see some teen boy with a crew cut and tee shirt, but instead I see an old gray headed or bald grandpa person driving. (Wait a minute, that could be me)

During my teen years, the teen boys made many trips to the junkyard to get parts to repair or modify their cars. Modern teens miss out on that satisfaction.

Chapter 7: ADVENTURES WITH POISONOUS SNAKES

 While living at our new house, my parents would still rent a cabin some place for a week or two during the summer. My most memorable experiences were at a cabin on a private lake with four other cabins in the Pocono Mountains. It had excellent fishing, swimming and best of all it had a rowboat and 2 canoes with it. I could use more of my Boy Scout training in rowing, paddling and canoe tipping. Sam would come along with us. I could not be trusted alone.

 We were always told to be on the lookout for snakes. We had often seen garter and water snakes in the area as walked around. Not seen as often were the poisonous copperhead and rattlesnakes but were there. One of our stupid stunts happened when we were out fishing and rowing around the edge of the lake. There were some low-hanging branches hanging out over the water. Our boat was drifting, and we hit some branches. Something fell off a branch, hit the side of the boat, and then fell in the water. What we saw swimming off toward the bank shocked us. It appeared to be a copperhead snake. I recognized the markings and triangular head from a copperhead in a cage at scout camp. A water snake looks similar, but a water snake does not have a triangular head. We got out of the area quickly, making our rowboat look like a motorboat. After that we were more careful about boating close to the shore, but our curiosity drove us back to see if it would show up again. Below is a copperhead snake and one in a kayak.

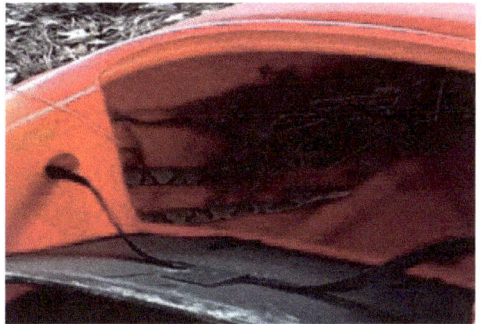

Several days later, we were out rowing again and saw it sunning itself on some rocks and tempting us to try something. Its triangular head peeked out of its coils and it seemed to call us with a tempting smile as it showed its fangs glistening in the sunlight. Our devious minds plotted how we could catch it. We got a fishing pole and make a loop at the end. We could slip it over the snake's head, tighten it and put it in a container. Perfect plan, I saw it used on "Ramar of the Jungle" with cobras.

We grabbed a fishing pole, made the loop, grabbed an old pot with a lid and headed back to the spot. We slowly rowed up to it and saw it was still there. We stuck the fishing pole out and slipped the loop around its head and then quickly pulled it tight. The snake jumped all around, wrapping itself around the pole, but we had it. We lowered it into the pot, put the lid on, released the line and then pulled the pole out. We had successfully caught a copperhead snake. Now, what would we do with it was the question? My brother-in-law was a hunter and fisherman, so I figured he would be impressed and know what to do with it. While we were rowing back to the cabin, we noticed the snake had pushed the lid up and now had its head out. It was looking at us with a very evil look; like I am going to eat you guys alive. You will wish your mother had beat the devil out of you when you were young.

It is question time again. What do you think happened when the copperhead stuck his head out?

A. Sam grabbed a reed, played it like a flute, and charmed it back into the pot.

B. It made a strange snake call, and a giant Anaconda came swimming toward the boat, ready to devour us.

C. Sam saw it was a female snake and sweet-talked it into giving him a kiss instead of a bite. He took the snake home for a pet.

D. It crawled into the boat with us.

Unfortunately, it was D. As we saw it looking at us, we both thought that we were in big trouble now. When the snake crawled out into the boat, we both realized that there was no room for the three of us in that boat, so we volunteered to leave. We swam as fast as we could back to the cabin, not knowing if the snake would chase after us or not. The boat eventually drifted to shore and my brother-in-law went out with his pistol to check it out. We saw no signs of the snake, but we did not know if it was hiding under a seat or not. We eventually towed it back to the cabin, and my brother-in-law filled the boat full of water to force out the snake if it was there. Nothing came out, and we all figured it was safe to use again. I do not think I enjoyed the lake as much after that. I had dreams about the snake coming after us. Here is one extremely terrifying nightmare I had. At the cabin, I slept on the top bunk bed because I had never done that before. My sister and her husband slept in another bedroom but had my niece sleep in a crib below my bunk. One night I had this terrible nightmare that the copperhead snake had swam up to the boat that my niece and I were in. the snake jumped into the boat, grabbed my niece and went back into the water. I must have partly woken up, sat up on the edge of the bunk and looked down off my bunk and saw what I thought was my niece below me in the water with the copperhead laying across her body ready to bite her.

Guess what happened next?

A. I pulled the covers over my head and went back to sleep.

B. I cried for my mommy

C. I yelled for my brother-in-law to come and start shooting

D. I dove in the water to rescue my niece.

It was D. The only problem was that there was no water, and my niece was not in trouble. I landed on the railing of the crib and there was a loud crashing sound, my niece started screaming scared to death and I was yelling because I did not understand what was going on. Everyone came running in and wanted to know what happened. I remembered the dream with every detail, and the water looked so real. The snake I thought I saw was a robe belt from a bathrobe in her crib with part of it laying across her body. You would think I would have learned to not mess with snakes after hearing the Adam and Eve story. Things could have turned out badly for us, but this was another time that our guardian angel did his job, but I am sure he was pulling his angel hair out. Maybe he laid on top of the crib to break my landing.

My brother-in-law, Ken, brought out much of the love I have for the outdoors. He was a hunter, camper and fisherman plus just loved the outdoors himself. He had hiked some of South Mountain himself and was aware of some places Sam and I had been. He showed me around the Mt. Pocono plateau where my grandfather used to hunt. He took me on my first camping trip in the woods at Mt. Pocono and helped me learn how to shoot a rifle and bow and arrow.

YIKES......A RATTLE SNAKE IS IN THE CAR?

About fifty years after this event, another poisonous Timber Rattlesnake would cause me to flee, this time out of my car. I was driving along a country road in Pennsylvania and hit a rattlesnake crossing the road. I heard the snake hit the underside of the car and then the engine speed up and the car coasted and slowed down to a stop. When hit, the snake must have hit my transmission linkage, disconnected it and knocked it in neutral. I was coasting helplessly to a stop. I looked in the rear-view mirror but did not see the rattlesnake on the road. A terrible fear raced through my mind as I remembered a giant rust hole in the rear floor of my car. Could the snake have got caught on my linkage, crawled through the hole and now was somewhere in the car waiting to get its revenge on me.

As I coasted to a stop, I prayed that the snake was not in the car. The car finally came to a stop in front of a house, so I jumped out of the car and ran like a man without faith that my guardian angels' job was to protect me. I was so full of anxiety I just kept running around. I am sure my guardian angel was trying to get a paper bag over my head to help with my hyperventilation. He deserves hazard pay.

A woman came running out and asked why I was running around like a chicken with its head cut off. I explained what happened and eventually she called my wife to come get me. I came back later, towed the car home, let it set a couple days and carefully checked out the car before driving it again. I sprayed all the bug killer spays I could find in the car. I never did find out what happened to the snake. However, the following year, I hit a Rattle snake at the same location.

This time I saw the rattle snake was dead, so I took it home and had it mounted after getting a permit to keep it. It is hanging up in my basement today. Was it the same one? Will it come back to life someday and get me when I am sleeping? Just wondering?

YIKES....A SNAKE IN THE BOAT

There was yet another encounter with snakes. David and Tammy were out in a lake rowing a boat when a snake crawled across the floor of the boat. They did not know what kind it was, so they jumped out and swam to shore. I went and got the boat and we filled it full of water to see if it was under the seat. It was just starting to get dark and to our surprise a big black snake came out from under the seat and swam across the lake into the darkness. Sudden, we heard a whoosh like a giant reptile flying over us. Then a big splash and there was no more snake. I guess an eagle, owl, or hawk must have seen it and had it for dinner.

YIKES……. A RATTLE SNAKE IN OUR YARD

About 30 years after this event, my grandson Zac screamed, Grandpa there is a snake in the yard a couple feet from him. I saw it was about a 5-foot-long Eastern Timber Rattlesnake, all curled up and rattling. I called different phone numbers to have it removed safely, but with no luck. It soon crawled out of my yard, down the road, hopefully back to the forest. When it turned into my neighbor's yard, I tried to keep it on the road with a broom, but it insisted on going where it wanted. I did not want to kill it if I did not have to, so I prayed for protection as I tried to reroute this snake.

I am sure my guardian angel asked why me again? I then asked my neighbor to get a box to put it in and he called the PA Fish & Game Commission. After a few attempts, I used the wooden broom handle to pick it up and put it in the box and tape it shut.

About an hour or two later, a PA Game Commission Officer came, and we carried it on a hand truck and turned it loose way back in the woods. It seemed to be happy away from those crazy humans. As it crawled away, I saw how well God made it to blend in with leaves, twigs, and other vegetation. No wonder it is so hard to see them in the wild.

They do try to avoid humans. After my other life experiences, that was a piece of cake. I think the rattler put the word out that there is a Little Devil on Forest Dr that terrorizes and puts snakes in a box, so keep away. I have seen none since.

A rattlesnake on the previous page that was in our yard and me holding a nonpoisonous snake while in Jamaica. All snakes will be safe to handle after Jesus returns to the earth.

YIKES......BABIES PLAYING WITH COBRAS

Poisonous snakes are something to be aware of and not handled except by experienced snake handlers, "like myself", with proper equipment and training. It gives me great hope and encouragement as I look forward to the day that I read about in the Bible. After Jesus Christ, the son of God, that will be king over the earth returns to this earth to rule it, he will change the nature of animals and reptiles.

In Isaiah 11:8 NIV it says" The infant will play near the hole of the cobra, and the young child put his hand into the viper's nest." It will be a time when it will be safe to hike and not worry about poisonous snakes. People can camp out and not worry about a poisonous snake climbing in their sleeping bag, being under something you pick up or being in your boat, car, or yard. Some people read in the Bible that many plants were given to the animals to eat. They believe until sin entered, that animals did not kill and eat meat, just like it will be after Christ returns. Isa. 11:7. Interesting concept. I cannot wait.

Satan, the devil, took the form of a serpent to tempt Eve. When tempted, the best approach is to do like Sam, and I did and flee. Also like I did when I thought there was a snake in the car, or like David and Tammy did when they saw a snake in the boat and swam away. It would be time to flee, swim, jump or run as far away as possible to get away from temptation and sin.

Chapter 8: PRE-TEEN SURVIVALISTS

About this time in my Boy Scout training, I was learning to build fires, shelters and what I needed to camp in the wilderness. After our thrilling adventure with the cave, it was time to move on and see what else nature had in store for us. During our hikes, Sam and I were always ready to explore, look for an adventure or just see what was out there. Our idols were other great explorers like Lewis and Clark, Kit Carson, Daniel Boone, Davey Crockett, and Jim Bowie. We wanted to be like them, to hike deeper into the wilderness and escape civilization to just see what was out there.

We hiked off trail, making our own trails as we went; scouting the areas deeper in the woods and found this area on the side of a hill with two springs flowing out of the ground. Fresh water was hard to find since most of the springs were lower down the mountain. This was a real no-man's-land, real uncharted wilderness. Just think, perhaps no human had ever put foot in this area before us. It was real virgin land, just like the "Wild West". This was one of those beautiful spots you just feel at home, and all that hiking made us hungry. Sam built a fire, and I filled our canteens with cold, fresh spring mountain water. We cooked our hot dogs, toasted our buns, melted the cheese on the dog and then added the onions, ketchup and mustard my mother would not let us leave without.

As we feasted on wilderness food and relaxed, we talked about what a beautiful area it was to camp in. It seemed like such a perfect secluded spot, away from everything, so we both agreed to do it. During the next several weeks we went back to the same spot, cut down small trees and built a tree house to sleep in. We used rope to tie the cut trees to other standing trees just like the pioneers before nails. It ended up with no roof, no sides, but had a railing and a ladder that we would hide when we were not there. It was now late spring and there were leaves on the trees plus some Mountain Laurel all around, but it was mostly clear for about a hundred feet all around. Our parents wanted us to wait until we finished school and then they would let us go there to camp a few days.

WILDERNESS CAMPING: BUT WE'RE NOT ALONE OUT HERE

Summer finally came, school was finally out, and it was time to try wilderness camping on a Friday night and see how it would work out. Sam and I had everything prepared to go. Our wilderness survivalist supplies included 2 sleeping bags, flashlights, hot dogs, bread, ketchup, mustard, cheese, eggs, pancake mix, butter, syrup, milk, snacks, peanut butter sandwiches, marshmallows, candy bars, cookies, Kool aid mix and my Boy Scout cooking kit. The two of us hiked out into the wilderness to our secluded camping spot tree house and set everything up.

As we cooked a delicious meal and sat around the fire, a feeling like we were real pioneers in the middle of no-man's-land came over us. Knowing we were on our own, miles away from any signs of civilization, just gave such a proud feeling that we could do this. We thought we were extremely brave to do this. This must have been the feeling the earlier pioneers and explorers felt. Since the spring water was ice cold, we took whatever food that needed to be cold and put in the spring and then climbed up in the tree house to sleep. It turned pitch dark quickly and became rather scary once the fire went out and then the thoughts of wandering if this really had been a good idea. It was too dangerous now to walk out in the dark and too far in the woods to go back home now.

There were no cell phones yet, no pay phones out here to call for my mother to come pick us up. We were stuck here and would have to stick it out for the night. In the pitch dark of the night, we started hearing noises in the forest we had never heard before. What kind of wild beasts are out here in the wilderness, making those noises, we wondered? How could we sleep wondering if some horrific monster or a giant spider would eat us alive or catch us and eat us later? Were there wild Indians out there waiting for us to fall asleep and then come in and scalp us? Had we wondered into the Land of The Lost and we were hearing dinosaurs, brontosaurus or pterodactyl following the human scent. We had seen no animals or Indians out here when hiking, so what was going on now? It was hard to sleep with all these thoughts running through our minds.

We also found the tree house floor to be uncomfortable since the branches we made the floor out of were rough and had stubs sticking into our backs and legs. I am sure we got some sleep that night, but not much. During the night, Sam and I woke up terrified as we heard awful screeching, screaming noises coming from the spring, like something was fighting and being torn apart. The first thing that came to our minds was lions, tigers, and bears, oh no. Maybe some prehistoric monster was out there eating our food. We knew there were bears, raccoons, skunks, opossums, and all kinds of wild beasts roaming in the area eating whatever was available. This was real wilderness, and we would not get up to see what was out there. We were sure it was safe to be in our tree house? Can a bear climb a tree? The movies never showed this part of the early pioneers. Daniel Boone always looked rested after sleeping on the ground in the wilderness movies. He looked healthy and was not afraid of noises. That was a night we did a lot of praying. We survived. I am not sure if my guardian angel helped any because it scared us to death all night. Maybe he protected us from being eaten by wild animals without us knowing it.

When it was finally light, we got up and checked the spring to see what had been going on there. What we saw made Sam's eyes as big as golf balls and my tongue drop into the cold spring water. There in front of us was our food scattered all over the ground, destroyed, eaten and gone. It devastated Sam and I to see all our food had been ravaged, even our milk was gone. Maybe Big Foot was here and drank our milk. The only food left now was some crackers, pancake syrup and snacks we had up in the tree house and lots of spring water. Sam and I ate what we had remaining and wondered what we would eat the rest of the day. We looked for tee berries, sassafras root and birch bark but we were spoiled, we wanted strawberry pancakes and fully loaded hot dogs, peanut butter and marshmallow sandwiches, not birch bark and sassafras root from the wild land out here. Roots and bark are not very filling for mountain men.

A DISCOVERY WORSE THAN WILD INDIANS, BUFFALO HUNTERS OR NEWLY HATCHED DINOSAURS

Tired and discouraged, Sam and I laid down to rest and think. We wondered how all this happened. This is not how it was supposed to be. I never saw in the movies that all this could happen. We were rudely brought back to alertness with harsh sounds coming out of the woods. We heard all this screaming and yelling coming from the top of the hill.

What in the world was going on now in this God-forsaken wilderness? We wondered what else could go wrong. Is this The Land of The Lost? The noise reminded me of a tribe of wild Indians or maybe a new hatch of dinosaurs. If it was Indians, they were on the warpath, ready to attack us. If it were baby dinosaurs, they would be hungry. What type of holy terror was up there? Carefully and quietly we crept toward the horrifying screeching sounds. We climbed up the hill to see what was going on. We peeked through the bushes and were terrified at what we saw. This was the worst thing I had ever seen. Sam's eyes were as big as golf balls and my mouth fell open as my tongue fell on the ground into some stickers. Our empty stomachs growled. We fell to the ground in tears, beating the ground with our fists from what we saw. This was worse than awful.

Here is another question. What did we see as we peeked through the bushes?

A. A tribe of wild Indians on the warpath.

B. A group of buffalo hunters having a party

C. A bunch of baby dinosaurs, newly hatched

D. Something worse than A, B or C.

It was D. Surprised, sobbing, and disillusioned; we could not believe what we saw. There, only several hundred yards from our uncharted wilderness camping spot that took hours to hike to and years of exploring, were girls in uniforms unloading from a bus and running all around screaming for joy. We looked around and saw what appeared to be a Girl Scout camp. Our hearts sunk. Sam and I had never scouted out what things were on top of the hill we were on. We scouted everywhere else but there. How could we be so stupid?

I bet my guardian angel had a friendly laugh for a change. I bet he made a video and sent it to "Heaven's Funniest Videos Show". We never checked it out, but that means there also had to be a road to the camp. We hiked an entire day to get into what we thought was a wilderness, and here there was a road a few hundred yards away. My mother could have dropped us off there and picked us up there. The thought makes me sick and stupid at the same time. That is a good point to learn. When you think you know where you are in life, just a small amount of additional knowledge can change your entire perspective.

We were probably about eleven or twelve years old, at the age when boys notice girls differently. I say that because we stayed and watched for a while and seemed to enjoy it. Was this predicting the end of our wild adventures? Would we be like those cowboys that fell in love after saving the beautiful damsel and then rode off into the sunset to live on a ranch happily ever after forgetting about their cowboy friends? This would be one of our last adventures together. We had reached the end of the wilderness and ran smack into more civilization. With no more wildernesses to explore and we had done everything we could in the area so there was nothing remaining for us to do there anymore?

Sam and I watched the activities of the girl scouts until we got too hungry to continue. I am surprised Sam did not go into the camp and sweet talk the girls into giving us food while I scouted for roots. (That is another story) With no food, it forced us to pack up and head back home with our spirits dragging, rather disappointed with our first wilderness camping trip. Little devil tear drops dripped from Johnny Angel's eyes as we humbly left the area.

The photos below show the girl scout entrance as I went back 50 years later and the digging through our wilderness which is now I-78 and Rt 309.

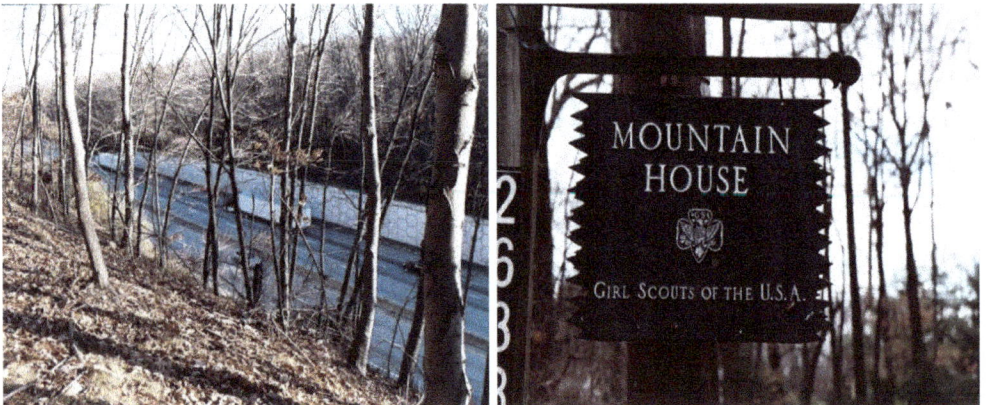

Chapter 9: HORMONES MORE POWERFUL THAN BLOOD

During the summer we often went back to the same spot to see what was going on at the Girl Scout Camp to check out the view. We took our Tony the Tiger or captain Midnight binoculars along with us, we may have gotten through the mail after saving cereal box tops Frosted Flakes or Ovaltine proofs of purchase. Things were changing; we used to hike to the top of high rocks to see the view of the Lehigh Valley, now we hiked up the mountain to see girls. I am sure it was Sam's idea to go see the girls more, since he was becoming a real chick magnet. I always hoped girls would remember me for my good looks, big muscles, and superior intellect, but it seems the girls remember Sam for that and remember me for being the tree climber and being a Little Devil. This will be the beginning of the end of our wilderness adventures together.

Later that summer, Sam went with us to our vacation to our summer cabin, we met a girl named Marta on the other side of the lake. She liked to watch us swim, fish, dive, act crazy and jump out of boats screaming when the Copperhead chased us, plus she had a friendly smile, a cute giggle and when she shook her head, her hair just flipped and flowed perfectly. She played it smart and seemed to like both of us, so that was fair and worked out well. Then one night she came over to our cabin and played cards with our family. When it drizzled, she asked Sam to take her home in the rowboat. I watched them row off as the rain came down. Being a gentleman, he then gave her an umbrella. Then the unthinkable happened. She moved aside of him and she covered both with the umbrella. I

did not understand why he allowed that and did not throw her overboard. My blood boiled as I wondered what they were doing under that umbrella since she was one of those city slickers from NYC. Can you imagine Sam allowing his hormones to take over and coming between blood brothers?

A few years later I went by the cabin and saw Marta outside, so I stopped to say hi. She did not remember me even after I hinted around that I was the guy with the white skintight swimming suit which showed off my tan. I told her I was the one who rowed and paddled around the lake with bulging   muscles she may have noticed, but she still did not remember me. As I reminisced, she remembered seeing two crazy boys dive out of the boat and swim across the lake when the copperhead chased us. She laughed as she remembered the events, but not my name, other than referring to me as "Snakeman". Then shockingly, she asked "how is Sam"? What did she say, I thought angrily?

What do you think happened then?

A. I said sarcastically, he is well

B.   My Little Devil wanted to punch her in her disrespectful mouth.

C.   I may have my guardian angel say in my ear, she is not the one that will notice you. Suck it up.

D. I pushed her in the lake and stomped away angrily.

It was C. If I had climbed trees with her, she would have remembered me. I wonder if a guardian angel has the power to dampen an ego, to keep us humble.

Later that summer we went to another cabin along a creek. Sam and I were having a good time doing all the fun things on the water until it happened. Another test of blood vs. hormones. Two girls showed up. They just watched us but did not seem interested in joining in on the fun since the water was cold. There was an above-ground pool at the cabin, and they were interested in sitting in the warm pool water with us. The chick magnet, Sam, asked them to come in the pool. The sitting turned into splashing and flirting and some talking, but I noticed something quite different about Sam and me. This was just the beginning of us starting to mature and putting other things in front of our shared adventures. There was a new adventure entering our lives, GIRLS. Now, we would really need a guardian angel for protection from the dangers that awaited us.

The following year, we planned to go hiking up to the Girl Scout Camp but were prevented from continuing our journey by a giant hole in the mountain that giant earth moving equipment had cut into the mountain during the winter. This equipment was tearing apart our hiking trails and our wilderness. It would become I-78 and Route 309 through the South Mountain. Even today as I drive along I-78 through the South Mountain, I look for the canyon where the cave is and wonder if it is still accessible and wonder if there are any signs of our tree house remaining. I drove up to the Girl Scout Camp which is still there and looked down the hill where we camped at. There are houses all around now. They do not know the genuine history of the area and survivalist kids that explored and tamed the area.

I do not really recall any other experiences with Sam after this, just some visits. Since it was obvious, we were maturing, it may have been the summer during junior high school when Sam moved to Lancaster, probably when we were about twelve or thirteen years old. We would, about age 16, get together again for an adventure.

About 50 years after all these things took place, I went back to our wilderness camping spot and the Girl Scout Camp to see if it was still there and take some photos. To my surprise there was a tree with Sam's name on it. Why would someone write Sam's name on a tree unless he became a legend at the Girl Scout Camp? Were they mesmerized by his good looks, big muscles, and superior intellect? He is my idol. The force of being a chick magnet is strong in him. I saw a sign with John written on it but it led me to toilet. Is there a message there for me?

A NEW ADVENTURE WITH GOD AT CHURCH CAMP

When I was about 10 or 11, I went to a church camp in the mountains with log cabins, hiking trails, a lake with all typed of slides, swings and jumping towers to help enjoy swimming. It was my kind of adventure. I really enjoyed the outdoors and rustic living. There was no running water in the cabins, so you had to walk to the bathhouses. We had a campfire every night, singing songs, telling jokes, and listening to a Bible story.

We did nighttime hikes where I got to show my bravery as the girls grabbed my arms for security. We hiked to a field that had an exceptional view of the sky with billions of stars showing. We saw the Milky Way, which was the outer band of stars in our galaxy. We were told that many of those further stars were galaxies like our own. As of present, it is estimated that there are 100 billion galaxies out there, thanks to the Hubble telescope. With new technology, it is estimated that the number will grow to 200 billion galaxies. Some estimate it at 2 trillion.

Now that is a lot of planets, suns, and stars. I cannot comprehend it. I just imagined all that territory out there, just waiting to be discovered, and explored. How long would explorers be gone? What an incredible creation it is. I wondered what the purpose of all this was. Later in life I would read about Christians being God's children and joint heirs with Jesus who inherited everything. Did that mean that someday I may have a planet of my own, how about my own galaxy?

I hope my human greed is not coming out. What an incredible destiny that is. I just felt so close to God that week and believed what I heard.

I already knew there was a God and had heard about Jesus, so one night at a campfire, I wanted to dedicate my life to God. When I got back to my church, the pastor said I was too young to make that decision, plus I was baptized at birth.

Rather discouraged, I just continued to get to know the God that answered prayers and made such a beautiful earth. My entire life, I would meditate and ponder that wonderful destiny and the purpose of this earth and the universe. I was so impressed with the chapel in the woods that later I would build my own.

AT WORSHIP IN CHAPEL-IN-THE-WOODS. GRETNA GLEN. MT. GRETNA. PENNA.

Chapter 10: THE MOST DANGEROUS ADVENTURE - GIRLS - NOW I REALLY NEED A GUARDIAN ANGEL

About age fourteen, I became interested in a girl in my Sunday school class, or maybe I should say she was interested in me and she seemed to be always around me. I think she enjoyed, I hoped, my good looks, big muscles, and superior intellect. When she was around me, I felt adrenaline flowing through my body just like I felt when climbing a cliff or being on a speeding locomotive.

One time she sat aside of me in church and grabbed my hand and then held it on her lap during the rest of the service. I had held a girl's hands during skating and when they were scared, but I never held a girl's hand to just enjoy the touch. It was a unique feeling. It felt soft and warm and I seemed to like it, but I was so nervous, I just kept sweating during the whole church service. Holding hands made me feel like we were special friends and there was a connection between us. Our parents must have noticed what we were doing and said it did not look good for us to be sitting so close in church.

The next week an older friend of mine volunteered to sit in between us and since we were sitting on old wooden pews, we could hold hands behind him. Anytime we were together in church she would want to hold my hand, hold my arm or just be close to me. Since we were holding hands, she said we were going steady and I should get her a ring to show other girls I was not available. Did that mean she knew of other girls who noticed my good looks, big muscles, and superior intellect. We exchanged rings, and we went steady, which meant we held hands at church or any other time we were together. This was going to be a new adventure. The teens normally sat by themselves in a corner in the back of the church during services. I could see my mother behind the organ peeking out to see who I was sitting with and if I were behaving. I had to be careful while in church because anything that was fun was a sin.

SINNING IN THE BACK SEAT AFTER CHURCH-THE DEVIL MADE ME DO IT

There were girls in my neighborhood, but they always seemed to be content to play football, baseball or go hiking, climb trees or swing on a rope in my backyard. None of them ever tried to hold my hand. The churches in Allentown had a combined youth roller skating party every month that we all went to. Normally my steady girl got a ride with another parent and my dad would take me. On one occasion I rode with an older boy from church who drove a 1955 Ford. My steady girl had no ride home, so we offered to take her. On the way home, we were in the back seat and the heater in his old Ford was not working very well. She said she was cold, so she grabbed my hand and moved my arm around her shoulder to keep her warm. This was another new feeling that I enjoyed.

This would be my first adventure of having so much physical contact with a girl. I felt like such a hero, keeping her warm and all, but I should have known to never be in a back seat with a girl if there is room in the front. She had moved awfully close to me and said she was still cold, so we covered up with a blanket was on the floor. She said she was still cold, so she pulled the blanket over our heads. I will have to admit when I was winter camping with the Boy Scouts and got cold, I went inside the sleeping bag and was much warmer once all covered up. She kept moving closer and pulling me closer to her. It felt good to be warm, but I felt uncomfortable, maybe because I did not feel in control. I was giving into my new feelings, hormones and emotions. Then she put her hands on my face and pulled it facing her and then kissed me on the lips. I pulled back and felt like I was going to throw up, gag and spit all at the same time. I had this funny feeling that I was in trouble, like lost in a dark cave, trapped on a speeding locomotive or panicking on a cliff, not knowing what to do and should pray for rescue, but I did not.

I was hoping my guardian angel was on a break. She asked what was wrong, and I said nothing. She asked if that was my first kiss and honest John said yes. She said that she really liked me and would like to kiss me more. Giving in, I let her teach me how to kiss all the way to her house. I felt guilty because I thought it was a sin, but I kind of enjoyed it. She was a Christian girl the same age as me, and I wondered how she became such a good kisser. I remembered what my mother said about kissing a girl was a sin and. would make her pregnant. I knew I was now a big sinner and she would become pregnant and I would be a father soon but at least I liked holding hands and kissing her. Maybe I could like being a father since holding hands and kissing were fun.

Through the years, I have seen many couples get married because they enjoyed the physical contacts and the feelings they got from that contact, even though they knew truly little about each other. Getting married for those reasons seems to end in divorce. Also, at that age, in the '50s, I would have to say I did not know any divorced people. I knew none that had a baby before marriage and never heard of an abortion. If there was any, it was really kept quiet. Later in life I would learn the correct way of dating, but not from this Christian girl.

DO STORKS DELIVER BABIES?

 The next week at church I avoided her because I felt so guilty and ashamed. She finally tracked me down and asked what was wrong, and I explained my fears of her becoming pregnant. Her sweet voice reassured me it was not a sin. She told me with a little laugh that she would not get pregnant from our kissing and that she had heard that babies come only to married couples. The couple must want a baby, the wife goes to a hospital, and a stork brings the baby. That kind of made sense to me since I heard of couples, once married, the wife went to a hospital and came home with a baby. I saw cartoons and heard about storks bringing babies to married couples while they were in the hospital. Maybe I did not sin after all, but why was I told that?

Just think about all the anxiety that was caused by that false thinking. The only thing I knew about relationships with girls was it did not look good to sit with them at church, and kissing a girl was a sin. After hearing that, I was relieved, and I took kissing off the sin list. I could not blame her for wanting to kiss me because finally someone appreciated my good looks, big muscles and superior intellect and she even remembered my name. Wow was that good for my ego, plus Sam had nothing to do with it. As time continued, she always wanted to hold my hand, kiss when we could and always be with me. On the occasions that we were alone it seemed she wanted to get more physical, but I did not feel comfortable plus did not understand what she wanted to do. It did not seem fittin' nor proper, as my southern wife would say. She kept texting me, calling my cell phone, kept tweeting me and sending messages on Facebook. I think she was stalking me. (Just kidding, not invented then, but I was thinking what teens do today) I felt tied down, so I backed off and shortly after that asked for my ring back. I had a strange feeling about our relationship which is hard to explain but was like being in a tree on a skinny branch ready to break or with an unsure grip or footing and the scary feeling I would fall and get hurt. It may have felt like swinging across some rocks on a skinny vine, and I had the feeling it was going to break, and I would come crashing down.

I was rather naïve since the subject was a rather hush-hush thing around my family and probably in society in the fifties and early sixties before the sexual revolution. I am not sure if there was a winner in that sex revolution. Back then I think the church and society just were not teaching any sex education and tried to keep the topic hushed up. That was wrong to do and had terrible results, but today the total opposite is being taught. There is sex education everywhere but still is not the correct way to do it. There has been a lot of talk about who should pay for contraceptives and abortions. Supposedly there is now even a problem with elementary age children being sexually active plus boys kissing boys and girls kissing girls in school. There are many abortions from unwanted or unexpected pregnancies.

The lack of sexual knowledge of the '50s did not work well at all, and the abundance of sexual knowledge today is not working well either. I believe since abortion was legalized in 1973, there have been millions of abortions. I think there is even more anxiety caused by today's teachings. If there was only an instruction book with a balance of sexual knowledge, we could use. There is, I found the Bible to be an instruction book for God's creation and it even has a troubleshooting guide and examples of what happens if we are not maintained correctly.

As a side note and looking back now, in a way my mother was right about kissing. The act of a kiss does not make a baby, but it can be a step in that direction. As I have seen nature work through the years and how beautiful God's creation is and how much pleasure it can bring if you follow the rules. I have found marriage to a rewarding, exceptional experience that God allows us to have. The lifetime adventure of getting to know someone more deeply than any other human being on earth and exploring what makes them tick. It first begins with an emotional attachment as a person reveals their innermost thoughts and then progresses to physical contact like holding their hand, a hug and then a kiss.

As I found out, physical contact too soon leads to special feelings for the person even though there may be no intentions of marriage or love. To save as many of these emotional and physical contact connections until marriage cannot help but make marriage more of an adventure and leave imaginations and expectations wide open for this new union of marriage. After 52 plus years of marriage, I am still amazed at what I learn about this wonderful woman I married. Somewhere out there is the correct teaching of sex and marriage but unfortunately not always found in our three educational sources and that is the family, the churches, and the schools. I believe the Bible has the truth but sometime is overshadowed by Hollywood, actors, and singers. We are like animals with instinct but are born with a blank slate and must be taught. Instead of teaching the correct way to get a desired behavior, many use fears, or an incorrect way to get the desired behavior.

I thought Santa Claus and God had something in common. People used both as a way of getting a certain behavior they wanted. If you did what your parents said, you got gifts from Santa, but if you were bad, you got a bucket of coal or nothing at all. The only thing that was confusing was that I always got what I wanted from Santa, regardless of how I behaved. I thought God and sin were the same way. I wondered if sin was something people made up just to get a certain behavior from others. Was I going to get to Heaven regardless of how I behaved since I was baptized as a baby? I believed I was, and even other adults felt the same way.

When I finally found out where babies came from, probably about age 16, I was disgusted that people would do such an act. I could not believe that my parents did that and my sister who had recently married and had a baby girl. I guess that was strange for a boy in high school to not know these things, but it was the early '60s. Everything about anything sexual was hush-hush. I was sick on the only day of sex education class in high school and knew nothing, so as I heard other boys talking about it, I did some research in an encyclopedia and educated myself. I think I was more of a Johnny Angel around girls, but there may have been times when a Little Devil showed up.

AMERICAN BANDSTAND AND DANCING WITH A BROOM

 My older sister used to watch American Bandstand, which I thought was stupid until I hit my teen years. I really enjoyed couple skating with girls and then in high school we had dance lessons in gym class, and I enjoyed dancing as well. Suddenly, I started to enjoy watching Bandstand; it helped me learn how to dance with a girl. As I picked out the most popular dancer and watched his technique and practiced it dancing with a broom.

Fifty years later, I still dance the same technique and my wife loves it, (I hope) thanks to American Bandstand and Dick Clark. We had dance lessons in gym class and I then had to dance with girls. Sometimes, the boys and girls lined up, and we had to dance with whoever they assigned. I was not cool, not very tall, my muscles were under my gym uniform and I had no chance to display my superior intellect, so the pretty taller girls gave me dirty looks. When we had to ask a girl, I was kind of bashful, shy, not very sociable and out of my wilderness surroundings, so I was hesitant about going up and asking a girl to dance. I tried to be a Johnny Angel and asked girls to dance that no one else wanted to dance with. I did not want to appear ignorant about dancing with a girl, so I practiced at home with a broom. The only difference in dancing at school and Bandstand was at school they played big band music and bandstand, they played Rock-and-roll music.

Another thing I also enjoyed was listening to and going to dances with rock-and-roll music of the '50s. Nothing like going to a dance wearing tight jeans, a t-shirt with rolled-up sleeves with my hair all greased up with a crew cut or wave in a car blasting rock-and-roll on the AM radio. There was a place called the Ritz in Allentown where all the teens hung out. It was so cool to drive through the lot with that AM radio blasting away on those cheap speakers. I waited for the girls in their poodle skirts to come running over to me, but they never did. I think my guardian angel may have put a screen over my greasy crew cut, my nice white T-shirt with rolled-up sleeves, my tan arm hanging out the window and my cool car with loud mufflers.

The screen made me look square, ugly, skinny, and boring. Hopefully, he used a screen or maybe I was that way. No one noticed my good looks, big muscles, and superior intellect then. It could have been my guardian angel protecting me from something not good for me, like a big ego or seeking worldly attention, by putting a veil around me. I should thank him.

I never became a person with a cool line that I could walk up to a stranger and start talking. Almost all my dates were introduced to me by someone else, or I knew them from church. I had no problem being aggressive and self-confident in nature, but not around people.

Chapter 11: MISCHIEVOUS BOY BECOMES A TROUBLE MAKING TEEN

 Like most teenagers in the '50s and '60s, I enjoyed rock-and-roll music and dancing. While at a dance one day, I thought it would be a good idea to share my love of dancing with the teens at church. I thought it would be cool to have a dance for the youth at our church since I thought our youth group was boring and it was time to have some fun in our huge basement meeting room. The next Sunday evening at the youth meeting, I asked the pastor's wife, who was the youth teacher, if we could bring in a boom box, iPod, cell phone or a laptop with iTunes on it and some big deep bass woofer speakers with a 1000 watt amplifier, some strobe lights and then play some rock-and-roll music to dance to one Saturday or Sunday evening. (Oops, all those devices did not exist yet. I would have had to bring a record player and the 45rpm records needed to dance to or maybe use a reel-to-reel tape recorder I recorded from the AM radio.)

When I asked the minister's wife, she turned pale, her eyes rolled back, she grabbed her heart, stepped back with a terrified look on her face looking like she was going to die right in front of me. Then after regaining her composure she got this shocked, disgusted, angry look on her face and immediately stuck her finger at my nose and asked me why I did not know that dancing was a sin and how I, the organist son, could ask that to be done in the house of God. I am thinking even my guardian angel fell backwards and fainted when he heard the answer. That was a shocker. No one ever told me that. How was I supposed to know that God did not like dancing? Dancing seemed like good, clean fun and through my adventures, I thought God created this earth and everything in it for us to enjoy.

I continued to dance but never again brought up any ideas that would be fun for the church to do. I just figured that anything that was fun was a sin and that to be a Christian meant giving up fun, which was everything I liked. I had to also "assume" that Elvis was a sinner and especially his dance moves. Those dance moves were nothing a Christian should look at and especially would never do. It appeared anything fun was a sin, and it appeared also that I was a sinner and unfortunately seemed to enjoy it. I wondered where all these ridiculous ideas like no dancing, no playing cards, no movies, no alcohol in your house, no kissing girls, no sitting in church with girls and not acting up in God's house came from. No one ever told me why these things were wrong. How about other traditions, were they what God required or what God liked? After that moment, I knew I would have to have my fun outside the church. I think I was becoming bitter.

I would continue to attend but just to meet girls. Sam would have been proud of me since I was becoming a real chick magnet. The only problem was that my chick magnet skills were turned opposite and instead of attracting girls, I was repelling girls like two north poles of a magnet repel each other.

Although, church picnics were fun when we played all kinds of family games like three-legged races, wheel barrow races and throwing water balloons (which was hard to fill since there was only a hand water pump at the church picnic grounds and a pit toilet as well). Those old "sticks in the mud", "funny-duddies", dressed in black suits, people at church had fun and were fun to be around. (But only once a year at the picnics) At church it was always don't run, don't talk, don't smile, don't be seen and don't interrupt but at the picnics, it was run, yell, scream, play and have fun.

I thought Christianity was dull and boring. At the time, I only could judge Christianity by my mother's church. Our pastor was always dressed in black as well as many men in church. There were groups of religious people in PA that lived not too far from us and they were living an austere, strict, primitive way of life, drove black cars, painted their bumpers black, some of them drove horse and buggies and they believed that was what God expected. Since the Bible said to not be part of the world, anything the world did, they did the opposite. The message seemed to be that anyone that gives up all the pleasures of was on their way to Heaven.

As I got older, I would have to say, unfortunately, that there was nothing that would make me excited about being a Christian except for a few people I had met at camp that set a good example. I was happy to thank God and Jesus for all they had created and for what little I understood about Jesus and he died for me. I did not feel a need to talk a certain way, act a certain way or give up anything without a good reason. I saw myself as a Christian and on the way to Heaven since they baptized me as a baby, and I was attending a Christian church.

I recently was talking with a man from a church in the denomination I grew up in. I commented that the church has changed a lot since I was a kid. He said he did not really see any changes. Maybe it was me that had changed. Now that is something to think about. Until God calls us, opens our minds, we want to accept God's way, allow God to change us after God gives us His Holy Spirit, we are hostile to what God says, His people and His church.

In my teen-age years, some would have thought I had become a real big sinner. It must have also been a real big sin when I went to see the movie "The Ten Commandments" since movies were a sin. I also enjoyed playing card games like Rook, Rummy and Canasta with my family. Another big sin. I remember my parents having a serious discussion about whether to see The Ten Commandments. Sam's parents would not allow him to see it with us. Sam's dad was a preacher.

Back then, there was a real shortage of true Bible knowledge of sin and how to live this life and face the real temptations that I would encounter. It just appeared as though the church and society were both influenced by the same ideas and traditions. Where did they come from? Was it the Bible? Later in life, while doing research, I found out where they came from.

As parents, we tried to explain why or why not our kids should do or not do what we believed the Bible taught. Like any other parent, we had limited knowledge, we can only teach what we know. That is what my parents did. Wanting to be a good parent, I will search for true answers and find it difficult.

THE 15-YEAR-OLD LITTLE DEVIL DRIVES

At age 15, my parents would allow me to start the family car for them and when they were not looking, I would back it up and pull it forward. I usually went along with my mother to Wednesday night Bible Study. It was boring and there was nothing for the teens to do so I would walk around Allentown for an hour. The family car was a 56' Chevy Impala, 2 door hardtop convertible, they called it, just like the photo but with original wheels.

Then I started sitting in the car and listen to rock-and-roll music and would occasionally move the car back and forth in the parking lot. To satisfy my hunger for adventure, I would drive the car around the parking lot and re-park it before my mother came out. There was another older teen boy with a license that helped me drive. He suggested we take a spin around the block so once I felt confident in driving it was time to adventure into the streets. This soon led to driving all over Allentown streets and coming back before Bible Study was over and hopefully finding the same parking spot. During my illegal driving, I was never stopped nor had an accident. Did my guardian angel protect me even when I was doing something wrong?

Once I turned 16, I went for my driver's license shortly after receiving my permit. I passed the test during the first attempt. That made me happy to drive legally. Then the trooper asked how I learned to drive so good so fast, so I said I practiced in our church parking lot. That seemed to satisfy him, but he looked as though he had doubt about possibly releasing a Holy Terror on the public streets.

WHAT A STUD? NOT ME AND NOT SAM

When I turned sixteen, I soon got bored with driving the family car and started looking for a car of my own. My parents wanted me to save and buy a good reliable car. That just is not what a sixteen-year-old did in 1960. I was in auto mechanics class and a friend told me about a 1937 Studebaker 4-door sedan his neighbor had for sale. Another classmate went with me to look at it. He was my neighbor that had moved into the house across the street from us, where I used to play in the foundation hole.

We loved it and bought it together. It would cost $30, so it was $15 each. We drove it home after freeing up the tires that were frozen to the ground. We eventually called it "the Stud". We got the title transferred, bought a license plate, and started checking around for insurance that would be available for two 16 years old boys. With much searching, we found a company that would sell us insurance. It was a black color which was the only color available in 1937. It was covered with rust and was a four-door sedan. It looked like something the federal agent, Elliott Ness, drove in the "Untouchables" TV series.

My parents asked who's old ugly car was in front of our house and I said it was Andy's car. They wanted him to move it in front of his house across the street because it looked bad in front of ours. We moved it over there, and his mother asked who's old ugly car that was, and he said it was mine. She wanted me to move it over to my side of the road. We kept moving it back and forth to hide the truth, that it was both of ours.

We finally sanded it and used a vacuum cleaner blow attachment to paint it, a dull black color in Andy's garage. A few runs on it, but at least it looked better. Andy's mother was not happy because the paint fumes went into the house through the kitchen vent fan.

We had a lot of fun with that car during our high school days. We stood on the running boards, pretending we were federal agents getting ready to bust a distillery, but most people thought we were more like the "Keystone Cops".

That was one tough car. During the high school years, I dated a girl named Sylvia who enjoyed having fun like me. She usually rode with me as we rode the car on dirt roads and on mountain trails.

We would drive it through wooded areas knocking down trees as we went, just like a tank. We put lights under the running boards and lights under the hood, plus a straight pipe instead of a muffler.

Under the back seat on the floor, it had a cover above the rear axle. We entered a parade in Allentown and planned to drive the Stud. (I believe a Saint Patrick's Day). My neighbor, Andy, took a date, and I took Sylvia along. When we got to the parade, we realized we forgot decorations, so the girls went out and quietly took a few decorations from the other cars that were parked there waiting for the parade to start. During the parade, we would pull the choke out which made it run terrible and put out heavy black smoke trying to make it look like a clown car.

Then to make it interesting, we would pour water out the hole in the floor, which made it look like we were leaking gasoline. To top it off, we then would flood it with the key off and turn the key back on, which made it backfire and send flames shooting out the tailpipe. People screamed and panicked, thinking there would be an explosion. As we went by the judge's stand, we did it again and the judges, ready to run, seemed to say, get that car and those Little Devils out of here before they kill us all. We all had a lot of fun and about two weeks later, I got a check in the mail, which was prize money for having the best clown car.

Sylvia enjoyed doing many of the things I liked, and we had similar beliefs, other than she was Catholic. We had a lot of fun together, became good friends and got to know each other very well but never got physically intimate other than the good-night kiss. She was a wonderful influence and helped keep me out of trouble. That fact allowed us to stay friends even when we met again about 30 years later. We were able to get together and introduce our mates with no guilt or shame.

When I met her, the first thing she said was I remember the "Stud" and how much fun we had. What a compliment, to remember me as a Stud. But then she went on to say the old Studebaker and when we went in the parade. She remarked about the times hiking and cooking out. What is it about me that no one remembers my good looks, my muscles, my superior intellect, just trees and cars? I do not even remember if I had good looks, muscles, and superior intellect; I just remember having good clean fun. Although, few people remember my devilish, mischievous moments.

I wish I still had the Stud. It would be worth a lot of money now. One thing about having an older car, like the 1937 Studebaker, was that parts were not easily accessible. Fuel pumps, water pumps, generators, transmissions, suspension, and everything else was repaired, not replaced. When something broke down, you took it apart and repaired it or replaced parts in it from a junkyard or new if you could find it. This led us to going to machine shops to have kingpins manufactured, junk yards to get parts or try to match up parts to make it work.

I mentioned before about driving by the Ritz at the Allentown Fairgrounds to show off our cars and there would be other teens there checking out the cars plus the other teens. But I do not recall teens just hanging out all day with nothing to do like you see today. It seems we were always busy trying to get our cars to go faster or just keep them running.

Probably because of my desire to understand how something works helped me to diagnose problems. That skill allowed me to be an asset in Vietnam to keep forklifts and generators running to provide lights for security. I spent much of my time around the Danang Air Base and smaller bases in Chu Lai. Occasionally I would be flown by helicopter out to a remote outpost to repair a generator or other piece of equipment. One time we disassembled a forklift small enough to load on a C-123 aircraft and landed in a remote jungle area and then reassembled it again. In Vietnam, if the lights were on, I was Pvt. Johnny Angel, number one Marine with good looks, big muscles, and superior intellect. If the lights went out, it was like everyone went insane and threatened to send me to where the devil is if I did not repair it quickly.

Even when I returned to the States, I was assigned an Engineer Battalion and made a mobile mechanic. My job would be to repair various types of heavy equipment that could not be easily moved to a shop around the base at Camp Lejeune, NC. This gave me an excellent opportunity to explore the rivers, swamps and forests of the base. I was lucky to mot be shot by a sniper in training, blown up in an artillery range or minefield, eaten by an alligator or bitten by the many poisonous snakes in the swamps.

I FOUGHT THE LAW AND THE LAW WON

One sign that I continued to be a Little Devil, was that I got into several scrapes with the law. After Sam moved out of town I kind of hung out with some other guys that maybe were not the best for me. Sam was like a guardian angel in the flesh to help me with my genuine passion of loving nature and keep me out of trouble. Although I would often take a date hiking or out for a picnic, I was not really seeking outdoor adventures anymore. To keep gas in my car for cruising around with the guys, we would count our pennies and buy a gallon of gas for $.12 or pull up to a closed gas station and let the drops still in the hose run into a gas can. A gallon would last an evening. Then one day someone suggested we siphon some gas out of parked vehicles, so we started siphoning just enough for an evening. One night the cops saw us and chased us, catching one guy as we ran off. The boy never gave our names, but the cops told the boy to tell us to voluntarily turn ourselves in and it would easier on us. No one else was going to do it, but I thought it was the right thing to do since we were busted. I and a few boys went up to the Whitehall Police and turned ourselves in. It was the Christian thing to do. They would not tell our parents if we paid for the gas and other parts missing, even though we stole no parts. Every week I had to report in and turn in some money until paid off.

You would think being caught would have taught me a lesson, but a few months later I was caught stealing car parts from a junkyard and taken to the Allentown Police station. My parents were called and had to come pick me up. That was a terrible thing to happen to any parent. I was afraid that the newspaper would publish a photo of me in a striped uniform and say Johnny Angel is the Devil in disguise, now in prison splitting rocks on the chain gang. (Mentioning striped uniforms, splitting rocks and chains, you know that had to be a long time ago. I saw that on the three stooges.)

Through the years I should have received a good spanking for what I was doing but never did, I would run away from my dad and hide. Unfortunately, I would remain a Little Devil, sneaky and mischievous. I was not protected from these incidents, so whether my guardian angel or God himself backed off, sometimes we are held accountable. Unfortunately, I did not think it was a big deal to have my parents called to jail. I did not like the idea that I hurt my parents. I got a taste of how my parents felt when my own kids got into trouble. Eve wanted to have the knowledge of what that fruit tasted like, try things on her own and not have anyone tell her what to do, and so did Adam. All of us are doing the same thing now, and we must pay the penalty for that knowledge.

My parents put pressure on me to seek other friends, and I think the Johnny Angel side agreed. This group of classmates were the same people that introduced me to beer, made fun of me because I missed the sex class and did not have a clue what they were talking about when they told vulgar jokes or belittled what God made wonderful between a man and a woman. My wife and I are glad I did not.

After this, I bought a 54 Ford and fixed it up for drag racing and then a 57 Ford convertible that I also did some modifications to. I continued to date Sylvia and did not get into any more trouble. Sylvia, like Sam enjoyed outside activities, had morals, wanting to do what was right and kept me out of trouble so I would not get too polluted to be of value to the one God chose to be my lifetime companion. The people we choose to be our companions or friends sure can make a difference in our lives and future. Although I wanted to be part of some group, I realized I could not be because I was developing a relationship with God and the two were not compatible. I would just have to hang in there until I found out where I belonged.

Chapter 12 ADVENTURES WITH ANGRY MAMA BEARS

I went camping several times with my sister and her husband at Promised Land State Park. He showed me a place where the Park took the garbage and dumped it in the woods. He took me there just before dark and we hid behind trees and watched as black bears came out of the woods to go through the garbage and eat what they could. We went up almost every night to watch them come out and eat. Some nights we would go there, and the bears would be out all ready, and then they would run off when they saw us. It was quite an experience to watch these large animals roam around and sometimes fight over food. I thought to myself, I must bring Sam up here and show him these bears. I was sure he would consider it quite an experience. Maybe we could even get some photos or make an 8mm movie.

AHHHHH..CUTE CUDDLY BEAR CUBS

Sam and I must have been at least sixteen years old since we were driving, and I had a car. He was living in Lancaster PA now, but we still had some contact with each other and occasionally got together for some adventures. Early in the summer, Sam and I wanted to get together and go camping. We went up to Promised Land State Park for a week. The only campsite we could get was amongst the Pines at the bottom of a hill, so we pitched our tent and like a good Boy Scout made a mattress out of Pine Needles. We laid our sleeping bags on the Pine Needle bed and it felt so soft.

I wanted to show Sam the bears, so we jumped in the Stud and took off into the woods to the trash dump. We hid behind some trees and waited for the bears, hoping they were still there and would come out. It did not take long to see the first bears coming out, but this time they were two small cubs that came out first and then the bigger bears followed. Wow, this was quite an experience; we had never seen cubs in the wild before. They looked so cuddly and cute, just like a stuffed animal bear. Hoping to see the bears this trip, I had brought my dad's 8mm movie camera along to make a movie of camping, but seeing the cubs made it so much better. I wanted to film the bears, but I knew it was too dark with all the branches, trees, and Mt. Laurel around. Plus, we were a little too far away. I needed to be a lot closer. We went back to the campsite, enjoyed a nice big roaring campfire, and then went to bed.

That night there was a thunderstorm with heavy rain. Water flowing down the hill and into our tent abruptly awakened us. There were already several inches of water in the tent and rising. Everything was soaked, including us, so we slept in the car. In the morning we hung our sleeping bags and clothes up to dry. I guess because we had a low campsite or a leaky tent; we appeared to be the only campers wet. Maybe it was because everyone else had modern-20th century air mattress or cots. We were the only true frontiersmen there.

During the afternoon, a couple girls drove into the campsite across from us. They appeared to be college age girls and seemed to giggle at our wet sleeping bags and clothes hanging up. They seemed to whisper to each other as they looked at us, and we wondered why. Then we realized what the giggle was about. It was not my good looks, muscles, or intellect but the fact that our sleeping bags had dried but still had a wet spot in the middle. They probably thought us young high school boys probably wet our beds that night without our mommies there to take care of us. Realizing how it looked, we quickly took them down and hid them.

We wondered how we could meet the girls since we were getting off to a poor start. We would impress them with our ability to break up wood with our bare hands and show of our wilderness skills of fire building. We figured girls could never start a fire so cold and hungry, they would come running to our big roaring fire and beg to come sit with us. We knew we would draw them to our good-looking muscular bodies, and they would eventually know our superior intellect.

We decided that I would drive off in my hot old car, figuring they would just melt wanting to come meet such hot guys. I would go get some rotten wood we could break apart by hand, then bring it back in my chick magnet car, show off our muscles as we broke it up with our bare hands. Sam agreed to stay behind to clean up the campsite, get some food ready and start a fire with the wood we already had.

When I drove back with the wood, that two-timing chick magnet Sam was over at the girl's campsite with a roaring fire going. Those cheaters used store-bought wood, newspaper, and charcoal lighter. They almost had a meal cooked and Sam said they invited us over to eat. So much for showing off our wilderness skills. We had a good meal with them and was soon time to go see the bears. Sam seemed to always know what to say to girls to befriend them. He seemed to enjoy hanging out with girls just as much as I enjoyed going on adventures. (For the sake of his wife, I am sure this was before he met her).

The girls were afraid of bears, so did not want to go. Sam, the chick magnet, thought roasting marshmallows with girls was more important than filming bears, so I went by myself. He thought he may get in the way if he went. Yea, right? I went up about an hour before sunset so I could get into a nice close position and make a good movie. I went into the middle of the garbage, so I could get a movie of the bears as they went through the garbage. I hid behind a tree planning on filming the bears and especially the cubs as they came out and went in the garbage. After waiting about forty-five minutes, my plan worked perfectly. Soon the cubs came out of the woods but this time they were a little closer to me than I planned. I started filming them as they played and ate things off the ground. They were only five to ten feet away, and I just kept perfectly still other than filming.

The smell of the garbage probably hid my scent, so they did not recognize I was there. (Some would say that camping garbage and I have the same wild scent, but I ignore them) I enjoyed archery hunting for deer, so I knew how important it was to be still and move slowly. It was amazing how close deer would get if I moved slowly and hid my scent. I figured when after filming, I would just jump out, yell, chase the bears off and then walk out. I kept filming as they were kind of playing around and chasing each other. It was great to be that close.

As I was filming, I heard some noise off to the side and kind of glanced over to see a huge black bear walking through and smelling the garbage, which I assume was the mama. I saw there were other bears coming out of the woods as well. When they got closer, I saw how big they were, how sharp their teeth looked and how long their claws were and were not as cuddly as the cubs, I wandered if this was a good idea. (Why do I always wonder that during my adventures instead of before? My mother would have said, "Johnny, that is not a good idea" but I never listened anyway).

Although it was getting scary being that close, I wanted to get all the bears on film just like those wildlife photographers on TV. I got the bear cubs first on film. I slowly turned around and filmed the other bears, but they heard the clicking of the camera and when I moved, one bear saw me and grunted. The others looked up at me and when they realized I had violated their space; they took off running into the woods. However, the mother bear did not run off, probably because I was between her and her cubs. She started grunting, swaying her body and then hitting the garbage with her paw. I knew this was not a good sign so I just kind of froze in fear and did not move. This was not the time to try to scare her off.

The bear then stood up and tore the bark off a tree next to it. I now saw that this stubby, fat bear was taller than I expected and with its claws in full sight was more vicious than I thought, and it was extremely terrifying. My heart was pumping so fast I thought it would explode. My adrenaline was rushing through my body getting ready to fight or run. My other body functions were preparing for flight or fight as they released excess weight. I knew this mama bear was not happy with me being there by her actions. This was another praying time and my guardian angel ready to run for the hills, probably said, "Not again", as he popped a nitro-glycerin tablet to prevent a heart attack.

Here is one of those questions again. What happened next?

A. I stood tall, growled like a male bear to chase her away, but she came to me, saw my good looks, big muscles, licked me and took me to her den for a mate.

B. The cubs ran up to me and licked me like I was garbage

C. Goldilocks showed up and sweet-talked the bear into eating some porridge as I escaped.

D. I pretended to be a bear cub and crawled up to her with the cubs, eating garbage.

E. Sam showed up with the girls and they made up a cheer, 2 bits, 6 bits, 8 bits, a dollar who wants the bear to eat Johnny, stand up and holler.

F. None of the above

It was F. When the mama bear stood up; the cubs ran past me back to their mama. The mama appeared to look right into my eyes as if to say, I would love to tear the skin off your body and tan your hide. There is chatter in the forest about a Little Devil crazy kid, and that must be you. Never do that again and then slowly walked back into the woods. I thanked God and went humbly back to the campsite to tell about my experience. They saved a few marshmallows for me. The next couple of days, we hung out with the girls, going swimming, hiking and we all went up to the trash pile at night to see the bears but with no luck. I do not think this group was as quiet as just Sam and me.

The photos below remind me of the nightmares I had about that moment. Even mounted bears seem to be after me and my grandkids for my shenanigans.

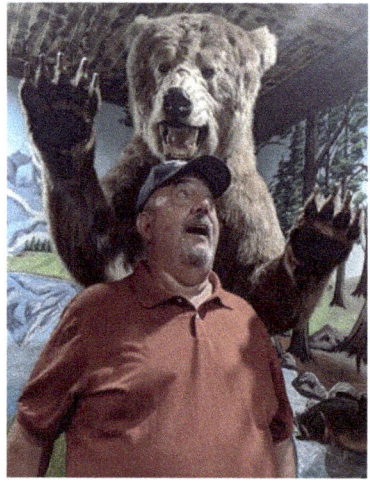

Bears swim in our lake and dare me to kayak. They swim into my yard, they turn over my trash cans and spread garbage all over the yard as if they are daring me to come out to join then in the garbage and make a movie of them. I imagine they are chasing me when I ride my bike wanting to eat a meal on wheels.

The last night of our camping trip I wanted to go see the bears once again, but I think Sam was busy with the girls and I am not sure if he went along or if I went by myself. I thought he went along, but he does not remember what happened so maybe this was one of my mono-mono devilish-stunts. When I got to the dump, the bears were already out and there were more than I had ever seen. I wanted to get this over with quickly, so I yelled and ran toward the bears.

The bears scattered all over the place, running in every direction. One ran down onto the dirt road I was on, stopped and looked at me. I yelled again and ran toward it thinking if he became aggressive and ran toward me, I would just turn around and out run that big old fat bear back to the car. Well, the bear took off running away from me rather slowly and I soon caught up to it within feet of it and thought maybe I would kick him in his butt. I yelled one more time. He turned his head around and when he saw that I was so close he kicked in the afterburner and it was gone out of sight in no time. I stood there in awe amazement at the speed of that enormous animal. My tongue fell to the ground on some wild strawberries, so I scooped them up with my tongue to quench my fear.

I just stood there thinking I was going to die of stupidity. I was ignorant to the fact that they could run so fast. I did not recall the Boy Scouts teaching me how fast bears could run. I thought about all those nights chasing bears and being close, thinking I could outrun a bear. From then on, I had more respect for all bears and never went back to the dump again. I recently heard that a bear could run 30 mph. I still wonder how I survived all these years doing the things I did. I learned lessons, but fortunately never paid the ultimate price. Once again, I think my guardian angel called the heavenly 911 for a flaming chariot ambulance pick up, using the code for an "angel down" because of a stress attack.

Of all the adventures in the wild, I have come across rattlesnakes, copperheads, and black bears, big bucks in the rut, bobcats, an alligator, sting rays and shark in NC and have found these wild creatures usually want to stay away from humans as much as possible unless cornered, bothered or have their young with them.

Another time, my wife and I plus my daughter and her husband were hiking a trail when we saw a mother bear and two cubs along the trail. We stopped and gave them some time to get out of there. We continued when suddenly, the two cubs ran across the trail right in front of us. We froze as we realized we were between the cubs and the mother bear. We stood there not moving and hoped the mother bear would cross in peace, which she did, and everything was fine. Only occasionally have I ever heard of a black bear getting aggressive. Usually they can be scared off with a yell or appearing bigger than they are. It is still best to avoid them when at all possible.

After this trip, Sam and I felt like seasoned campers and wanted to try another wilderness camping trip. Through the years of hiking, camping, bike riding and cross-country skiing we have had more trouble with loose dog attacks than bears.

A BARE MAMA CHASES A MAMA BEAR

Many years later, after marriage, we were staying at a cabin at World's End State Park. I had to go back home, and Diane had just gone inside the cabin after taking a shower at the shower house. She started to cook breakfast when suddenly, she heard a banging at the door. As she turned, she was startled to see a gigantic bear staring at her towel wrapped body. The bear probably smelled some of that delicious breakfast. The bear was now intruding into Diane's space so she would protect her children to the death.

What happened next?

A.   Showing no fear, she scared it off by yelling at it and threatening it with pots and pans.

B.   She cooked some porridge for it.

C.   She threw some food out the window and the bear left.

D.   She called Sam to come sweet talk it.

It was A. Because now Diane was the angry mama and protecting her young. The bear thought more of its life than it did of food, so it ran off.

PAWS AND CLAWS

Another time we were at Promised Land State Park at a cabin and a bear came strutting through the cabin area. Parents and children gathered to see it and take photos. A child ran toward it and threw a kickball at it. The bear struck the kickball with its paw and claws, causing an instant deflation of the ball. Everyone just slowly backed away from the bear. We followed it into the woods where it stood up against a tree and ripped the bark right off it like it was putting up a No Trespassing sign. We all obeyed. Ripping off bark must be a universal sign of do not follow or do anything stupid.

Most of the information I have read about Black Bears is that they try to avoid humans unless attracted by people feeding them. When we go wilderness camping, we try to be sure no food is in our tent. Any food we have is hung in a tree away from our tent. I have heard that Black Bears do not attack humans. Grizzly, Brown, and Polar bears are a different story. Again, in the Bible bears are mentioned after Jesus Christ returns to be king of the earth. In Isaiah 11:7, it says "The cow will feed with the bear, their young will lie down together, and the lion will eat straw like the ox." The nature of animals will be changed, they will be safe, and it appears they will no longer be meat eaters. That is an interesting concept and gives me something to think about when I am out kayaking or sitting on top of a mountain. The Bible says in Gen. 1:30 that animals were not meat eaters at creation but became that way after sin.

CHAPTER 13: WILDERNESS CAMPING AND GETTING LOST

Sam, another boy, and I got together during a summer school break and go on a 3-day wilderness camping trip and live off the land. We planned to catch fish, eat wild plants and berries, and drink lots of mountain spring water. My mother said she would pack a few extra snacks for us because we could not find watermelon, hot dogs, peanut butter and marshmallow sandwiches, cheese, rolls, onions, ketchup, mustard, pancake mix, butter and syrup in the wild so we carried a large cooler on our wilderness survival trip.

We camped at Mt. Pocono, PA, where my brother-in-law had taken me hunting and had taken me wilderness camping when I was younger. There was a mountain stream full of native trout and a deep area to swim and fish in. There were remains of a log cabin close by with apple trees and blueberry bushes. Everything else was thick woods with no one else around for many miles. While hunting, we walked all day and never saw a road or a house. The stream eventually flowed down into a deep canyon called "The Devil's Hole". (I should feel right at home there) There were other streams flowing down into the canyon and made beautiful multi-level waterfalls.

It was a beautiful area to camp and enjoy. I would, years later, take my wife there to camp on our honeymoon and again several times after that until the area got built up in the 1970s.

We parked our car on a dirt road and started hiking the several miles to the camping spot. For the most part we followed a dirt road to a boundary trail that was marked with white paint to the creek and then follow the creek to the fishing holes and a suitable spot for camping. On the way there, the handle on the cooler, that had my mother's snacks in, broke. It was too awkward and heavy to carry with all our wilderness camping equipment, so we agreed to leave it there and come back for it later. Sounded like a plan. We hid it and marked the spot.

When we finally got to what looked like a great camping spot, we unpacked and set up camp. We planned to find firewood, pick some fresh berries, and do a little fishing before dark. Sam volunteered to go back and get the cooler while the other boy and I would get the camp ready. He said he remembered the way back, so I reviewed with him what to look for to find the trail again. He would follow the stream to the trail with the white marks on the trees and follow the trail to the cooler and return the same way. He nodded and walked out of sight.

I went and picked some blueberries and some green apples, gathered some wood and prepared the campsite. I figured it should take about an hour to get there and back. When the hour had passed, I got concerned. Since it would be dark in a few hours, maybe I should go looking for him. I grabbed a flashlight and ran off into the woods toward the trail. Since I had hunted there, I was familiar with the area, so I took a shortcut to the trail. When I reached the trail, I called out to him, but with no answer. I ran up the trail toward the point where we had left the cooler. When I got there, the cooler was still there. Now I worried since he had never arrived there. Did he miss the trail and keep walking up the creek? Did he turn the wrong way on the trail and go deeper in the wilderness? Did a bear chase or attack him? Did a rattle snake bite him and was laying somewhere in pain, not able to walk? I grabbed the cooler and head back down the trail, calling out to him as I went along. I figured if I did not find him by dark, I would go get help. I rushed down the trail calling out "Sam, Sam" but with no response. I hiked back to the camp and there was still no sign of Sam. This was the worst moment of my life, not knowing but imaging all the bad things that could have happened. (It prepared me for being a father of teenagers) I think I had tears in my eyes as I cried out to God to protect him and to help me find him.

After all the things we had been through, hopefully this was not the end. I tried to imagine what he would do and how he would handle himself. We had been through a lot together and I knew what he would do. I figured if he missed the trail as he walked along the creek, he would eventually come to a swamp and recognize he went too far and return down the creek. The creek would lead him back to the campsite. We both knew that rivers or creeks always lead to people, and you always have water to drink along the way. If he had gotten off the trail or was just wandering around, it could be hopeless. I knew he was not familiar enough with the area to use the sun to know which way to go. Other areas we hiked in always had a road within an hour of whichever direction we went. Here, there was only one direction that would take you to a road. Any other direction would just go deeper into the woods and all around the Pocono plateau.

After being friends for eleven years, I knew how he would behave. If he missed the trail, he would walk up and down the creek until he found it or head back to the campsite.

I walked up the creek calling his name and looking for signs he had been there. I continued up the creek past the trail looking for him and yelling out but with no luck. Eventually there were No Trespassing signs, and I knew he would not go beyond that point, so I knew he was not beyond that point. I was getting so worried and discouraged; I did not know what else to do. It was getting dark, and I thought it would be best to go back to the car to get help. I wandered what was going through his mind as he was probably wondering around lost, scared and hopeless. We had been through a lot of dangerous and questionable situations but always seem to get out of them OK. It just seemed like there was someone or something out there looking out after us, despite all the stupid things we had done. I may kid around a lot about guardian angels using my imagination about what they do, and I know we are told in the Bible that we should pray directly to God the Father in Jesus' name, not to angels. I know it is God who answers prayers, so I always give Him credit. Looking back on my life at an older age, I really see God as a very patient, loving God with a sense of humor who allows us to decide and experience the results, but steps in if it gets to a point that does not fit into His plan for us. Through these adventures, Sam and I were building a bond, but I was also developing a relationship with the One who had created everything that we were enjoying.

Here is another question: What happened next?

A. I had to call the police, rescue squads, and National Guard to find Sam.

B. Some Amazon women found and adopted Sam.

C. Sam used his chick magnet skills, found some girls camping, and they made him a meal.

D. I found Sam at the local Girl Scout Camp.

E. Marta was out hiking and found Sam, so they sat under an umbrella until I found them.

F. None of the above

It was F. After praying for my best friend and blood brother, something came over me. The fears evaporated, and I had hope and peace. I just had a feeling he was fine, and I would find him somehow. I had renewed energy; I called out again and again. Then I thought I heard something. I yelled again and yes; it was Sam answering. It was distant and hard to tell which direction it came from, but I kept calling out until I knew which direction it came from. Then, I saw him, he was, alive and well, no bite or claw marks from bears, no snake bites, no lipstick stains from Amazon women, no broken bones, not holding any Girl Scout cookies and no signs of Marta and her umbrella. He was well, why would I doubt? I did not know whether to kiss him or punch him. Turns out he missed the trail, then eventually found it, like I figured he would, but then could not find the cooler, because I had taken it all ready. He ended up back at the car, so he headed back to the trail and just kept looking for the cooler. He did want to go back without the cooler, so he just kept looking. Maybe we were close when I went back or maybe I missed him when I took the shortcut or maybe I made it hard on him when I picked up the cooler. Anyway, he was not really lost; he knew how to get back to the car if needed. At least, that is what he told me. I am not sure that either of us would admit we were ever scared or especially lost, because we were the modern-day mountain men, pioneers, explorers, and frontiersmen. They never got lost. (In the movies, at least)

We gave thanks to God for being reunited with no injuries and our fears being unfounded. The rest of our wilderness camping trip went on as planned. We caught some beautiful colored native trout, went swimming, slid down some rapids into pools of water, hiked and ate some excellent food. While fishing some young fawns walked up to the creek and that was a beautiful sight to see but we knew there could be a protective mama or a jealous buck with sharp antlers around so we let the fawns see us so they would run off.

This may have been the summer we graduated, and I would soon go into the Marine Corps and Sam would join the Navy. We originally planned to go in the Coast Guard together, but plans changed when the Marine recruiter walked into school with his dress blues on. I figured that uniform would make me a chick magnet like Sam and beautiful women around the world would be impressed. I never became a chick magnet like Sam, and the world of impressed women was in Vietnam. I probably was never satisfied who I thought I was. I always wanted to be someone else or be accepted as part of a group. I thought dress blues were the answer, but they were not. I believe God put that desire in us to seek Him and want to be like Him and feel like we are pleasing to Him. Jesus made it possible for us to be part of His family and have that security that he loves us.

Chapter 14: BEER ALTERS MY THINKING AND LIFE

My parents always said that drinking beer and any alcohol was a sin. I heard them talk about people in church that were sinners because they had seen them with beer in their refrigerator. It confused me since I saw a bottle of wine in my parent's refrigerator, although it seemed to last forever. One time I tasted it and it burned my mouth, so I left it alone. At Christmas and Thanksgiving, we had this special sauce that would-be put on mincemeat pie that gave it a kick. They allowed me a spoon full. When my parents were not looking, I would add more, and I noticed it made me kind of happy and giggly. Eventually I found out it was whiskey in an unmarked bottle.

After turning sixteen, some high school friends invited me to a New Year's Eve party. My parents tried to tell me about the friends I made but, as usual, I did not listen. They wanted me to have church friends, but one of these church friends made me sin by kissing me. Then there was the Christian boy from church that drove the car and suggested we sit in the back seat, and it was his idea for me to drive my mother's car at church. Just a few months before this party an assistant counselor from our church camp, two years older than me, that counselled me and helped me with my Christian life asked me to stop over at her house to talk. When I got there, she wanted me to take her for a ride in my 1937 Studebaker and she moved close to me. I felt kind of awkward since she was my mentor. It turns out; she wanted to do more than talk.

She wanted to kiss and get more intimate, but I was rather naïve and did not feel it was right, so I ran out and went home. Through the years I have heard people going into various jobs to meet or abuse children or teens. Could she have been one of them or what? At that point I was not impressed with church friends, plus I was not strong enough to stand firm on what I believed if I even knew what I believed. From that point on, I gave up on trying to be a Christian. Christianity was something you did on Sunday and then did whatever you wanted during the week. I knew there

116

was a God, but I did not understand why more people that claimed there was a God acted like there was no God.

There would come a day after God changed my life through Jesus Christ that I would stand so firmly in my beliefs that they would fire me from 6 jobs in 10 years' time for my beliefs. One such case was when I refused to forge another person's name to some warranty papers to make the company more money. They let me go the next week. Being unable to find another job, I ended up cutting grass and raking leaves for a living, which began what my wife calls the tribulation years. She wrote a book about those years called "A Family's Journey Through Prayer". In the book, she describes many a healing and miracles of providing our needs when we were in need.

Back to the New Year's Eve party. At this party there were snacks and sodas served, but then a parent brought out some beer. I was only 16, not legal to drink, but I eventually tried one and it tasted good. I eventually drank two or three beers and I found myself and others were more fun after a few beers. I saw it gave me the courage to say and do things that I normally would not do if that was possible after all I had done. It also made me feel like one of the guys. I had the confidence in myself in the outdoors and survival but did not possess the social confidence to be one of the guys or to be social with others. Beer seemed to help me accomplish that, and I felt like I was part of the group. This would be the beginning of enjoying alcohol and the effects of it to help me (what I thought at the time) enjoy life. From here on out, I would seek parties or places where beer was. When the party was over, I was able to drive home without killing myself or others somehow, although it was hard to focus and concentrate. I quietly crept into the house and went to bed so my parents would not see me stumbling around. As I lay on the bed, I saw the entire room was spinning and I felt kind of seasick, but I fell asleep anyway. If someone only could have told me ahead of time what Proverbs 23:33 says about drinking: "Your eyes will see strange sights and your mind will imagine confusing things. You will be like one sleeping on the high seas, lying on top of the rigging."

I woke up during the night and felt like I was on the high seas, lying on top of the rigging. I felt nauseous. Since my bedroom was on the second floor, with no bathroom upstairs, I opened the window and got sick out the window. The next day I was outside and looked up and saw my beer, plus all the other food I had eaten that night, had frozen on the outside of the wall all the way to the ground. That was difficult to explain to my parents and neighbors. I did not care for getting sick, but I had fun at the party and again found it hard to believe that all these things were sinful when they seemed to be so much fun. That is the hard part to teach our children that sin can be fun but has awful consequences, either immediately or eventually. As a Christian parent, we also must separate what is an actual sin and what they pass down as sin. Shortly after that a boy at the party who was part Russian introduced me to Vodka which his family had in the basement by the case. He carried a bottle in his car and we often had a drink. As a teenager I was finding a whole new exciting world out there and I could not think of any reason, whether from my parents or church, not to explore it. I looked at my parents and church people as being out of touch with this younger rock-and-roll generation. I did not have any legitimate reasons to avoid these new thrills. I would just have to determine what behavior was right and wrong myself, but I still saw no problem thinking myself as a Christian and acting the part when I was at church or around church groups. I did not have to make any testimonies or confessions. I just had to dress up and attend church to be part of the church group.

I have found out that there are no shortcuts to happiness or self-esteem. It takes preparation, hard work and working together and is a lifetime battle. Any mind-altering substances just hide the problem and sometimes destroy future attempts at happiness and do a number on self-esteem.

GOD HEARS A YOUNG FARM GIRL'S PRAYERS IN NC

About the time I turned sixteen and made some wrong decisions in my life, including choosing wrong friends. There was a young twelve-year-old farm girl in North Carolina, lying in a field, praying for her prince charming to come and take her away. She had dreamed of seeing what was beyond the farm and having adventures like she had read and dreamed about.

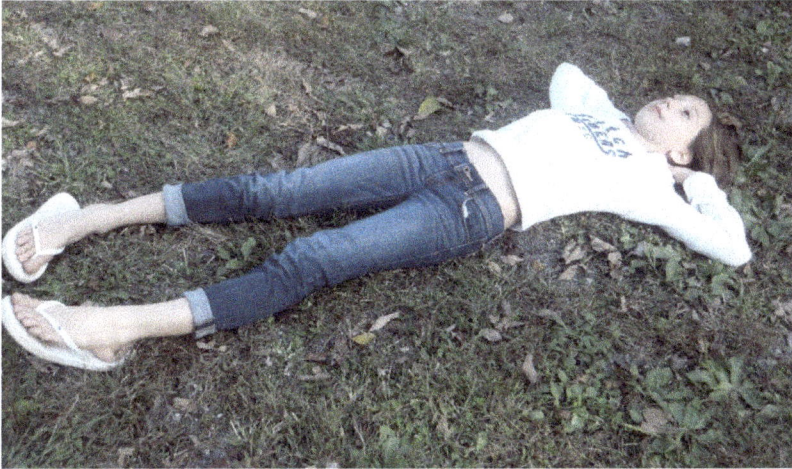

I believe these prayers had an influence on my life because eventually I would have to account for and pay the penalty of my poor decisions. I would also get to know more about this God I believed created all the things I enjoyed so much. I would finally come to establish a Christian belief system. Once God would set the scene, Prince Charming and Cinderella would meet, get married, ride away in their carriage to their castle and live happily ever after as they shared adventures together and with others.

I would like to recognize other prayers for me, like my mother, grandmother, my aunt, sister, cousins, and many others. I am sure there were others who knew what was going on in my life but still considered me a Johnny Angel.

Chapter 15: USMC YEARS: JOHN WAYNE OR GOMER PYLE

Sam and I had talked about joining the Coast Guard together after high school, but somehow, I ended up in the Marines and he joined the Navy. I think it happened when the Marine Corps recruiter came to the school and I pictured myself traveling the world with many adventures and how good looking I would be in those dress blues, how my muscles would stand out and with that dignified look everyone would know I had superior intellect. It turned out that Marines were not issued the dress blues but had to buy them and after buying them, I only wore them for a couple dates, to church and for our wedding.

Since I did not have a car the first year in the Marines, a Marine friend and I would often hitch hike from Camp Lejeune, NC to Allentown, PA or occasionally to Washington DC. That was a real adventure, having to depend on other people to give us a ride for a distance and then start over walking and thumbing again. We found that if we carried a bag that said USMC that we stood a better chance of being picked up. We dreamed of being picked up by two beautiful young girls that would give us a ride anyplace we wanted to go and reward us for our service to our country, but that never happened. We needed a chick magnet like Sam to get us girls or else enough money to buy chick magnet dress blues.

Most people that picked us up were vets that understood our circumstances. During pre-Vietnam War days, it was a lot easier to hitch hike and get a ride safely. Occasionally a trucker would pick us up and give us a long ride. Once we were thumbing on I-95 and a state trooper stopped and said it was illegal to hitch hike on I-95. He told us to get in the back seat and we were sure we were going to jail. Instead of jail, he drove us to the end of his territory but dropped us off on Rt. 301 instead of I-95. We had to do most of our hitch hiking on Rt. 301. I-95 was not complete and only had short stretches that were open.

Occasionally we would get dropped off in center city Philadelphia. We were usually unsuccessful hitch hiking in the city, so we would walk through downtown Philadelphia during the night to a road, like route 309, that eventually would lead to Allentown. In 1964-65, it was safe to walk downtown streets of Philadelphia at 2am.

When we went to Washington DC, we would normally sleep on the grass at the Washington Monument or any other park we could find. (Later, after marriage, I would stop at the Washington Monument on the way to PA or NC to nap there while the kids ran around.)

In Washington, we could find free meals at various places for vets. A church group normally operated them. We would have to sit through a brief presentation on salvation before the meal, like a high-pressure time share presentation. I do not think high pressuring someone to win them to Jesus is the correct way. It was probably a quota to get numbers of servicemen saved, regardless of what they really believed. I felt the same pressure later in life when I was helping pass out church pamphlets on the street. I was told I was not handing out enough and needed to be more assertive. Instead of asking people if they wanted a pamphlet, I put one in their hand. I handed out boxes of pamphlets and the church was happy with me.

When leaving, we found many of the pamphlets in the trash can. That way just did not seem right. I usually reject something that is forced on me. Back to the food. The sooner we would admit that we had Christ in our hearts, the sooner we could eat. Since they baptized me as a baby and accepted Christ's sacrifice at camp, I thought I was a Christian, was saved and had Jesus in my heart, but I was not living in any way a Christian life. I knew there was a God, and I prayed for protection while hitch hiking but did not understand what living a Christian life was. Once admitting I was a Christian and prayed with the people, I could eat. Not very Biblical. After my negative experiences with so called Christians, this added to it.

After a year of various training, I was on my way to Vietnam on a ship. On the way there we stopped at Hawaii for three days. I thought this would be an excellent opportunity to try surfing the rolling waves of Waikiki

Beach. I noticed immediately how clear the water was, even at four or five feet deep, and how far the waves would roll in. I rented a surfboard and off I went. How hard can it be? I could ride waves laying, sitting and kneeling but every time I stood up, I would fall off. Many native Hawaiian children were flying right past me and making it look so easy. I eventually tired of being humiliated and went back to the beach and just did some swimming.

That night I had a few too many drinks and stumbled into a Hawaiian policeman. I guess I became a little obnoxious again, and he took me behind a building and using his wooden baton began teaching me a lesson in respect, the Hawaiian way. Not even the Marines did that at boot camp. I never was disrespectful to a policeman again. I guess I needed that.

We also stopped at Japan for an overnight stay. I went out to the town wherever we were and had a few drinks and then returned to the ship, not impressed with Japan. After leaving Japan on our way to Vietnam, we went through a typhoon. Now that was frightening. Once again, I found myself hanging on for dear life. At the worst of the storm, we could not go above deck to see anything, but since there were civilians aboard, I had guard duty to be sure no civilians ventured outside. I was stationed by a door leading out on the deck, and it was very frightening to look outside. I did not understand that waves could be so big, and a ship look so small in them.

As the ship came out of the water at the top of a wave and crashed to the bottom of the wave, crashing and sinking into the water as we did with water washing over the entire ship. When the ship turned to go down the wave, the propellers came out of the water making swishing noises and vibrated the entire ship until they were back in the water. I realized we were seconds away from being at the bottom of the sea. I was reminded of those enormous waves many years later as I watched the movie "The Perfect Storm". There are some substantial forces at work in Nature. Not all nature is fun and exciting. There are many beautiful things about creation, but we are still under a curse from sin. Being in such a severe storm made all of us seasick including my guardian angel I am sure.

Thinking about such a vast ocean that it takes 30 days to cross it on a ship and the depths of it that if we were to sink, we would never be found. That reminds me of when I became a true Christian and my sins were forgiven and were like at the bottom of a deep, deep sea, never to be found or heard of again. Sometimes it is hard to not go scuba diving or deep-sea fishing to find them again. It is hard to believe that I would go looking for my past sins but I do. The devil makes me do it or my own sinful human nature. I am sorry to report at age 74 plus, I am not a perfect person yet. My wife said she knew it. We have to wait until we are changed to spirit.

We also made a stop at Okinawa but only allowed off the ship one half day, so it was a quick sightseeing tour and back to the ship.

Finally, we arrived at Danang harbor in Vietnam after thirty days at sea. They assigned me to a unit right outside of Danang where the mountains began. It was a unit that unloaded ships, distributed supplies, and did some construction work. They trained me in auto mechanics in high school and the Marines trained me as a heavy equipment and diesel engine mechanic, which meant I would work on forklifts, bulldozers, cranes, and generators.

In fifth grade, I took trumpet lessons and played in the school band. I then played in the junior high school orchestra and band and in high school marching band. We used to play during the football game half time and do shows with precision turns. Sometimes, just for a laugh, I would turn the wrong way and act like I goofed and then quickly turn around and join in again. People in the stadium just asked themselves, who is that devil of a kid that messed up the band routine? I probably caused my band director to have a stress attack. I also played with a string band that performed in parades like the Mummers, walking down the street with plumes of feathers attached to me. I also played bugle calls at Boy Scout camp and had a merit badge for knowing all the bugle calls.

While at the Marine Corps boot camp, I auditioned for music ability and had qualified to play the trumpet in the Marine Corps Band but I turned it down to become a heavy equipment and diesel engine mechanic. I liked mechanics more than music. When my gung-ho commanding officer checked my records and saw I played the trumpet, he made me his personal driver and told me I was to play the bugle calls: reveille, mess call and taps. My primary job would be a mechanic but would play the bugle calls at the required times and be on call if he needed a driver. I wanted to be in the jungle fighting the enemy, not a bugler. I thought maybe I could roam the jungle and become a sniper or be scout out the unknown territory.

Instead, I got a gung-ho CO (commanding officer) who liked to hear live bugle calls. Once I played the bugle calls, it caused every dog from the nearby villages to run in our compound and attack me. I guess the noise hurt their ears. Eventually, I had to have an armed guard to accompany me. The Marines in this unit would not remember me for my good looks, big muscles nor superior intellect, but the boogie-woogie bugle boy that disturbed their sleep with bugle calls and howling dogs. I think they may have used a few other vulgar adjectives for me as well. The photo below is my dad and I in my high school marching band uniform and me playing bugle in Vietnam.

During the day, I had an interesting job of driving the officers around or running errands for them. Driving the Colonel's jeep gave me permission to go places I could never go on my own. I would sometimes have to take papers, supplies or other people out to other outposts deeper in the jungle. This was my chance to explore the jungle roads and see what was out there. It was like riding my motorcycle in Japan and seeing the sights. Except in Japan, I did not need a loaded rifle by my side. In Japan, I did not hear helicopters overhead, nor artillery, explosions and rifle fire around. In Japan, I saw no Marines marching down the dirt roads loaded with gear, nor tanks and trucks forcing me off the road.

I still had a curiosity to find out where various roads went and was intrigued to see how the Vietnamese live. It was embarrassing to write home and tell my friends I was a bugler and not running through the jungles like John Wayne winning the war. At least driving a jeep through the jungles was a little more thrilling. Driving a jeep on muddy, pothole filled roads reminded me of driving the Stud through the PA dirt roads and woods. It also gave me a chance to stop at a local village or go into Danang to buy an ice-cold drink like a bottled coke. At our compound we got our water out of large water bags which were often heated from the hot temperatures and not very refreshing. Occasionally we got a cool flavored water drink at a meal to go along with our food, which was usually warmed up canned vegetables. Later it became dangerous to buy bottled sodas because the Viet Cong would put bits of glass and poison in them.

Sometimes, after talking to other Marines in the outposts and the action they had seen, I would feel like I was not using the combat training the Marine Corps had given me. Occasionally requests would come in for volunteers to go on search and destroy missions to rid an area of Viet Cong and North Vietnamese soldiers. I always volunteered to get out and see more action but was always turned down because the CO said I was too valuable to him. He said there was a shortage of heavy equipment mechanics and it also cost the Marine Corps too much money to train me. Besides, he needed someone to blow the bugle. Looking back, I can give thanks for being protected from the major battles and fighting that took place in Vietnam, especially later in the war.

One day after being in Vietnam about nine months out of a thirteen-month tour, my CO called me in and said he was being transferred. He also asked if I was still interested in getting more involved in the war since he had received a request for volunteers to join an infantry unit to go live in a Vietnamese village. This meant I would live out in the jungles in a village, working with the local Vietnamese soldiers to protect and defend their village. He said if I wanted to live in a village, he could guarantee the assignment, but I would have to extend my tour of duty by three months. I agreed and extended my tour in Vietnam three more months to have the opportunity be in this Combined Action Company (CAC). Later would become CAP and CAF.

LIVING IN A VIETNAMESE VILLAGE

I packed my belongings and off I went to a village along the Danang River. It was a different way of life for me, although one I had no trouble adapting to. The village people lived in a one or two-room hut and slept mostly on a mat on the ground. They worked in the fields all day and maybe had one water buffalo to help do the work. Their existence was much like the simple life of the early American settlers and those that settled the frontier. It amazed me as I watched their ingenuity. I could just imagine that was the way they did things in the wild west.

There was one squad of twelve Marines with a corporal in charge plus a Navy Corpsman. There was also a squad of twelve South Vietnamese troops. We lived in tents on a wood platform, ate C rations, had water delivered to us in a tank and used a homemade shower much like a camping shower with a barrel on a platform. Many years later, as I looked at the photos, I saw it was an Agent Orange barrel someone had got us. I was eventually diagnosed with exposure to Agent Orange. It was one of those things that no one told us how to recognize the markings. I knew they sprayed defoliant but had no idea what it was or that is was dangerous. We probably traded the Vietnamese for it since they salvaged much of our trash from the dump and made items to sell back to us. I found the country of Vietnam to be beautiful and the village people friendly, at least around 1965-66. The people had been at war for many years and just wanted to live their lives in peace. Much like the people in the USA. We just want to work and provide for our families with as little government control as possible.

We ran regular patrols around their village with the Vietnamese soldiers to be sure everything was safe. We were basically an early defense for the Danang Airfield to be sure no enemy was sneaking in mortars or troops. During the day, I watched the people working in their rice paddies or working in their villages. During a day patrol, the villagers would often invite us in for some hot soup, share some fish or other seafood. The food came in handy since we only received a delivery of C-rations once a month and sometimes ran out early. I learned how to speak Vietnamese and learned some of their customs, which made my experience more enjoyable. The area around the village was often used to shoot mortars at the Danang Air Base so we always were on the lookout for signs of Viet Cong infiltrating the area, especially at night. Fortunately, none of the patrols I was on had any problems, other than watching for various traps that awaited us. We depended on the local soldiers to tell us where the traps were since they saw or heard about them first. They attacked our compound several times at night, which was always scary. When we went on patrols at night, it created a lot of anxiety since we would move along trails or through jungle with no light. Often, we hiked out along the trail or road, then spread out and sat for several hours and just looked for any movement of the enemy.

There were a lot of creepy things that would crawl all over us, so it was not very pleasant to be out there and even harder to be still and try to stay quiet. There were many poisonous snakes crawling around, so we just hoped they did not crawl over us. Although, all those camping trips when I was young prepared me for strange things and sounds, I heard at night. The Vietnamese soldiers knew what to look for as far as boobie traps go, so they warned us where not to go or step. It was a frightening realization that there were people out there that meant to cause us pain, suffering or death. I think that is why veterans have trouble when they returned to the USA. In a combat zone, your adrenalin is flowing all the time trying to spot a danger ahead of time, prepared to hit the ground if attacked suddenly, being suspicious of everyone just being tense and on guard all the time.

Below are photos of our tents and bunkers, me with some children from the village and my assigned guard bunker when we were attacked. Notice how close the bob-wire and jungle are, making it easy to be attacked.

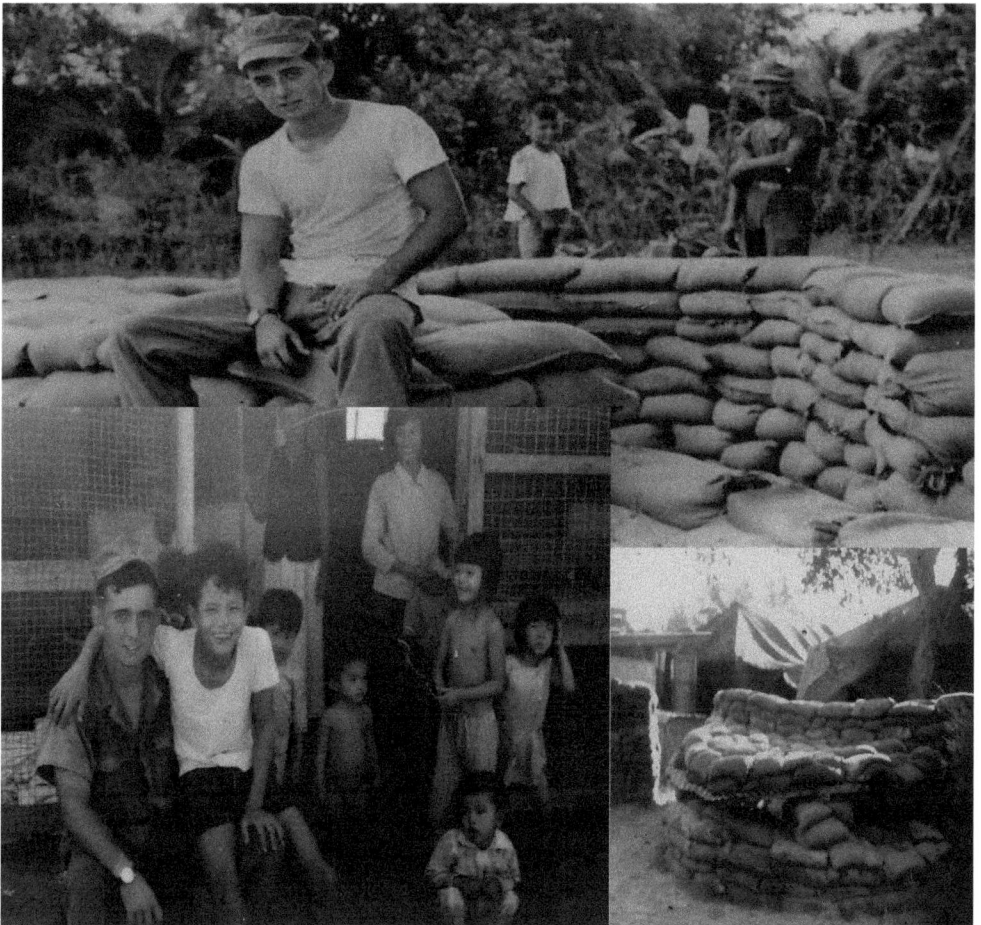

A FIREBOMB IN A CARE PACKAGE

Knowing I was in a village with children, my mother often sent items in like a Care package, for the children. Sometimes the packages were rather large since she got collections from churches. The children loved me because of what my mother sent. My mother also wanted to be sure I ate my favorite foods, often sent various food items not available in Vietnam. Just like she packed all the stuff for us when we went hiking or camping.

I often received my favorite homemade moist chocolate cake with a can of icing in what we called a care package. She would wrap the cake many times with aluminum foil to keep it moist. My fellow Marines did not know about my Little Devil tendencies but also did not know me for my good looks, muscles or superior intellect. They only knew me for my mother's cake and cookies. One day I received a package from my mother with several containers of Jiffy Pop. It was one of those camping Jiffy Pop foil covered pans with oil and popcorn in them that had to be heated over a fire. At the time we were eating C-rations or would buy cooked food in the village or seafood or crabs along the river. We had no stoves or microwaves to cook in. The only way of cooking it was over an open fire, but it was not allowed.

Around the perimeter of our living area compound, we had dug foxholes about three to four feet deep and big enough for two people to be in. They left some as just a hole in the ground and others had sandbags around the top to be used in the event of attack and a frame to lay a roof on if there was a lot of rain. It then became more like a bunker. One day when everyone was on patrol, they left me behind to "protect" the compound. HA HA. I gathered some dry wood and build a fire in the foxhole to cook the popcorn on. I figured no one would see it there, and there would be no danger of catching anything else on fire.

I would cook all of them, maybe 4, at once so everyone would have popcorn, as a surprise, when they returned, so I built a large fire. Maybe they spoiled in the heat or something, but it did not seem to cook right and not popping, so I kept adding wood to make it hotter. I was down in the hole, shaking the containers over the fire, getting hot. Soon they started to pop, but there must have been a small hole in the foil of the Jiffy Pop and the grease caught on fire. It soon flamed up and got so hot with flames shooting all over the fox hole that I think my guardian angel yelled in my ear to get out of there, you fool. The fire flared up as the grease continued to burn, catching the others on fire which produced a real thick black smoke and lots of popping sounds. There was burning popcorn flying all over. Soon the usual village kids gathered around laughing as they asked each other, what is going on, is it a holiday with fireworks, was it a secret weapon, will this little GI devil burn down the village, or "who is this guy that caused this funny scene?" All I had was a canteen full of water, so it took a while, but eventually I put the fire out, but it burned the popcorn of course to a crisp.

I probably looked like the Road Runner as I ran back and forth getting water to put the fire out. As the patrol came through the village later, they heard the exaggerated stories of gun fire and smoke coming from our camp. Maybe the patrol wondered if there were any survivors after an attack like described on our compound. When they ran back into the compound, they acted anxious about what happened. After I told them what really happened, I think it amused them. My squad leader told me to have my mother just send cakes and cookies from then on, no more Jiffy Pop. I was not the most popular Marine around after that. If we had a Marine reunion, I do not think I would be remembered for my good looks, big muscles, or superior intellect. In Germany in WWII, Marines were called Devil Dogs for their fierceness in taking a hill. I may have been called a Devil Dog for a different reason.

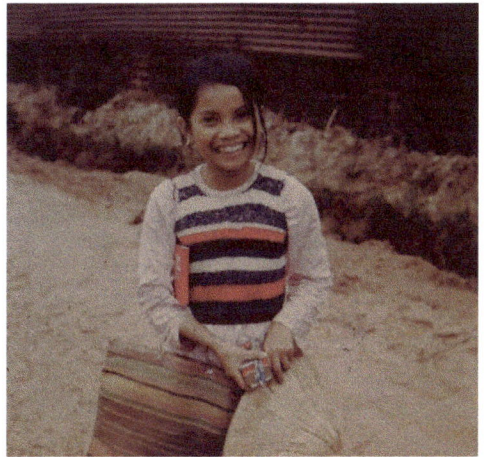

One day, we heard our squad leader arguing with the Vietnamese squad leader. As it got more heated and louder, we gathered around as well as the Vietnamese soldiers. Our squad leader was accusing the Vietnamese of stealing some of our supplies. Suddenly our leader drew a pistol and pointed it at the Vietnamese causing all the marines and Vietnamese soldiers to draw our weapons and point them at the other side.

There was much arguing, and I knew if anyone fired that first shot, we would all fire and we all would be dead. I think that was the scariest moment of my life. Things became very tense and I was praying as hard as I could. Fortunately, a Vietnamese soldier spoke up and admitted he stole the supplies. We relaxed our weapons, and the Vietnamese took away the transgressor never to be seen again. Our relationship with the Vietnamese was never the same. There was a couple of Marines that just kept up accusing the Vietnamese of every little thing and that kept things tense. I am not sure if that lead up to the next event.

One night after finishing my guard duty in a bunker which was basically a hole with sandbags around it, I returned to my tent which was a wood floor with plywood up the sides about two feet and then screening up the walls to the roof. The roof was a canvas tent on a wood frame with the side walls rolled up. I hung up my shirt and flak jacket and bent down to take off my boots when suddenly there two ear busting explosions, one after the other which sounded like it was right next to my tent. I felt the concussion of the blast and heard shrapnel and debris hitting the plywood next to me and shrapnel ripping through the screen and canvas around me. Debris was flying past me, so I dove on the floor and grabbed my rifle and ammo belt when another explosion rang out hurting my ears.

Then I heard rifle fire both going out and incoming rifle fire as I heard bullets ripping through our tent. As I ran frantically outside to my bunker, there was a few more ear deafening explosions from grenades and I saw flares being shot up in the air and tracer fire going out and muzzle flashes from the wooded area on my side of our compound. As I ran to my bunker, I returned fire toward the muzzle flashes in the woods. I looked around for the Marine that was on duty when I saw him outside the bunker wounded and in pain. I called for the Corpsman and did what I could to help him while trying to return fire at the same time. After about an hour, it was over.

An interesting question I have always had. At training, it teaches us to hate the enemy so we can kill them as I will point how later. Living in the village, I felt sorry for the Vietnamese plight and always showed respect for their customs and way of living. I enjoyed talking with the people and learning from them. I especially enjoyed playing with and talking to the children.

Sometimes when I was on guard duty, children would come up to the barbed wire fence and we would talk. Maybe they were impressed by my good looks, etc. or maybe because my mother sent over candy and other treats for them. We had a small compound in the backyard of a Buddhist Temple and the barbed wire was only about 5 feet away from our bunkers and tents we slept in. So, kids often came up to the fence to sell things, receive free goodies or just talk. Sometimes we paid them to come in our compound and clean up or do other chores.

They always seemed to know when I was on guard duty somehow. A day before the attack, some children came up to the fence, and we talked and joked as usual. When leaving, they said they would see me tomorrow and wanted to verify when I would be on duty. That was unusual. The attack happened just a few minutes after I got off duty. I just cannot help but wonder if these kids knew about the attack and wanted to be sure I was not in that bunker.

Did my guardian angel protect me that night? Lots of interesting questions to ask some day. Not to judge anyone but the two Marines injured were excellent Marines and combat trained but did not belong in a village working with people they hated. They were infantry taken off the front lines and assigned to the village. I am sure it was hard for them to work with and help the people that probably killed some of their friends.

They were the two that kept accusing the Vietnamese about every little thing. The hard part of fighting a war with an enemy who lives in the village you are trying to help, dresses like everyone else with no enemy uniform but at night becomes a terrorist. Marines, to kill the enemy, were taught to hate the enemy but then somehow had to separate that from the peaceful villagers. That was a lot to ask of the men and women who wanted to defend our country and Vietnam. WW II was different since you killed those in uniform and helped those in civilian clothes.

The two injured Marines never returned, and we never heard about their recovery. Our relations with the Vietnamese were better after those two were gone. I wondered if it was just a spontaneous attack or a targeted, planned attack. Whatever the case, I gave thanks for protection.

After we were attacked, and since I had no problem with creepy crawlers, they chose me and another Marine to go out into the jungle at night close to our perimeter to watch for Viet Cong trying to sneak closer. We went out too far and were out of sight of those in the compound. We must have fallen asleep and were awakened by noises close by. It sounded like someone coming through the jungle. In the moonlight we could make out several silhouettes with a straw hat on, like the VC wear were carrying something which appeared to be rifles. We could not tell how many there were, but our hearts were pounding. When it appeared, they were too close for comfort. We shot off a flare into the air, jumped up and aimed our rifles at the intruders and yelled Dung Lai which meant stop. Thinking we had caught some VC returning or going to an attack, we felt proud. The men almost had a heart attack.

Turns out we had positioned ourselves near a trail that the fishermen used to get to their boats, while still dark, and they were fisherman carrying poles and had papers to prove it. We had failed to look at our watches after waking up to see that it was almost dawn. We were supposed to go back in the compound during the night and before dawn. No one was ever sent out again. The men we stopped were talking a lot of fast Vietnamese and I am sure it was not complimenting my good looks, muscular body or superior intellect.

Shortly after that some of us were transferred to a new village was with the same unit and needed some experienced Marines to help get it going. This village was deeper in the jungle and further away from Danang. It was basically the same; we lived in tents with a wood frame and floor and plywood about 2 feet up on the sides. We ate C rations, drank tanked in water and bathed in the same spring fed pool of water the local villagers washed clothes in and bathed in. No shower at this one. Someone had concreted the area where the spring was and was about the size of a bathtub. Their idea of a bathing was to bring a pan, fill it with water, wet themselves, wash with soap and then pour water over themselves to rinse off.

We did the same thing, but occasionally I would sneak out into the pool and soak in it. The water was not cold like PA mountain spring fed water but was at least cool and felt good in the hot Vietnamese sun. Occasionally some Vietnamese women would come up to the pool to wash clothes and see my naked body in the pool as I quickly scrambled for a towel. Some just laughed, but once again, I heard some language I never heard before and I do not think it was complimentary.

I did not think this village was as friendly as the other village was, maybe because we were further away from Danang. I think it caught these people in the middle of the Viet Cong and the Americans. They did not want to be seen helping us or being friendly to us. There were no friendly children hanging out at our fence. Everyone just kept to themselves. I wondered when we received sniper fire into our compound or at a patrol was to sidetrack us while Viet Cong snuck through another area.

ADVENTURES IN THE PHILLIPINES

During a tour of duty in Vietnam, Marines would have the opportunity, every few months, to get away from combat and choose a place to get a brief rest and relaxation. When my turn came, I chose the Philippine Islands for 5 days.

I spent a day or two hanging out with some other Marines and going to bars and clubs. Their idea of rest and relaxation was to drink all day, get drunk and head back to the hotel. I tried that the first day and night, but it

133

seemed to be such a waste of money. If I remember right back in 1965, I was making about $2000 a year, as an E-2 or 3, so I wanted to not waste it. I felt like I was being taken advantage of.

I figured this was the only chance I would ever have to see the sights in the Philippines, so I just preferred to do something different. They gave all of us a list of things to do or see while we were there, so I found a place that offered tours and I signed up. This was an all-inclusive service which assigned me a taxi to go where I wanted and gave me liberty to choose the tours I wanted to go on. There were day tours and evening tours, so I signed up to see some WW II battle grounds and cemeteries where US servicemen were buried after the invasion of US troops to chase out the Japanese. It was amazing to see what appeared to be acres of white crosses, all in perfect alignment, where all those heroes were buried. Imagine men fighting and dying on foreign soil, for the freedom of other people and then not returning home but being buried on that foreign soil. It was a totally different war than Vietnam.

I asked a lot of questions to our guide, which was a young girl about my age. Her name was Julie. I told some of my family jokes and she just kept laughing and did that giggle thing when she looked at me. It was so nice to be around a girl instead of Marines after being in Vietnam. It was especially nice to see a girl dressed up, clean and just had a pleasant appearance without worrying about grenades, poison, knives and other means of death. Most of the women I saw around the village wore clothing like black pajamas and had no running water to bathe regularly, but neither did the Marines.

Julie asked if I enjoyed dancing and listening to bands, and I did. She then asked if I would like to go see some night clubs with some other tour guides and that was a big yes as well. We went to clubs with live bands, and I showed off my American dance skills. Everyone got a kick out of the way I did the twist, mashed potatoes, and even did a few splits. We were all laughing and had a good time. I had a few drinks but did not get drunk. I was happy that no one was trying to get my money or use me in any way. My meal was paid for and people bought me drinks. It may have been because I showed interest in their culture and way of living.

I noticed the tour guides were talking among themselves and Julie eventually came to me and explained about a tour guide training adventure the next day which involved a jeep ride through the jungles along a river to an area where there was a waterfall and then canoe some whitewater on the way back. She said it was just for tour guides to get familiar with and be trained on how to guide this adventure.

She said she had got permission for me to come along if I wanted to. The real reason, I figured, was that all the female guides liked my good looks, big muscles and superior intellect. Realistically, she thought it would be something I would enjoy and wow, was she ever correct?

The next day taxi took me to the meeting place. We went on a bus trip to a place along a river where we got in jeeps. Now this was my kind of adventure, riding through jungle without worrying about land mines and ambush, although I could not help but be anxious and on the lookout. That was a problem vets had as they returned to the USA after war. They were always on edge, anxious and on the lookout for signs of danger ahead.

At the waterfalls, we were given a history of the area and were encouraged to look around to find something of interest to add some talking points when tours were taken there. I looked and explored the area and found a hollowed-out area behind the waterfall. I encouraged Julie to go behind the falls to see this area with me and she went along. She was scared, but I held her hand like a true gentleman.

It was exciting to be there with water crashing down at the entrance in front of us. Years later, when I would see the movie, "The Last of the Mohicans", I would remember this waterfall and the cave, just like the one in the movie.

Below are photos of a similar waterfall and the fun my family is demonstrating that you can have. That includes standing around the falls, being in the falls or sliding down the smooth rocks like a water slide.

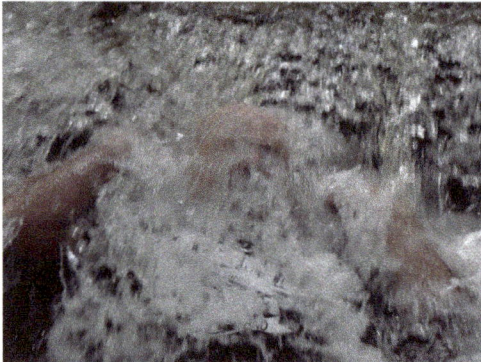

Most of the trainees just looked around, took pictures, and some waded into the river. Not me, I dove in and swam around and then climbed the rock cliffs to jump off into the pool of water at the falls. I did my Tarzan yell as I jumped into the falls. I went behind the falls and dove into the water through the falls. There was not a big hydraulic effect from the falls that would have pulled me under, but I was careful anyway. Julie just stood there smiling and staring at me like what is wrong with this crazy

American. I bet she was thinking we are a quiet group, and he is like a Holy Terror among us. I figured I would give them something to talk about and remember me by. They all remarked how I had given them some ideas of what to do at the falls to make it fun for the people that would visit there. I always wondered what they allowed on the tours.

We had a picnic lunch and then got into the canoes to ride the rapids downstream. These canoes were huge, not like what we had at Boy Scout Camp, they held 6-7 people, were wider and deeper. They looked like canoes I had seen on Tarzan movies that the natives made. Instead of seat they had cushions on the bottom. I sat down and Julie sat in front of me. We all took turns paddling, even though some did not do very well. Although I wanted to show everyone my canoe tipping skills, I learned in the Boy Scouts, but I refrained from my desires and just enjoyed the trip. As we went down the river the guides paddled, and I just enjoyed the ride, dodging rocks and going through rapids. As we went through the rapids, Julie got scared and leaned back against my chest. Once again, it felt good to protect a young lady in times of fear. I wished that chick magnet Sam was there to see me canoeing with a young lady. I would make him sit alone and watch as I put my umbrella over the two of us like he did to me when he rowed off into the darkness at the cabin with Marta.

At least I should have taken a photo of her under an umbrella with me and sent it to him. Once again, I felt a bonding to her because of the physical contact and fun we had, even though she did not take part in the fun part of it. After being in Vietnam a year, this kind of bonding was dangerous and could lead me to thinking I was in love with her and that happened. It is amazing what loneliness and physical contact can do. If you are feeling bad, a hug can make you feel better. Holding hands while praying can bond you to a group or an individual. When experiencing loneliness, physical contact and enjoying someone's company could bring on emotions that may cause you to not evaluate your emotions correctly and think you are in love.

That evening there was a picnic when we returned and a wrap up for the guides. Julie was a lot of fun and I really enjoyed being with her, but I knew I was going back to Vietnam the next day and we had to say our goodbyes. Before leaving, we exchanged addresses, and we promised to write each other which we did. Many of my US friends were no longer writing, so a new friend sounded good.

We started writing each other, and I really seemed to think about her a lot and missed her even though I knew little about her. As we wrote to each other the rest of the time in Vietnam, I was thinking I was in love with her. How could I be in love with someone I only knew for three days? I knew nothing of her religious beliefs, work ethic, morals, family history or anything else about what she thought about or hoped for. Later I would find out she hoped to go to the USA and may have been using me. I thought she was a lot of fun, but she just laughed at my jokes, made me feel good because I impressed her with my spirit of adventure and she leaned against me like she couldn't get enough of me. I thought she was mesmerized by my good looks, big muscles, and superior intellect. I hoped so anyway, for my ego's sake. Besides that, I had no fun with another girl since leaving the states.

As we were writing each other, she mentioned she was in love with me and she hoped we could get together again and maybe even get married. Alone in Vietnam, I thought maybe I loved her and continued to write in those terms. About 2 years later I had returned to the USA, Julie wrote me and said she was going to California to see a relative and asked if I could come see her. I agreed and made plans. She was limited in time with her stay in the USA and mentioned that if I still loved her, we could get married and she could stay here in the USA with me. I cannot say I really loved her since I did not know much about her. I may have also felt sorry for her plight and just wanted to help her stay in the States, but during that 2-year period, I was dating other girls. I was not in love with her.

When I asked around about getting married, some older Marines informed me about girls overseas who just want to come to the USA and will do anything to get there and that I should be careful. That was a shocker and a hurt to think there was a possibility that Julie was using me and not mesmerized by good looks, big muscles, and superior intellect. More about that later. Right now, it is back to Vietnam.

HIDING IN SHADOWS PAYS OFF

After several months in that village, I was transferred to a new location in Chu Lai, about thirty miles south of Danang, to defend a small airstrip in the jungle. It disappointed me it was not in a village with children. They needed an experienced mechanic to keep generators running at a small landing strip for single engine spotter planes. These planes often came in all shot up from flying low, looking for the enemy or calling in artillery fire. I saw quite a few planes crash as they landed and helped rescue wounded pilots which sometimes did not survive.

This little airstrip was out in the jungle with no villages nearby. Kids came from somewhere to receive handouts and to sell things. In this area, it was not safe to buy things from the children or allow them in our fenced area. Sometimes women and teen girls showed up to try to entice Marines to come out of the compound with them. I was told that some Marines snuck out at night and were never seen again. The people could not be trusted in this area. We ate C-rations and drank warm water from a water tanker once again. No ice and no cooked food, but no patrols either. The local people were not friendly, so we were not allowed out of our compound except in a truck or helicopter.

They were getting regular attempts of the Viet Cong trying to get into the airfield to destroy the planes and fuel. There were portable lights on trailers and generators that we took to places that could be attacked. They hid everyone else in bunkers except for me since I had to refuel and keep the generators going. I did not like being in the open and being a target, but a Marine does what he is told. Just like when we played hide and go seek as a kid, I knew if I moved in the shadows, no one could see me. Playing cowboys and Indians plus going hunting taught me how to move without being noticed, hopefully. The lights seemed to have its desired effect, there were no more attacks, just the common sniper fire to knock out the lights or damage a generator. All part of the job.

After spending sixteen months in Vietnam, it was time to say goodbye. I extended my tour overseas to spend six months in Japan to experience one more overseas adventure.

Chapter 16: NOT THE LAST SAMURAI BUT A FIRST OKI SAKANA

They stationed me at an air wing at Iwakuni, Japan and worked as a mechanic of jeeps, trucks, forklifts, and other equipment. It was a pleasant duty after being in Vietnam. We had real beds, a real barracks building with heat and air conditioning, running water, toilets, showers, mess hall with cooked food, movies and a town full of Japanese people just waiting to see my good looks, muscular American body and experience true superior intellect and it was safe there or at least it was until I arrived.

I enjoyed going out into the town in the evenings, drinking at the different bars, talking to the girls. They appreciated my attributes because as soon as I came in; I saw the girls talking to see who would be so lucky as to meet me. Each time I went in a girl would come right over to me and say Hi, you big strong, good looking Marine, you are number one GI. Wow, finally someone sees me for who I am. Being a gentleman, I would ask her to sit down and buy her a drink for recognizing my attributes. She was so in awe of my superior intellect that they would just sit there with me all night listening to my stories but listening really make her thirsty. I just kept buying her drinks, and she kept saying, "Oh John-son, you are number one Marine" which I was glad someone finally noticed. I should have had her write a letter to my CO so I could get a promotion. Once my money was spent, she would excuse herself to go powder her nose and I would never see her again. I am sure it was exhausting being around a person like me.

After spending a lot of money, I found out they hired these girls to talk to the Marines if they kept buying them drinks. One time a girl said the other girls called me Oki Sakana, which meant "Big Fish", like a big sucker. う お She wrote it in Japanese, so I would always remember. Being taken advantage of was just the normal life in military towns. It may be true in life; if you have money, you have friends. However, they seem to disappear when the money runs out. That is the incredible relationship with Sam; we have been friends since kindergarten through thick and thin, with money and without money. My wife is my best friend through the good, the bad and the ugly since 1968.

NO FOOD AT THIS DRIVE-THRU

One day I was doing maintenance on a vehicle that towed aircraft around. I was driving this gigantic heavy monster of a vehicle to the maintenance shed to refill all the fluid levels. I had the pedal to the metal and was moving fast. As I headed for the shed, I was playing chicken with the other Marines working there. I put my foot on the brake pedal to slow it down, and the pedal went to the floor. I pumped it frantically with no luck. This monster was too heavy to steer away from the shed.

What DO you think happened next?

A. I turned so hard that the vehicle turned over and over.

B. My guardian angel picked up the vehicle and flew it over the shed to a safe stop.

C. I laid down on the seat and crashed into the shed.

D. I jumped off before the crash.

It was C. I had no choice but to lay down on the seat and hope for the best. As I crashed through the building sending oil cans, tools, parts, and lubricants flying into the air. When it finally came to rest, I remember being trapped with a lot of debris on top of me, but then remembered nothing until days later. I may have been unconscious for a while. Everyone was glad I was not injured severely, but they thought it would have been better if I had died in the accident, rather than face the CO when he found out. They thought perhaps the CO would take me up in his airplane and throw

142

me out at 30,000 feet over a volcano, run me through with a Samurai sword, do away with me by firing squad or feed me to the sharks in the nearby waters.

When I finally appeared before the CO for destruction of government property, he acted mad but later told me he wanted to tear it down and build a bigger one, anyway. He just wandered why the vehicle was not marked that it had no brakes. He mentioned about my driving skills and why I was going so fast. I am sure he thought I was a hazard to his equipment and did not want me to drive anymore vehicles.

Maybe he wondered how someone allowed a Little Devil into the Marines. This was another case where those Marines would not remember me for my good looks, muscles, or superior intellect or even my mechanic skills.

SEEING THE COUNTRY OF JAPAN

I shortly grew weary of the bar life in Iwakuni and I remembered how rewarding it was to learn Vietnamese, live in their villages, eat their food, learn their way of living and travel around seeing their country. I decided to take advantage of my stay in Japan to learn about and see the country. A Japanese man that worked on the base with me, had a motorcycle and took me into town to look at some motorcycles. I bought a Honda Scrambler to drive around the base and go into the town of Iwakuni. I had to get a Japanese driver's license to drive off base, so it took some practice driving a cycle. By this time in my life I had learned that all military towns, around the world, are just about the same but have different faces. If you want to see and learn about the culture of the country you are in, you must get away from the base and the bars.

There were some Japanese people working on our base that spoke English and Japanese, so I started spending time with them intending to learn the Japanese language. I also bought a Japanese-English book to study the language on my own.

My Japanese friend would take me off base to visit Japanese dance halls where American music was popular and ate at a Japanese restaurant. I learned that to make an impression with the locals; you had to ask for hot

Sake (a rice wine) and be able to eat Sushi and other Japanese food. The town of Hiroshima was about an hour away, so we went there often. Not too many servicemen went there, so people were a lot more friendly to Americans than the base town was. Possibly I was the first American they had seen and often wanted to use me to practice their English with. Instead of trying to take my money, they often bought me food and drinks.

At a club away from the base, he introduced me to a Japanese waitress and bartender. She spoke some English, and I spoke some Japanese. We seemed to hit it off, and I continued to go there. She was not out to get my money and only spoke to me when she was not busy.

One day my Japanese friend arranged for this girl to be my date, to go along with him and his date to go sightseeing during the Cherry Blossom Festival. We had a splendid time and I really the beauty of the Japanese culture. My date brought her young daughter, but I never asked why she did not have a husband. She was a beautiful sweet young girl about 4 or 5.

To make a long story short, this girl invited me to various private parties and dances at the club, and I got to see more of the customs and learn more Japanese. At one party they did the bunny hop, which was right up my alley. I was trying to save some money, so I did not go to the clubs or bars much. Whenever she invited me to a private event, it was free for me. Eventually, she asked me to baby-sit her daughter when her mother could not watch her when she worked. I jumped at the chance since I loved kids and gave me a chance to learn more Japanese. When she got home from work, we talked some and then I would leave to be back at the base by my curfew. She taught me about how to live in a traditional house, but she never taught me about public bathing and that would be a problem for me later as I toured Japan.

We remained good friends the remaining months I was there. Because of the emotional bonding taking place, I probably felt like I was in love with her. Here I was writing to Julie, thinking I was in love with her and feeling in love with this Japanese girl. Was I becoming a chick magnet like Sam or like a sailor, having a girl in every port? What was up with that? There really is a lot to learn about the feelings we get when around the opposite sex. We really must be cautious and be prepared for those feelings of a good friend and be able to separate them for genuine love and knowing who we want to spend a lifetime with. I knew she would never leave Japan, so I never kept in contact with her after leaving.

CRAZY DRIVERS - WRONG SIDE OF THE ROAD

One of the biggest challenges I had was driving with traffic in Japan. They drove on the opposite side of the road as we do. They drove fast and crazy, passing on the right or left or anywhere else they could. I was a safe, careful driver and would have died if I continued to drive so safely.

Before the cycle, I often went to Hiroshima by train. One visit took me to the ground zero of the first dropped atomic bomb and a Peace Park they built there. Inside a museum were horrible photos of people and the actual town affected by the bomb. There were photos of body parts that were melted together, images like a shadow on building left behind as a person was vaporized and many severely burned adults and children. I know the bomb ended the war sooner and saved American lives but added new meaning to the saying "War is Hell". I would also visit the museum at the other atomic bomb dropping in Nagasaki. It sure made me hope the Vietnam War would be over soon and there would be no more atomic bomb drops. Unfortunately, the war would go on for another 8 years and even more powerful nuclear bombs would be developed.

One night we were in Hiroshima, and after a fun night, it was time to head back. I may have enjoyed my hot Sake too much or maybe we were running late, but we were in a hurry to get back to the base. I was following my friend and to keep up; I had to become an aggressive driver, just like he was. We made it back safely and in good time. From then on, I had a drink before driving to ease up my safety consciousness, and thus I could drive wild and crazy and got along fine. This was not a good thing to do. It would be the beginning of using alcohol to do things I normally would not do.

My friend and I talked about touring Japan on our motorcycles, it sounded like fun, so we started planning. I had fifteen days of leave coming so I put in for 15 days leave to get approved. We were planning to camp along the road as we went down to the southern island of Kyushu and then up to Tokyo and then back.

My commanding officer wanted to see me about this trip, so I explained it to him. He thought it may be dangerous and rather unbecoming of a Marine to camp out along roads. He said he would only approve the leave if I would stay in youth hostels and hotels, so I agreed. Since at a youth hostel, I would need my bedding, I took a sleeping bag along. I found out where all the hostels were but thought once off base, I would do what I wanted as usual.

When the trip was planned and only a few days away, I was informed by my friend that he could not get the time off and could not go. This was a real disappointment since I was looking forward to going on this trip. Since the plans were in place and my leave approved, I went by myself. It would be a real wild and crazy adventure for an American on a motorcycle, with limited Japanese skills, touring a land where the Japanese spoke very little English in the mid-1960s and try to figure out the road signs to know where I was going.

HEADING TO KYUSHU TO RIDE UP A VOLCANO

The time came for me to leave after changing some money into Japanese yen, getting a sleeping bag, camera, and some extra clothes. I was on my way to the southern island of Kyushu, where I heard there was an active volcano, and you could ride right up to the rim and look in.

I had planned to tour Aso National Park to see the volcano and go to Nagasaki, where the second atomic bomb dropped. After riding all day and was exhausted, I pulled off the road in a grassy area and under the stars, spent the night in a sleeping bag. I was awakened around sunrise by bright lights, a lot of Japanese talking and the sound of motorcycles. I thought, oh no, it is a Japanese motorcycle gang coming to do me in. When I finally could see, I found it to be two policemen on motorcycles, my first run in with the law. I did not understand what they were saying but understood enough to figure out they allowed no camping along the road; it was too dangerous. Because I was an American, they seem to give me some leave way and said to get going. Later I found out it was not a familiar sight to see anyone camping alongside the road. From there on, I would get off the road and camp in the woods.

My first couple days were exciting but uneventful, other than seeing some sights and seeing how the Japanese people lived out in the countryside. I was pleasantly impressed with the Japanese and the care they took of their property and how they used a lot of flowers as decorations.

I thought Japan was the most colorful and beautiful country I had ever seen.

I was traveling through a mountainous area of Aso National Park and came across a small town with what appeared to be volcanic hot springs. I must have been getting close to the volcano. That night I spent the night in a hotel, motel or whatever they called it. It was in the hot spring area. What caught my attention was that people were cooking various food items in the hot boiling water pools. I bought two hard-boiled eggs and meat and had my supper. I returned to the hotel ready for a hot bath. The owner gave me a towel, soap and showed me the central tub and I was ready for soaking. It was in a separate room with a little pond and a lot of flowers and an area that looked like a shower without a shower head. The tub was a built in the ground stone like tub, big enough to sit up and put your legs out. I did my soaking, washing with soap and rinsed in the tub. I thought I would be helpful and drain the water and clean the tub. When I went out the room, the owner went in and I heard all this commotion. The woman came out and I could tell she was furious with me, but I could not understand what she was saying. Later I found out I was supposed to wash by hand in the tiled area, rinse off and be nice and clean before entering the tub. The tub was filled with the volcanic hot mineral water from the local hot springs and was considered having therapeutic valuable and healing ingredients. I guess I did not do much to make an impression of my knowledge of the Japanese culture, improve diplomatic relations or be remembered for my good looks, muscles, or intellect of any kind. The word was out to not let this Holy Terror in any hotels. The photo below is me by a steamy boiling volcanic pool of water.

The next day I wanted to drive my Honda up Mt. Naka-dake to see the volcano. It was an exciting trip with lots of beautiful scenery. I think

147

the most exciting event happened when I got to the volcano parking area where people parked to walk up to see the volcano. While there, a busload of schoolgirls drove up and parked next to me. When they saw I was an American, they got all giggly and seemed to want to ask to take a photo of an American. Finally, one asked, and I found myself in the middle of this group having a lot of photos taken. We could not go up to the top from that point. I had the impression the wind was causing the toxic gas to come down the mountain. The photos below are the school girls and me in a traditional robe to wear around town.

Later, I would see the same group of girls on a ferryboat crossing a large body of water on the way to Nagasaki. The girls were busy sneaking, trying to get photos of me. I am sure they recognized my good looks, big muscles, and superior intellect. When I reached Nagasaki, I remember being disappointed at what I found. I toured the museum and visited the Peace Park but found it to be too much of a tourist town and I did not care for tourist towns. After riding across the lower island of Kyushu, it was time to head back to the main island and head north toward Tokyo.

HEADING NORTH TOWARD TOKYO AND MT FUJI

On the way there, I mastered the art of finding a camping spot in the woods. I had no more trouble until one night; I was trying to drive as far as I could and had driven until late at night. I started looking for a wooded area and finally saw one. I walked my motorcycle into the woods on a trail until I found a soft grassy area and spread my sleeping bag out and went to sleep. I was awakened by a lot of Japanese talking once again. When I looked out my sleeping bag, I saw it was daylight and there were about eight Japanese children around my sleeping bag.

When they saw I was an American, I got the surprised looks and the giggling once again. I looked around and what I saw this frightening sight. I had walked through the woods right into someone's backyard and was only a few feet away from a house. When I greeted them in Japanese, I got even more giggling. I packed up and walked my cycle back to the road and started my journey once again. As I got closer to bigger cities and the more populated areas, I found it harder to find safe places to camp. Although I did some more camping out along the way, I recall no more exciting events with camping. There were many historic areas to see, like enormous castles with gigantic walls and moats and Buddhist temples with gigantic statues of Buddha. I especially enjoyed the gardens of flowers, cherry blossom trees and beautiful colored buildings and bridges.

I was going through one city when I decided it was time to stay in an American style hotel with bell boys and all. The bell boys spoke a little English and seem to be around my age, about 19 or 20, and seemed to be intrigued by my adventure. They invited me out on the town with dates for them and for me. We rode some place on a train and then went to a club where there was American music and dancing. It gave me a chance to show off my moves with splits and all again. Beatles imitation bands were extremely popular, and other bands that played American '50s music.

My favorite was Land of a Thousand Dances, and I learned how to request it in Japanese. It was something like Dance ten goku. That would impress the bands. They especially were interested in the twist. It was a delightful change to travel and not be on a motorcycle. We eventually returned to the hotel and went our separate ways. It was nice to eat American food, soak in a big tub, drain the water out without getting into trouble and sleep in a large soft bed.

The next day, the bell boys took me out to their residence, which was like a college dormitory. On the way back from Tokyo, they would invite me to spend a night at their dormitory, which I did to save some money and see how they lived.

I had now been on the road for seven days and I had to go back to base to renew my fifteen day leave and check in with my CO. I took a high-speed train back to Hiroshima and a slow train to Iwakuni, and then a taxi back to base. I was getting good at maneuvering my way around Japan. Most train stations had Japanese and English city signs, which made it easier.

I checked in and reported on my trip up to that point. I did not tell the officers about my Gomer Pyle experiences, just my John Wayne ones, and how impressed everyone was with the United States Marine Corps. That impressed them and sent me back to continue the outstanding work of being a Marine Corps ambassador.

I reversed my trip back to the hotel and was on my way to Tokyo once again. The train ride gave me a chance to see even more of the country and the beauty there. Even to this day, I enjoy seeing the beauty that man has made from the natural resources. I so much more enjoy and am so humbled at the magnificent beauty that God has created. His creation overwhelms me.

"JOHN - SON, YOU SHOULD BE PRESIDENT OF USA"

Next stop was in Kyoto to see some attractions and castles. Nothing wild and crazy happened here, but I met a Japanese man that changed my life. I was in a Japanese bar before going to look for a hotel or an available field and ordered my usual hot sake. Some men made some casual conversation, but then a man came over and could speak a little English and started asking questions. Some questions I could answer in Japanese and some not. It turned he was the owner of a chain of restaurants and there was one right next to the bar. He invited me over for a meal. There was a choice of an American or Japanese menu, and I chose Japanese and placed an order. I impressed the owner by showing respect for their customs.

After the meal and more talking, he said he had an apartment type building where all his employees stayed and asked if I needed a place to stay the night. I said yes, and he seemed happy that I accepted. Here was another employer that provided housing for his employees. Most of them were young and single, anyway. I spent the night in his apartment in the same building on a mat on the floor. You would think he would have had a king size mattress for visitors somewhere. We spent the next day touring his restaurants, talking, and eating. He showed me maps of the USA and wanted to know exactly where I lived, so I showed him PA and my hometown. His employees had a lot of questions. The life changing question was what I wanted to do with my life once I was back in the USA. I said I wanted to be an auto mechanic. I never saw such a shocked look on someone's face.

They wanted to know why I did not want to be President of the USA or a CEO of a large company. Now my face looked shocked. They wanted to know how a person with enough courage and ambition to tour an unknown country with limited language skills would not seek a higher ambition than an auto mechanic. The USA had the best opportunities and freedom in the world; they could only wish to be an American. I would never become President nor have a desire to do so, but I thought about my goals and taking advantage of all the opportunities I had in the USA. I eventually would want to become the best husband, father and citizen I could be, but I would also learn that Christians are in training to work with Jesus Christ who is, I guess you could say, the CEO of the entire universe.

Maybe someday I will have a position more important than the President of the USA. I hope to see this man again someday and tell him how he changed my life. Below is a photo of me on my motorcycle and the Japanese family that owned the restaurant chain and invited me into their house.

I would stop on the way back from Tokyo to spend another night with this family and then keep in touch for a few years after that. Considering this man was a rich, successful man, he did not have a big fancy house like I was used to seeing successful Americans have. He believed in investing in his business and savings. He also provided housing for his employees. My parents growing up during the depression learned to work hard and save money and had little debt if any. The attitude this Japanese man had must have been what the early settlers and pioneers had when they built this great country.

Whenever I became discouraged or dissatisfied with my position in life, I would remember this man and then try harder to reach my potential and achieve as much as I could, trying to stay within God's will for me which I had no idea what that was. I just seemed to believe that God was shepherding me through life. Looking back now, I believe that was true.

On the way toward Tokyo, I saw an amusement park, which reminded me a lot of Disney World. I was running low on money and decided to just take photos of it rather than going in. While taking photos, a young man came over and started talking in English. He was a college student taking English and wanted to practice his English on me. He paid my way into the park and we spent the day talking and going on rides. These days, I call that a blessing. I also practiced my Japanese on him. One thing I found was that people knew what area of Japan I came from because, much like a New Jersey or a southern accent, I had learned Japanese in an area that had an accent and people recognized it right away.

Below is a photo of an amusement park with Mt. Fuji in the background and the man that paid my way into the park.

While on my tour, I tried all kinds of Japanese food. I especially enjoyed Sushi and learned to eat with chopsticks.

Fifty-four years later and I still love Japanese food, eating Sushi and still eat with chopsticks. I introduced the family to Japanese Hibachi food, and we all love it, especially on my birthday. In 2020 all 6 of our kids, their mates and 16 grandchildren, plus a few guests were there.

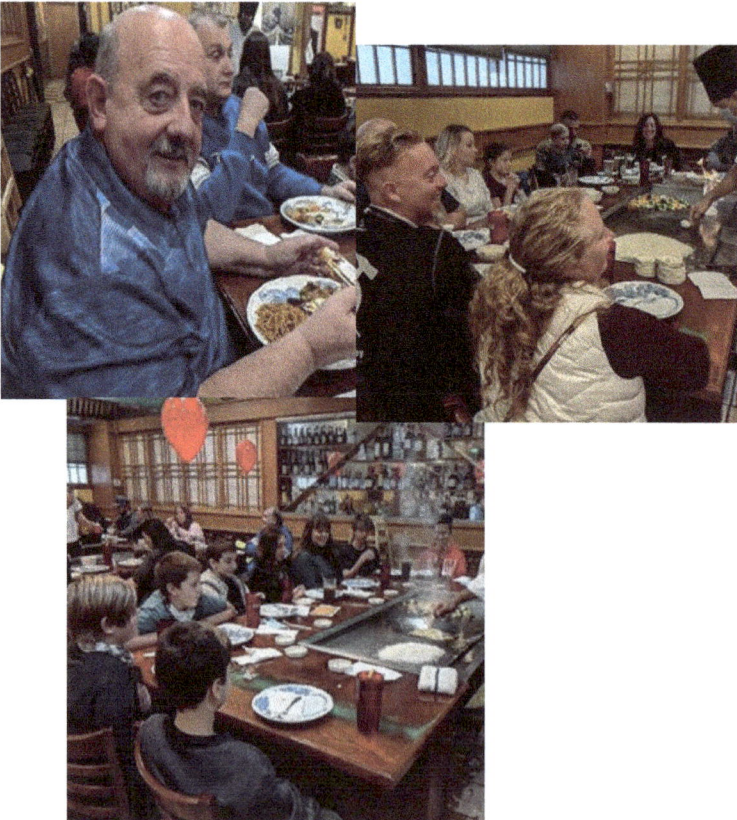

NOW TO TOKYO AND THE GINZA

When I arrived in Tokyo, I drove through town and walked through the Ginza, a popular shopping area. I saw quite a few Americans and a lot of servicemen there, and now I was just another American tourist with American dollars. Everything was much commercialized there, and I just did not feel comfortable, especially after the friends I had made on the way there. I rode out of town in a cloud of dust saying "hi yo Silver, away". (For those of you that remember the Lone ranger) I rode off into the sunset to one more attraction. Before going back to the base, I spent the night in a Japanese style motel.

It comprised one room with a delightful view of a Japanese garden and pond with goldfish swimming in it. As usual, it had a mat on the floor and a table about the height of a coffee table that people would kneel around to talk, eat or read. I had trouble kneeling for long periods of time, so I usually sat down with my legs under the table. When it got cool, there was an electric blanket over the table to provide some warmth while sitting since there was not much heat in the rooms. It also had a TV with all Japanese speaking channels. It had a public bath and toilets down the hall, as usual.

I never had a problem picking food to eat at a Japanese Restaurant. It was easier than choosing a dinner at some fancy restaurants I have been to. Unless you know what, you want to eat ahead of time, it is difficult to know what to order. One good thing about a Japanese restaurant was that instead of a written menu, there was a display case out front with plastic models of their food. I just picked the one I wanted to try and showed the waitress. Ordering Sushi was easy also since they displayed it, and I just picked something that looked good. The one with octopus suction cups looked interesting but was I did not care for it.

RIDING UP THE HIGHEST MOUNTAIN IN JAPAN-MT FUJI

When I woke up and looked outside, I saw an unbelievable, amazing sight. Even though I was still a day's drive away, Mt Fuji soured up majestically into the blue sky with its snow-covered peak. It stands over 12,000 feet high and was a well-proportioned volcanic mountain. It was a pleasant drive there with a lot of views of the mountain as I got closer, very impressive. I could thank God for such an inspiring, beautiful view. I arrived later that day and rode up the dormant volcano to an area where the snow started and there was a lot of black ash. I found out it was possible to hike up to the summit, but I did not have time since it was getting dark and I wanted to get away from the snow and the cooler temperatures. I camped in the woods at the bottom of Mt. Fuji and the next day started back to the base. I made a stop along the way to see the restaurant owner, who gave me a wood doll as something to remember him by which I still have. I also spent a night at the bellboy dormitory and then headed back to base. My trip was over as I approached the Marine base at Iwakuni but keeping a lot of memories for life.

Chapter 17: BACK TO THE GOOD OLD USA

In Viet Nam, Marines were now being flown back to the USA in passenger jets. However, when my six months was up in Japan, I was so lucky as to go to Okinawa for a few days and then get another Pacific cruise back to the USA aboard another troop transport ship. People would pay a lot of money to be on a cruise ship for 30 days and see nothing but ocean, but I got two of them for free.

It was so hot down below deck; I spent much of the day on the deck looking out at the vastness of the ocean unless there was a good movie playing. I was not one who was comfortable sleeping in bunks 5 or 6 high and packed in like Sardines, so I mostly slept on the deck with an inspiring view of all the stars on an unlighted dark section of the deck. Of all the places I have slept in my life, sleeping on a hard steel deck with a shirt on a pipe or hatch was the worse. However, as I looked up into the dark night sky with what seemed like endless stars, it made it easier to think about what I had experienced in Viet Nam, the Philippines and Japan. I thought much about life and all the questions that were entering my mind about life. I thought about the many good and exciting times I had with Sam. I thought about what a good friend he was, wondering what he was doing and where he was. In school, I had read a book about someone on a raft following currents in the Pacific Ocean, and other people had sailed across the ocean. Now that would be a real adventure, but I had no desire to raft, kayak or canoe the Pacific. I was more interested in being like Louis and Clark rather than Columbus and Magellan.

I thought about the Vietnamese people I met and how simple a life they lived but were still happy and willing to share what they had. They seemed to be very content with the necessities of life. This differed from the way of life I had experienced in the USA of trying to accumulate all the possessions I could. Then there was the Japanese man who thought I should want to be president instead of an auto mechanic. I came back with the attitude that I would be content with whatever I would have but try to become the best I could. Both were life changing experiences.

Also, what entered my mind were the many wonderful experiences and travels in Japan and the Philippines. It was hard to comprehend the Japanese families I had met and how impressed and knowledgeable they were about the USA. What drove a family to be so interested in another country?

I eventually became an auto mechanic then an auto body repairman, had my own business for a while and along the line taught auto mechanics, auto body repair, small engine repair and diesel engine mechanics. I retired from teaching after thirty-three years and feel I lived a rewarding, fulfilled life. One goal I had and fulfilled was to become one of only a few hundred across the United States to get Master ASE Certification in Auto and Light Truck Technician, Diesel Engine, Heavy Trucks Technician, Auto Body Repair and Paint Technician. I understood the theory of how the automobile and heavy equipment worked, so I continued to study trucks. Maybe I really did have a superior intellect. But maybe not.

I thought about some near misses and fearful events in Vietnam and how blessed I was to leave there alive and with no injuries. There were too many that did not leave that way and would have their lives or their family's lives changed forever.

I thought about life and all the questions I had. What I would do when I returned to the States? Would I find anyone to date and share with? Little did I know that as I was looking up into the stars at night, there was a teen-age girl walking the beach of Topsail Island NC looking up at the stars and wondering about the same things? Was there a possibility that God would bring us together later? Keep reading to see.

I also thought about Julie and the Japanese girl I had met. I wondered if I would see them again. Were they in my destiny? I wondered if the girl I dated through high school, Sylvia, was still available and would we start dating again?

I also thought about the horrors of war and the suffering of everyone on both sides. Someday, I would read in Ex. 23:28, that God offered the Israelites a way to escape war by God chasing out the enemy with hornets. But Israel wanted a king and an army to fight, realizing they would suffer the pain of seeing their sons and daughters killed or injured during war. In front of the United nations Building there is a statue of men beating their swords into plow shares which was found in Isaiah 2:4. I look forward to that time of no more wars but only Jesus returning to the earth to rule it as king of kings can accomplish it.

MARINES LAND ON THE BEACHES OF SURF CITY, NC

Instead of a military beach landing craft, these two crazy Marines landed in a canoe.

I arrived in California during the summer of 1967. There was a small group of people, probably family members of the Marines returning, and a band to welcome us home. Later in the war, ships and planes were met by protesters and cursing and throwing things at the vets. I did not come face to face with any protesters until later in 1967.

I flew to camp Lejeune, NC, checked in and then went on a 30-day leave. The first thing I noticed was that a lot had changed during the two years I was overseas. Many of my friends were now married and now had children, some friends were at college and some were working and had no time for adventures.

Most of my 15 days were putting my Honda motorcycle together since I had it disassembled and shipped to my house. I did not notice any Vietnam protestors at that time in 1967. I was too young to buy beer or alcohol off base, but I did have a fake ID if I needed it. I remember dating Sylvia and riding motorcycles with her brother. I have photos of Sylvia, her brother, his date, and me having a picnic in the woods by a creek. I always enjoyed dating Sylvia and the good, clean fun we had together. She was a good influence on me, and her high moral standards kept us out of trouble. I had a hard time talking about personal thoughts, so I do not recall us talking about religion or personal goals or beliefs. It would be harder for us to date once I went back to base since I often had some type of duty or training on the weekends. I preferred dating her if I could, but I did not expect her to wait around for a call. I do not recall going on any adventures in 1967-68.

My mother sent me brochures on the '67 Camaro, and I loved it. While home, I had planned to buy a '67 Camaro SS 350 engine with a 4-speed floor shift transmission. I had about $1500 to spend and the price tag was about $2500, so I bought a 1963 Chevrolet Impala convertible instead. It had a 283-cu. in. engine with 3 speed stick plus an overdrive. It would be the perfect car for the "swoop". The drive from NC to PA.

After my leave was over and I returned to base, I had to wait until Friday to see if I had duty during the weekend so if not, I often went to PA. The Marines called it the "swoop". It meant leaving Camp Lejeune about 4pm on Friday, going to a central place on base where the MP's announced who was going where so a driver could get riders to help pay for gas and provide a way for more Marines to go home for the weekend. It was illegal to go further than Wash. DC for a weekend so the MP's were indulging in other Marines to do an illegal event, that was strange. That is the way many people think. If no one knows, it is not illegal. But if you get caught, you were in big trouble, as I would find out someday. Quickly and aggressively driving to PA, NYC, or New England by like 2am, sleeping and having fun until about 4pm Sunday and then driving back, getting a few hours' sleep, and getting up for muster and calisthenics at 6am Monday.

Once back at Camp Lejeune, I noticed the people around the base were more hostile toward the Marines. Maybe returning Marines turned into real party people. I spent many a weekend working on my Chevy and now could buy beer on base. I started drinking more, trying to adjust to all the changes. There were no counselors, no testing, and no help for the problems returning vets would face. There could be a possibility that God made us incomplete, feeling like we are missing something, unhappy with our selves, always looking for something that we are not. I believe the only way we can be complete is to have God's Holy Spirit in us and being made into something that God wants for us.

One factor in my starting to drink more was the attitude of many people about the war later in 1967. Returning servicemen were not welcomed home as they deserved, they were called names, disrespected, harassed and denied entrance to some businesses. Around Camp Lejeune, there were signs on some people's lawns that read "Dogs and Marines, keep off the grass". Unknown to me, but many years later, I would be diagnosed with PTSD, which also had led me to drinking. Probably another factor in my drinking was that I was not happy with myself and alcohol gave me courage to be the guy I wanted to be. Eventually, I would come to see who God created in me and be happy with that.

I recall going home to PA some weekends, but I do not recall dating many girls or how I met them. My dad fixed me up with a girl from a business along his mail delivery route, but she did not help with my wanting to live a Christian life so I always preferred Sylvia, the girl I dated in high school. After arriving home, I called her to see if she was available for a date. She often had a date, so I often went a weekend without a date. Maybe she was not interested in dating me anymore. When I could get a date, we still enjoyed dancing, roller skating, hiking and picnics. Without a date, it was a lonely, frustrating time for me, which led to more drinking. I rarely knew if I would have to work on the weekend until the last minute, so it was hard to plan to arrange a date. I had a fake ID, before I turned 21, so I could buy hard alcohol like whiskey anytime.

VIETNAM PROTESTERS AND CROWD CONTROL

Most of the time I was a heavy equipment mechanic but later in 1967, Marines were being trained crowd control in case the protesters came to the base or the possibility that we may be called to go to a city to control the protests. The training included us in full gear with gas masks, rifles with bayonets. Other Marines dressed as protesters calling us names and throwing things at us. Those of us that were Vietnam vets were having a hard time with anger. There were times they called us to control protesters, and it was a difficult situation. We wanted to use the butt of our rifles and bayonets to solve the problem, but we had to restrain ourselves. In the evening we released that frustration by getting drunk and if we were out among civilians became a short fuse. During the last few months of 1967 and into 1968, I started drinking all the time. I had a bottle in my car, in my work truck, and even started drinking on the way to PA. That period may have been the worst time of my life. Being called names when off base. Not allowed in certain businesses if they knew you were a Marine. Going through training on base where we were called names, had things thrown at us and just made to feel bad about living. No veteran should have to go through that.

During this time, they also promoted me to sergeant, and I could now live off base. A friend and I rented a house near Surf City, N.C. It was right on the intra-coastal canal in a seasonal area. People showed up just occasionally, mostly during the summer. There were four Marines sharing a two-bedroom cottage filled with all kinds of alcohol. I started spending more time there at night and on the weekends.

MARINES PLAY COWBOYS AND INDIANS END UP IN EMERGENCY ROOM WITH AN ARROW IN LEG

One day a Marine Sergeant. Living with us bought a BB rifle to target practice with, and before long I became the target to practice on. I did not really mind since it only stung a little and besides, I could run, climb up on top of other houses and hide amongst all the vacant houses. Soon it became a game of the hunter and the human prey. I would climb on roof tops and run all around hiding in bushes or anywhere else I could. There was a swing rope tied to a branch of a big old tree in the back of our house that reached to our roof. I would climb up on our roof, swing off the roof and then jump off and run.

Fortunately, no one's property was ever damaged, and I never was hit in the face with a BB. That was a dangerous game for grown Marines to be playing, but for a change, that guy was a real holy terror. One weekend I went home to PA and brought back my bow and arrow I used to hunt with. This added a new challenge to our game, I was now armed, and I put him in my sights. Also, it was time for revenge.

Now it was cowboy and Indians, not just target practice for him. We continued to run around with him shooting me with BB's and I would shoot arrows at him intending to come as close as I could to him. I could usually put an arrow where I wanted it to go. It was exciting to see him scared and running from my arrows. The only problem was that eventually I would run out of arrows and then I would have to go collect them. It was not like the movies where I would never run out of arrows, although it seemed he never ran out of BB's. I did not use a full pull when shooting just to be safe; I knew the potential of hurting him. I just wanted to scare him, not kill him.

Then one day it happened; I was on someone's roof and he was behind a tree. He was shooting at me every time I would stand up to shoot an arrow. I shot arrows into the tree and in the ground all around the tree. I shot an arrow to hit the ground aside of the tree, but about that time he stepped out to run and the arrow hit his right thigh as I heard him scream. He quickly pulled it out and fell to the ground. I jumped off the roof as he looked at his leg (fortunately it was a target tip and not a hunting tip). There was a nice hole with much bleeding, so we wrapped it to stop the bleeding and off we went to the base hospital to get treated. That was a very humiliating experience to explain why two grown Vietnam vet Marines were playing cowboys and Indians. Fortunately, no actual damage occurred, and we were still friends however we never played cowboys and Indians again. 50 years later, when we met again at our anniversary, he reminded me of the scar he had.

I know you are probably asking yourself; how can this guy, that foolish kid, this Little Devil do all this crazy stuff and not get killed or kill someone else? I have no answer. Are there guardian angels and did they work overtime with me? Was I kept alive for the sake of my future wife and kids? It may not seem fair to our standards, but God is all powerful and does as His will is. Was luck involved or protection from God? Even my own kids have ended up with broken bones, burns and other scars from doing crazy things. I have also seen others trying various stunts and ending up in not so good a result, and I do not know why. The only thing I know is that we all have done wrong things and deserve the penalty of death, but we just must give thanks for the times we do not reap the penalty of our actions. I can only give thanks for the love, grace and forgiveness of an Almighty God. We do not deserve grace nor this great planet with all the pleasures we can get from it if it were not for a loving God caring about humans He created. Eventually there will be a new heaven and earth, and I cannot wait to see it.

THE 3 STOOGES FIGHT A FOREST FIRE

One day, at our Surf City house, we smelled wood smoke and went outside to investigate. It shocked us to see the forest across the street on fire. There was no 911 available, so we called the local police department and reported the fire.

We were told they would notify the forest department. A short time later, a single pickup truck drove up with a single Forestry Ranger in it. We asked if he needed help, and he said he could use the help. He fitted us with water tanks on our backs, gave us a handle with a patter on it to hit the lower brush with and a mask. We got in the back of the truck and drove down a dirt road toward the fire.

We figured we would never see this man again, so we thought we would give him something to talk about when he got home. We began making siren sounds and yelling out "Clear the road, fireman coming" and anything else we could think of that concerned firemen. When we got deeper in the woods, we found it was mostly the underbrush and smaller trees on fire. We began spraying water on the actual fire and patted the lower brush until it was out. Once the fire was under control, we played war. We started shooting each other with the water guns and pretending the fire was an enemy. We would hide behind a tree and shoot at a fire and then maneuver our way up to it and BANG, shoot it dead.

It was like the Three Stooges; I was Curly, the other Marine was Larry, and the Forest Ranger was like Moe, the serious one and always yelling at us and maybe ready to poke our eyes out or hit us on our heads. We eventually got the fire out, having fun along the way, and we figured we gave this Forestry Ranger some stories to tell others about these two crazy Marines that helped him. I am sure he thought other adjectives to describe us, but Little Devils were kind.

He thanked us for our help with a brief grin, a strange look, and drove off. We figured we would never see him again. He went home and told his family about the crazy Little Devils loose in Surf City disguised as Marines. I am sure he hoped to never see us again. Little did he know what God had in store for his future. Several years later, he would become a deputy sheriff and have my car towed to the junkyard because I ran out of gas. When he found out it was my car, he paid to have the car released back to me without poking my eyes out. We met again one more time in the future.

Chapter 18: THE CREATOR DOES A MAKEOVER

I was going home to PA almost every weekend to get a date and basically to get away from the base. While driving home late at night the only thing on the AM radio was religious broadcasting. For the first time in my life, I was hearing different views of Christianity. It was interesting to listen to. I thought about the life I was living and desired to go back to my Christian roots, but just did not have the courage to make changes by myself. Some preachers were saying things I never heard before, and one weekend I picked up my old childhood Bible and took it back to NC to see if what they said was true. I started ordering some free literature offered on the radio broadcasts. Occasionally, I would read my Bible, but was not making any genuine effort to make changes. I remember reading that to lust after a woman was a sin. That was not my mother, that was Jesus. Wow, I never heard that. My favorite song was "I'm A Girl Watcher".

Although, many memories run together in my mind but I know from my military records that early in 1968, I was sent to Instructor Training School and hoped to be transferred to the Heavy Equipment School where my friends were and the school that I had attended. After graduating school, I was told I was going back to Engineers to be a mechanic and not to the heavy equipment school. That also meant more of the dreaded crowd control assignments and more facing protesters. I was extremely disappointed and depressed. This was the tipping point, I tried to ignore the protesters tried to adjust to all the changes back home, the lack of friends and now the Marine Corps was going to deny me an instructor position in what I wanted and put me into something I hated. I went drinking that night and decided to not go back to the Engineers. I had my orders with me and figured the Engineers would not miss me for some time. I saw an opportunity to take off and end this misery I was feeling, and then later I could decide if I would go back.

I figured I would go home for a week or two and then go marry Julie and disappear. I packed my important items and took off. Unknown to me, my guardian angel must have reported my actions to God, and they must have agreed I was going a little too far. I think God said it was now time to do "The Hokey Pokey" and turn my life around. After feeling the pain of my actions, God would open my mind so I could see my actions were not producing the results God expected from me. He would bring to memory my Christian upbringing and the commitment I made at camp when I accepted Jesus as my savior.

I headed to PA, and while drinking, I ran into the back of a truck. The truck driver was a former Marine and told me to leave and quit drinking. It could have been worse, but maybe was a warning to go back. When I got home, I called Sylvia to get a date, but she was not available. I went to see a married high school friend, and he said he could arrange a date with a neighbor of his. He forgot to mention she was separated but still married. We double dated, had a fun time, and did some drinking, but the evening did not end up very well after her jealous husband showed up.

My friend also forgot to mention that her husband was a golden gloves boxer, and he thought my head looked like a punching bag. I never was into fighting much unless I had been drinking, after which I had a short fuse. He would not go away so I hit him first. He somehow pulled my sweater over my head where I could not move my arms or pull away. I got one lucky punch in and knocked him down. He got up, walked off and drove away. But a neighbor had called the police, so I had to give my information to them as they asked for my pass. I knew they may contact the base and they would catch me. A few months later, after realizing that drinking, fighting and dating married women was not who I wanted to be. So when I saw her husband again while driving one day, I apologized to him.

After a few days of recuperation, I then tried to arrange a date on my own with a girl I used to know. I remember going to the girl's house with a few bottles of liquor. The girl would not date me since I had been drinking, and I got mad and depressed. She was a nice girl I knew from the cottage my parents rented. I only have pieces of memories after that. I remember being at a bar with a pool table and getting kicked out because of being drunk and fighting. I remember getting hit by a car and getting into a fight with the driver. I remember throwing a bottle at a car and then some guys chasing me. I also remember hearing police sirens and then driving off quickly toward home, and that is the last I remember.

I woke up the next morning in a cornfield about twenty miles from where I started, with no idea how I got there. I must have had like a black out where you are awake but have no recall of what you did or how you got there. Parts of my body were black and blue, bruised, and sore from being hit by the car. My hands were sore, probably from fighting, and my face was still sore from the boxer. I did not like the idea that I drove a car and did not understand how I got there, plus had been out of control the night before. That kind of adventure I never wanted to repeat. I spent the next few days reflecting on what had happened. I decided this was not the way I wanted to live, it just was not me, so I would go back to the base.

I would deal with my new assignment, quit drinking, and straighten up my life. I was content being a Little Devil, but I did not want to be controlled by the Devil. (Actually, I have learned that our own selfish human nature is enough to control our habits and desires and causes us to have miserable and unhappy lives) I spent the next few days recuperating and then headed back to Camp Lejeune.

On the way back, I was listening to a preacher on the radio and just started feeling disgusted with myself. I pulled over and started crying and asked God to forgive me through Jesus' sacrifice for me. I told Him I needed His help to live the Christian life I thought He would want me to live. I gave up on Christianity because it seemed like I could find no one living a Christian life. I never saw an authentic example of Christianity. I asked God to make me an example to others and show others that being a Christian can be fun and not just black and austere. Almost immediately, I realized I could not be a perfect example of Christianity because I was not perfect, I would be a hypocrite even though it would not be intentional. Only Jesus was without sin.

I went back to Camp Lejeune, feeling good, and checked into my new assignment, and it appeared as though I was not missed during that week. I started thinking about my life and what changes I needed to make. A week later my CO called me into his office and said he got a police report about the fight and asked what I was doing in PA since I did not have permission to be away. I ended up telling him about my frustrations, my party life and everything else that made me leave. I was charged with an AWOL (away without leave). My CO said I was a good Marine but said I allowed depression and the party life to get control of me. He also said that he would help end it. No room for a Little Devil or any Devil in a Marine's life. He would help stop my party life with the punishment of forfeiting half my pay for three months and they put me on restriction for two months with no more liberty to go anywhere but work, my barracks and my off-base house. He said he would also help find me an instructor position that was not with the crowd control.

After describing my feeling about using Vietnam vets for crowd control, he agreed and did not think we should use them in that position. Unfortunately, sometimes vets were the only ones left on base since new Marines were not around long before going to Vietnam. That was great to hear. I was happy to hear about the instructor job possibility and happy about the restrictions since I needed a kick in the butt to help overcome the party life. It caused me to hang around our house and not do much of anything except read the Bible. Looking back, I am glad that I was caught and punished. It helped stop and protect me from a lifestyle that could have harmed others and myself. In the last 52 years since then, I have never abused alcohol again.

Being charged with AWOL and giving up pay, I ended my party life and not drink again. I also came to see the life I was living was not what I wanted for myself. I was not enjoying life when I allowed alcohol to rule me. I just started thinking about my life once again and where I was going. I had no problems or withdraw symptoms giving up alcohol and did not have a desire for it again. (That was a miracle) I had a toast of champagne at our wedding and a small glass of real wine at church for the Lord's supper but had no desire for more. Eventually with the help of the ministry I learned that the Bible does not condemn wine or strong drink, just the improper use of it, like drunkenness or using it to be someone you are not.

I also cleaned up my mouth and street talk overnight. My hatred for protesters hateful people around the base, and hypocrites Christians were gone. (Another miracle) A great calm and peace came over me. I was ready for a peaceful adventure.

I did come to believe that God was working with me and showing me I was lost (like when we were in that dark cave feeling lost and blind) and wondering around looking for something that I would never find. In the next several weeks, I would study the Bible, to find out what it meant to dedicate my life to God, and what it meant to accept Jesus Christ as my savior. I wanted to clean up my life, find some good friends and have some good fun like Sam and I used to do. I quit going out with the Marines and

168

quit dating all girls. Once my restriction was over, I would start to attend a local church. At our off-base house with four other Marines, I hated alcohol so much I poured my alcohol and their alcohol and beer down the drain. Going cold turkey and forcing my way on others was not the best way to win friends and influence people.

I was sure once they heard my story, they would want to change also but that never happened. I thought maybe if I preached harder, they would hear. I was doing to them what I hated others doing to me. I was pressuring them, condemning them, preaching to them like I hated others doing to me. After that, my fellow Marines and friend's kind of deserted me with my changes, I was now living even more of a lonely life. I started hiking through the woods around our cottage and found a place I could go to, be alone, and pray. It was like impossible to study and pray in a house with three other Marines, so I ended up clearing the land and building a little chapel like we had at Mt. Gretna church camp and would go there regularly.

I asked God to forgive me through the sacrifice of Jesus Christ and I read out loud Psalms 51 as I wanted to be cleaned up and get a new clean heart. God was changing me, and it felt good to live the life I wanted, but it was difficult being alone and not having money to do anything. I needed a friend to share with and have some good clean fun with. One day at the chapel, out of extreme loneliness, I just cried out to God for Him to provide a Christian person who I could share with. The photo shows the chapel I built in the woods patterned after the one I saw at Mt Gretna Camp as a preteen.

BECOMING AN INSTRUCTOR AT AN INFANTRY SCHOOL

I do not remember exactly when, but somewhere along the line, my CO came through and got me transferred to an instructor position, not at the Heavy Equipment School but teaching military subjects to Marines on the way to Vietnam. I started teaching weapons and how to use them to kill. I told my supervisor I did not have much infantry experience and did not feel comfortable teaching without experience. He gave me a Marine Corps manual on weapons and said to read the book and teach it.

I read the manuals and taught from them, but I did not feel comfortable about it. As a growing Christian, the Bible appeared to teach love and forgiveness, so how did teaching to kill fit into that. I thought about my experiences in Vietnam and how when doing maintenance on a generator at a field hospital, I would sometimes be asked to help unload the wounded and dead from helicopters landing at the hospital. I had mixed emotions about that. One emotion was to feel sorry for the wounded and to kill the enemy. The other emotion was to stop the pain and suffering on both sides and end wars.

Also, while in Japan and visiting the Peace Museums at both Hiroshima and Nagasaki, I saw the effects of the atomic bomb on the Japanese. I know that the atomic bomb saved many American lives by not having to attack the mainland. Those photos were horrible to see and made me want to find a way of ending wars. Realistically, I read in the Bible in Mt 24 that there would always be wars right up to the time that Jesus returns to this earth to end Satan's rule over this earth. To me, it meant praying more for Jesus to return to earth and become the king he said he was.

The Gunny Sgt. in charge of the school, used to put photos of Vietnamese children around the school with word "kill" over the photo. I did not like the photos promoting the killing of children, so I tore them down. I understood children were sometimes used to throw grenades, sell poisoned drinks to Marines, and offer to sell sex to Marines, but often led Marines to injury instead. However, not all the children did that.

I also taught another course about surviving if you become a POW. It included how to endure torture techniques that the Viet Cong used if captured and resisting and planning an escape. Before each class, all the instructors were put through a short torture period by our Gunnery Sgt. to let us know how it felt so we would not overdo the torture on the new Marines. He used to say if we abused the young Marines, we would find ourselves in the torture box. He also said if we went against him, he would lock us in there overnight.

Since becoming a Christian and changing my life, I had been preaching and witnessing to my fellow Marines. I told them how happy I was to quit drinking, stopped the party life, quit using vulgar language and how rewarding it was to give my life to God. I was sure once they heard the message that offered them a change, they would eagerly accept it like I did. I was wrong.

For some reason, I did not understand; they wanted nothing to do with my message. It was that God did not open their minds to be receptive to the message, just like me. They were furious with me, and I had a feeling that I would need my guardian angel. I was hoping he did not leave because of the heat, humidity, and mosquitoes in the area.

PREACHER JOHN - IN THE BOX - TORTURE TIME

One of the torture techniques the Viet Cong used was to put a prisoner in a small wood box in the ground, like an orange crate only big enough for a man to squeeze into. It created claustrophobia and the VC would then pour water, sand or anything else to cause pain to the prisoner. We had one of those boxes we used on the Marines so before each class the Gunny Sgt. put us in there for a few minutes and then let us out. He wanted to be sure that we experienced what it was like to be in there before we put others in. When it was my turn, I climbed in and they shut the lid. They designed it to create claustrophobia and fear of not being able to move. They did the normal, flooding my face with water and then kicking some sand on me. Normally they opened the lid, and we all had a big laugh.

This time the Gunnery Sergeant, said the men were complaining about me preaching to them and they did not like it. He also mentioned that he found out it was me who was taking down his photos, and he did not like that either. He said there was peace and unity before I came, and Marines cannot be effective unless there is unity. They thought it may be a good idea to live this new life for a year and then preach to them how it worked. He said they would let me think about it overnight and let me out in the morning and then walked off. I did not know what to think, but I felt I could not survive that box until the morning. Rather terrified, I was praying when I heard voices approaching. The men came back and let me out, kind of laughing, but said they did not care for my preaching at them all the time. They liked the way things were before I came. I gave that some thought about how I did not like being preached at all my life, but I wanted to see an example.

All the preaching in my life made no difference in me, it was God calling me, opening my mind so I could understand, and then I listened to preaching. So, I backed off preaching and concentrated on living a Christian life. I remembered at my conversion; I told God I wanted to be an example, not a preacher. Some people have said it is better to be a light rather than a foghorn, but we need both.

After that incident, I never had another problem, but neither did I have any friends there. They kind of kept to themselves. I enjoyed teaching and thought someday I might like to teach auto mechanics in high school. Eventually, the gunny Sgt. Put me in charge of the POW part of the school. I enjoyed my stay there and would have extended in the Marines to stay there. We had two week-long classes a month and two weeks to prepare, so it was good duty.

DISCOVERING AN AWESOME CREATION OF GOD

As a young boy and teenager, I did a lot of roller skating and really enjoyed it. I think I may have met Sylvia at a roller-skating rink or at least she was an excellent skater, and we went on many a date to the roller-skating rink. Then I would take her out to McDonald's and buy a 15-cent hamburger, 15-cent soda, and 15-cent fries for her. A date did not cost much in the '60s. She still dated me after spending only $.45 on her.

So skating was the clean fun I was looking for. I found a roller-skating rink on Topsail Island close to where my off-base house was and skated there regularly. My Little Devil lifestyle never ended since I was still on restriction and the MP's drove by house to see if my car was there. So, I would sneak out and drive my motorcycle to the rink. There were five or six young boys there that I had fun with, especially when they played games on the floor. It was the clean fun I remembered and enjoyed. I never took an interest in girls that went there, but one night a young girl caught my eye. I would have liked to have met her, but she was beautiful, and I was kind of shy. I felt like I needed to get to know her, but my body would not go over to her. I wished that chick magnet, Sam, was there to introduce us.

God was trying to answer my prayer, but I made it hard for Him to do so. I was skating around when suddenly; she ran into me and fell. (Is not that the oldest trick in the book? I think she could not resist my good looks, muscular body, and superior intellect.) Not the case. It turns out her brothers grabbed her and whipped her into me. I helped her up. She smiled, said thanks, and skated away. As she went on her way, I just melted with my mouth open so wide my tongue got caught under my wheel, but no words came out as usual. I saw her removing her skates, so I thought it is now or never. I asked her to couple skate and found her extremely easy to talk to, and we spoke a lot about God. We skated and talked the rest of the night.

It seemed we had a lot in common. We talked about life, family, and especially about religion. I told her all about my sinful past life and how God changed me. She understood and seemed to be happy for me. Later, she said she never heard of anyone confessing all their sins the first night they met. That may have helped her realize that I wanted to be honest and truthful. She usually worked every night and did not go skating, but her boss made her take a day off from work to have fun with other teens, so she came with her brothers. She had 4 brothers and 2 sisters and spent a lot of time working after school at one of the local ocean pier restaurants, walking the beach, and occasionally went to the same church I did. I offered her a ride home, but she said her dad was coming to get her.

Then, I remembered I brought my friend's car instead of mine, anyway. I was still under restriction, so when the MP's came by my house and saw my car was there, they kept going. Still being sneaky, I drove my friend's 1957 Plymouth four-door sedan that did not look too good. He used it for drag racing, so it was dented, muddy, and loud with the seats out except for a bucket seat for the driver to sit on. I had already impressed her with my good looks, muscles and superior intellect and now could have impressed her with my 1963 Chevy convertible. I tried to quietly drive off in this piece of junk and hope she did not see me. However, just as I drove by the skating rink, she came out and waved and said bye John. Later she told me she was not impressed with my good looks, muscles or my superior intellect but was impressed with my ideas of God, family, adventures, and the plain car I drove. It disappointed her it was not my car.

There goes my ego again. She also liked the idea that I was not so macho that I did not mind playing with the kids there and cutting up with them. Even to this day as a father and grandfather, I enjoy cutting up with the kids, even if it is very hard to do now as I get older and my muscular body is paying the price for all those Little Devil shenanigans. Since she worked at a restaurant and often had Marines coming in there to hit on her and offer her rides in their hot Mustang, Camaros and GTO's. Some could afford the new cars. She was used to good looks, muscles and superior intellect, but she liked plain down-to-earth guys not trying to impress a girl. Turns out that she told a lady at the roller-skating rink, that I was the guy she was going to marry. How prophetic.

I drove off realizing that this could have been an answered prayer, and I did not have her phone number, address, last name, (email address, Facebook page, twitter account-HAHA, not invented yet) or any contact information. How stupid of me? God would have to bring her back again. But in the meantime, I would do my part and search for her like a lost treasure.

I drove my Honda (same one from Japan) up and down the beach looking for her every day, hoping to run into her, but never did. I checked out all the local restaurants but could not find her; I wondered if I would ever see her again. I even went to church to search for her. Then one day I got off work early and was working on my car when a school bus pulled up to drop off the neighbor kids when I heard someone yell out "Hey good looking." I stood tall and smiled; finally, someone noticed my attributes but then as I looked up and only saw the bus driver who looked to be about seventy years old.

Disappointed, I looked down the bus windows and there she was just like a special angel sent from heaven, hanging her head out the window and said, "Hi John". It was Diane from the roller-skating rink, the girl I thought I would never see again. I stood there dazed, my eyes bulging as my tongue fell on the ground into some sand stickers. I may have tried to wave and mumble hi as the bus drove off. After all the searching I had done to find her, here she was driving by my house every day. I jumped up and ran to the neighbor kids to see if they knew her. I asked what she was doing on a school bus and they said she was a junior and was 16 years old and was their babysitter. She looked and talked much older than being 16.

I thought to myself, oh no, she was next door as a babysitter all this time. I am ruined. Did she see me drinking, swinging on our rope, see me shooting arrows at other Marines? Later that week, the neighbor kids gave me a message from her and that if I wanted to see her again, she would be at the Moose Lodge dancing the next Saturday night. I did, and this would be my chance to impress her with my exceptional smooth dance moves. I went, we danced, we talked, and I knew I was in love. This was God's answered prayer to me and what an answer, WOOOO. God is an awesome God.

We agreed to meet at church next time. I still had no contact information other than the bus. I tried to get home early as often as I could just to wave to her. I think it was the next week she showed up at church and ended up sitting with me or me with her, not sure how it was. She told me she was a waitress and short-order cook at Paradise Pier on Topsail Island and invited me up some time. The next day I went to the pier after work and we talked, I ate there, and watched her work and serve the customers.

Although I may have felt neglected, I was glad to see that she had an excellent work ethic and put her responsibilities above her pleasures. (That is assuming she found it pleasurable talking to me). Her father dropped her off and picked her up. So, I had to be gone before he came. H did not trust Marines.

I went to the pier every day I could, and she went to church whenever she did not work. We continued to get to know more about each other and observe each other in various circumstances. Our relationship was growing fast. I asked if I could take her home since I usually stayed there until close to closing. She said I would have to ask her dad.

She said late at night when he picked her up was not a good time, so one day, she invited me to her house to meet her mom and dad. I already knew her brothers and sisters from the roller-skating rink. I agreed, and we set a date for me to meet her parents.

HEALTHY MARINE HAS A HEART ATTACK

Finally, the day came for me to meet Diane's parents. After Viet Nam and all my scary adventures, this should be a piece of cake although I was a little anxious. I knew her dad was a Yankee and married her mother, a southern girl. I also knew the local girls were not supposed to date Marines. Returning Vietnam Marines had a terrible reputation for drunkenness, fighting and seeking to party. I was quite aware of that fact.

I went in and met her mother and we talked awhile, and everything was going fine. Then I heard a truck drive up and a door slam. As I looked out the window, the truck looked familiar, but from where? I saw a man in a uniform through the curtains and asked Diane where her father worked. As he was opening the door, she said he was a _____? The door opened and in walked her father. When I saw him, I could feel the blood draining from my face, my heart fell into my stomach and my knees gave out and my mouth opened; my tongue hit the clean floor Diane had just swept.

I almost collapsed as I looked into the eyes of who?

A. A Marine Colonel, my CO.

B. A Marine Major doctor that stitched up my friend's arrow wound.

C. My Gunny Sgt.

D. Moe, the forest ranger.

It was D. Could this be the man I had helped put out the fire with across from my house and played the three stooges? OH NO. When he stuck out his hand, I expected him to say pick two and poke my eyes, but he did not.

Instead, Diane introduced me, and I said hi as I shook his hand, hoping he would not remember me, but then he said, "We already met". He turned to his wife and said this is that stupid Yankee Jarhead I told you about at the forest fire on Little Kinston. I thought to myself, I am so stupid; there goes any hope of ever dating her. Why do I do the things I do? (Jarhead was a derogatory term used about Marines and it was not good for him to call me that.)

We talked awhile, and he seemed friendly. Finally, he said it would be OK to take Diane to work and bring her home again. He said, anyone that acted so stupid in a forest fire could be trusted with his daughter. (That may have been a compliment?) He then added, and that means right home. He said he knew how long it took to get home and if I stopped anywhere, I would be sorry. (I think it meant tying me to a tree and setting a forest fire) After leaving, I jumped for joy, screamed, yelled, and thanked God.

A PARTNERSHIP MADE IN HEAVEN

To make a long story short, I continued to visit her at the pier restaurant and taking her home and to work when possible. We talked a lot, and I noticed she was a wonderful cook, a good cleaner, and had a good work ethic. I also noticed she gave most of her money to her family to help them out, cleaned around the house doing chores and watched over her younger brothers and sisters. Hard to believe she had time to talk to me, but her actions were louder than words.

Her responsibilities came before the great pleasure of talking to me. As we talked, we found we had similar beliefs and had so much in common that our relationship just kept growing fast and we found we really enjoyed being with each other. We talked a lot about my family and things we did as a family. We went swimming at the beach with her brothers and I got to see her after any makeup was watched off and I saw who she really was. She was still exceptionally beautiful, but I just really loved her for who she was inside.

I was still a Marine and could not be alone with her other than the 30-45-minute ride home from the pier and we better not be late. When I visited the house, her brothers sat across from us as we talked and if I got too close to her or tried to hold hands, I got the evil eye from her brothers and threats of "I'm going to tell daddy". I never saw her yell at or get mad at her brothers and was always respectful to her parents. I had seen many girls be so sweet and nice when in public but yelled at her family or got disrespectful toward them. I saw Diane as a respectful young lady to her family.

We met in March 1968 and when Easter time came; I wanted to go to PA to visit my family and my mother asked if I would play my trumpet in church. Because of losing half my pay and being on restriction, I had not gone home in a few months and I was still on restriction but asked for a pass, anyway. My immediate officer said no because he did not trust me, and I may get into trouble, plus I did not finish serving my time.

I requested to see my CO and explained to him that I was behaving better, and my mother wanted me to play the trumpet in church. That must have been odd to hear that a Marine wanted to please his mother, playing the trumpet in church. Maybe he thought I could not get into trouble in church, (if he only knew) or maybe he was glad I found religion. He approved my pass.

I received a four day leave of absence over Easter to go to PA legally. Wow, what a change for me, God is real. I spent the entire time thinking about Diane and if I should allow the relationship to continue considering her age. While home, I told my parents about Diane and our growing relationship. I got my dad alone to ask for his advice, which may have been the first time I ever asked for his advice. I told him about Julie, who was expecting me to marry her in a few weeks.

I told him about Diane and how I felt she was an answered prayer. I also talked about Sylvia who I dated through high school and always enjoyed being with her, but it was harder to see her since returning from overseas, plus now my restriction kept me in NC. Also, Julie and Sylvia did not know about my change of life so I did not know how they would take it. I do not recall any advice that helped me, so it would be a matter of prayer and turning it over to God. After a lot of prayer, talking with a pastor, I decided God had brought us together, and this was an answered prayer for both of us. Turns out she was praying for someone like me and I was praying for someone like her. When I returned, she let me see her journal of what she was thinking while I was gone. It thrilled me to read that she felt the same way about me that I felt about her.

After this point, we knew we were in love with each other. Sorry to say, I was a little skeptic about her feelings. Why would such a beautiful and perfect girl have an interest in me? My pay was cut, and I had no savings, I had no way of offering her physical security although we talked about living in a tree house and being happy. One time while taking her to work, I ran out of gas about two blocks from a gas station. Since she had no driver's license to steer while I pushed, she got out to help push my 63 Chevrolet while I steered to the gas station. I then proceed to count out my pennies to get a gallon of gas. During our married years, we pushed many a car broke down or when out of gas and counted many a penny to get necessities.

Diane was not like many other girls I had dated. She was not a touchy, aggressive girl seeking physical contact. Actually, I don't remember when we started to hold hands or when I first put my arm around her for the first time, probably in church, but I do remember the first quick goodnight kiss outside her house by a big tree.

We finally had one date to go to a drive-in movie, but we had to take her dog, my dog, and it seems another dog along as chaperones since our dogs were jealous and would not allow us to get close. I finally bought a couple hamburgers and threw them in the back seat. Both dogs jumped in the back and we scooted close together. I was finally alone with the love of my life to enjoy the movie. We even snuck in a few kisses now and then. Shortly after that, the movie language became rather vulgar and being a newly born-again Christian, I did not want to hear that, nor did I want this precious sweet young girl to hear that either, so I took her home. She wanted to stay because she said she heard a lot worse from her dad.

Because I took her home early, her parents thought I had done something to hurt her or that we had done something wrong and felt guilty, so I had brought her home early. What a shame, we do something right and we get accused of doing something wrong.

After watching my married high school friends and listening to religious broadcasts, I had made a checklist of what I wanted in a mate and Diane had passed all of them. I thought about asking her to marry me. In May, we went to her Junior-senior prom. Her parents allowed us to go since her brother was a senior and would be there as well. After the prom, we walked on the beach and I asked her to marry me; she accepted. I was overjoyed and of course thanked God once again.

At that time, Julie was still planning on me coming out to Calif. to marry her. When I was home for Easter, I called Julie to talk to her but she was out on a date with another man so I wondered if the other Marines were correct that she may be looking for a USA citizenship. I had learned what genuine love was and felt Diane was a gift from God. I knew I loved Diane, but I would have to tell Julie I would not be out. I eventually called Julie to tell her about Diane and she of course cried and how much she loved me. I felt bad, but I knew little about her and now that I was a Christian, I had no idea what her religion was. I finally stuck to my guns and said I was sorry. A few months later I called again to check up on her and found she was married so I will never know her true ambitions.

I had no money to buy a diamond engagement ring for Diane, but I did have access to a machine shop at Camp Lejeune, NC. I handmade a ring and soldered a jewel covered cross on it. I thought the cross offered a better pledge of love and security than a diamond. She loved it and was proud to wear it. Her friends and family were not quite as enthusiastic. I was right about feeling the cross offers more love and security than a diamond, but at our 45th anniversary, six children and fourteen grandchildren later, I finally bought her a genuine diamond ring.

Her parents were not too happy about us wanting to get married, and since she was only 16, we needed her parents' approval. My parents were not too happy either. They thought we did not know each other long enough. She was too young; she was too far south, and they had not met her.

Diane kept asking her parents, but I also needed to talk to her dad. But he worked all the time. He was now a county deputy sheriff, so I decided to leave the base early one afternoon when I knew he would be working at the jail. I would have to talk to him at his work and I hoped he would listen and not chase me out, lock me up or shoot me. I hoped my guardian angel was not on vacation or out fishing.

We had a friendly talk together, and I explained why I wanted to marry his daughter. He also asked a lot of questions to see how much time we had been alone and if we had done anything to break his trust in us. I was very happy to say that the only times we were alone was on the way to work and back which he kept track of the time from his family and one time we dated and I did not feel the movie was good for her so I took her home early. He was happy and said he would think about it.

After a few weeks of not hearing anything, I went back to see her dad at the jail again. Once again, he said he would think about it. I made a habit of going back to the jail every week to ask him again.

At one of our conversations, he also asked if I knew about her health problems, I said I did not and asked what he meant. I knew she was thin and looked anemic. He said she had some female problems, was anemic, often felt sick, tired, and the doctor said because of internal problems, she most likely could not have any children. I had loved to play with my niece and nephew, playing with the children in Vietnam, Japan and enjoyed her brothers at the rolling skating rink and had looked forward to having children of my own. I loved Diane and thought I would just leave it in God's hands to heal her if He wanted us to have children. One of the other deputies suggested her dad throw me in jail to shut me up and keep me from coming up every week, but he never did. One deputy said she could do worse. That may have been a compliment?

Diane and I went to church together every Sunday and on one Sunday in June 1968, we were both in a surf city church when at the end of the sermon the pastor asked if anyone would like to renew their commitment to Jesus Christ. We had talked about it, so we both raised our hands.

The pastor had us come forward and asked if we would like to be baptized. We had studied baptism and felt it was an outward sign of our inward feelings, so we agreed. We were both baptized on June 23 of 1968, shortly after she had turned 17. Some fears of baptism were unfounded, I did not drown or choke; I did not speak in tongues and basically at the time felt no different from before. Gradually, though, I saw it was easier to change my ways, and it seemed like it was easier to understand what I read in the Bible.

My Marine buddies thought I was baptized to impress Diane and thought I would do anything to get this girl hooked, to conquer her, to win her like many of us guys do to get a girl. Sometimes getting a girl becomes a challenge to prove we are men. I hope my granddaughters watch out for that as they start dating. I hope they take their time and get to know that special person very well before marriage.

My Marines "friends" took any opportunity they could to get her alone and tell her, I was a fake and what I was really like, but she already knew what I had been like before because I told her that first night at the roller skating rink. I told her all about my past and my sins and the way I had changed and how I felt now. After hearing all that, she still wanted to see me again. It sure appears that honestly is the best policy. In modern terms, we should always be transparent and let God work out how others see us.

 We recently celebrated our 50th anniversary and asked one of my Marine buddies who was our best man to come to NC for the celebration. He was living in California. was surprised but happy that I was still with Diane, that we had a great family and were still committed to God. He was now living alone after several marriages. This was his first anniversary party since he usually was only invited to divorce parties.

Obviously, we got married in July 1968. We were both persistent in prayer and asking her parents until finally they gave in and said "YES". I do not know if it was possible back then, but if he did a background check or checked with my neighbor, who was the Police Chief to find out more about me and my family. He sure had other officers monitor us when we were out on the road. One day in my convertible with the top down, I put my arm around Diane and almost immediately lights and sirens came on. The patrolman said something like, keep both hands on the steering wheel, you Little Devil.

Another time, we stopped to walk on the beach and my car got stuck in the sand. We could not free it, but in a matter of minutes, a police car and tow truck were there, which I did not call. Maybe it was my guardian angel or someone else, like a spy policeman, watching over us.

While planning for our wedding, I mentioned to Diane that I was scheduled for 15 days of leave and had planned to be a counselor at Mt. Gretna church camp July 21-28. I asked if we were married before that, would she like to go along? She loved the idea, so we set a date for marriage for July 19, 1968. I called the camp and asked if I could bring my wife, and they said she could come and be a counselor as well. WOW, that was outstanding. We thought this would be an excellent way of showing our thanks to God. We would give our first week of our honeymoon to serve God and then go wilderness camping for a few days before coming back to NC. I was so pleased to hear that Diane would want to share these adventures with me.

Chapter 19: SAM'S ADVENTUROUS REPLACEMENT

My parents came down, and we were married with a nice little wedding at Surf City Baptist Church. My father played the organ, and my mother sang. I think my mother told the pastor I played the organ because he asked me to be their organist. My parents paid for a motel room for us and the next day we left for camp.

I mentioned before how Diane's father told me about her physical problems. She was having female problems, was underweight and was anemic and was told by doctors that she may never have children. We were disappointed but did not think about it very much. We just prayed that if it was God's will we have children, that He heal her. On our wedding day, Diane later told me she was feeling much better and some of her symptoms had just disappeared, much like my conversion. Although I was happy to hear that, again I did not give it a lot of thought. As the next few months would progress, we would learn that God healed her on that day as she gained weight, lose her anemic look, have more energy and her female problems disappeared completely. We would also have our first child fourteen months later and would name him John Elijah which means "God is love" and "The Lord is God". He would be followed by five more children, four boys and two girls.

Getting married young and having no savings, no job security but only owned a '63 Chevy, a Honda motorcycle, a dog, and our Bibles with a commitment to each other and God. We knew life would not be easy, but we loved each other and believed we could live on love and that God would provide our needs. We wanted to show our gratitude and commitment to God by giving the first week of our marriage to God. Although I know there is nothing, we can do to earn our salvation or have our sins forgiven by doing something good for God, we just wanted to do it.

I do not recommend living on love. It worked for us because we were in love and willing to sacrifice to be together. I believe God would prefer a couple to date long enough to get to know each other thoroughly in all situations. It is also best to be well established in an occupation and have a plan with some savings. Below is a photo of our wedding and reception.

OUR HONEYMOON AT A CHURCH CAMP

Our honeymoon week at Mt Gretna Church Camp, near Lebanon, PA., was so wonderful and fun filled that we did not think of it as a sacrifice. We slept in separate cabins and instead of taking her home to her parents' home every night like we were used to; I escorted her to the girl's cabin and said goodnight without even a kiss. We thought it might be inappropriate in front of the teen campers. I noticed how good she was with other teens and I learned so much from her. Watching and learning as she related to the campers was the best adventure I had ever been on. Some girl campers were the same age as Diane and would often flirt with me to make her jealous. One time we took the campers boating in the lake and a bunch of girls jumped in my boat to be close to my good looks, muscular Marine body, and my superior intellect. The boys jumped in Diane's boat, wanting to be around such a beautiful angel. I guess I must have appeared to be enjoying the flirting from the girls because when we got back, Diane pushed me off the dock into the lake.

It was dinnertime and since I had to escort my group into the dining hall and eat with them; I had to go in wet. Everyone got a friendly laugh out of that. We both put our full efforts into the campers and mostly gave up on any pleasures for ourselves for that week. The campers would often play tricks on us and were constantly watching us. Often at dinner, there was a song they sang "Around the Lodge You Must Go", which ended up with a boy and girl having to walk around the lodge together. I think we walked around the lodge together every meal, which gave us a chance to hold hands or sneak in a quick kiss. Occasionally they sent Diane or me around the lodge with someone else. We went along with the fun they were having at our expense. Sometimes they sang the song "In the lake you must go" to remind me what happens if I step out of line. They seemed to love her being jealous and doing things to me like pushing me into the lake.

We shared our story of how God changed me and then brought us together, and all the answered prayers involved. We also shared our testimony with the other campers and expressed our love for God and Jesus Christ. We encouraged them to not learn the hard way. Our message was that God loves them because he sent his son to die for their sins so they could be a part of his family. He shows His love in creation and everything we see around us from the beautiful sunsets over the mountains to the exceptional sunrises over the ocean. God also wants to show even more of His love for them if they believe that His son, Jesus, has died to cover their sins and has a plan for their lives, including after this present life. We said we all want the same thing and that is to have peace, happiness, and security. Diane and I have found we get it all from God, not the world. 52 plus years later we still believe the same thing. Diane and I only knew the God we found in creation, or should I say that he found us.

When I first asked the director of the camp if I could bring my wife along, he did not know that we were married only two days before. When we arrived at camp and he found out, he later told us he had some concerns about that especially with my history of being a rather wild and flirtatious Little Devil at camp. After seeing us during the week and hearing about my conversion, he said he was overjoyed to have us there and we could come back whenever we wanted. The next few summers, she was pregnant, and we were never able to return.

On our 50th anniversary, we went back to visit Mt Gretna.

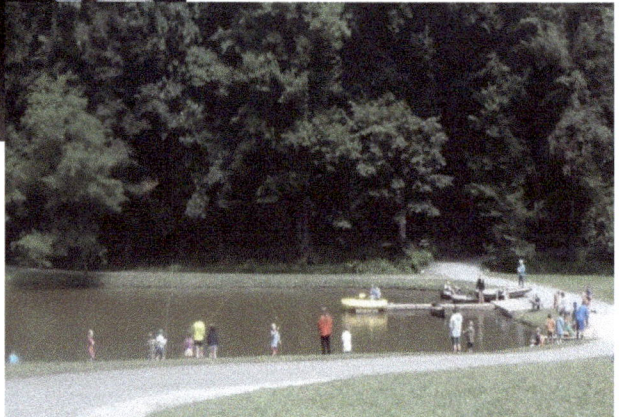

OUR HONEYMOON CAMPING IN THE WILDERNESS

After camp was over, we hiked and backpacked into the wilderness of the Pocono Mountains and camped by a stream for three days. We were even deeper into the woods than Sam and I had gone. It was a favorite hunting spot of mine since it was close to many cascading waterfalls. For food there was a wild blueberry field, apple trees and a deep hole in the spring-fed stream loaded with native trout and a great place for a dip in the ice-cold mountain spring water. Again, we had an outstanding time, and I was really impressed by how much we enjoyed doing the same things together. That fact is still true today, even after fifty-two years of marriage. We have enjoyed learning how-to cross-country ski, downhill ski, kayak, canoe, backpack, go wilderness camping and hiking and even winter camping.

The photos below show our wilderness camping spot. It had wild blueberries, nice trout stream, cascading waterfalls, a deep swimming hole and a beautiful, peaceful, quiet environment. Other phoots show that we went back to the same spot several times even after John was born.

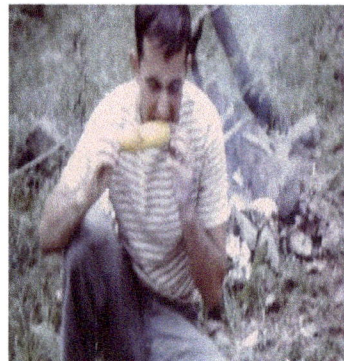

When we returned to NC, Diane moved into my house and there was only one of the Marines remaining. They scheduled him to get out of the Marines at the beginning of September, which he did, and moved to California. During the month he was there, we got along well, other than he did not like the idea that Diane converted his bachelor pad into a house. When he left, we had the house to ourselves.

THE MOST THRILLING ADVENTURES OF MY LIFE BEGIN

Diane and I are planning on writing a joint book of our married life, so I will not go into a lot of detail about our married life but just hit on a few of the wildest adventures we shared.

I may have had some adrenalin rushes in my life between growing up with some of the shenanigans I pulled and being in combat but being married sure was about to beat them all. God sure knew what He was doing. Getting to know each other more intimately, exploring each other's

190

thoughts, sharing fresh adventures together and getting to know the great God even better would be the greatest adventure of my life and when in trouble, we still cried out to God for help.

As we became more physically intimate and exploring each other's bodies, it was amazing. We would take lipstick and make drawings or put words on each other's bodies. One day I was working on base in my T-shirt when another Marine said my back was bleeding. I took my shirt off to see forgetting Diane had drawn and wrote various things on my back. I was totally embarrassed when the other Marines started laughing and commenting on what they saw. After that the other Marines wanted to meet her, so I had to keep her hidden but kept my bow and arrow handy in case they charged the cottage we were staying in. To be safe, I put boobie traps around the entrances and yard. It was like Vietnam all over again. I had trip wires attached to a bucket full of tin cans and a trip wire attached to a light. That was the beginning of motion detector lights. At the school, we made detonators with a small amount of gun powder in them that gave a small bang when you stepped on it. I put a few under our house. Some would say that is a sure sign of PTSD. She was safe. During the day, she was in school and was safe. Maybe she had her own guardian angel.

One thing I loved about Diane, when we were dating, how she was a good listener, had good empathy, sympathy and was very encouraging. She seemed to be everything I was not. Strange as it may sound, she said I was everything she hoped to be in my love of the outdoors, my strong family background and all the adventures I had been on. I could not help but give thanks to God and love Him more because He had done the perfect matching job of two people. We would share many adventures together, and I would make attempts at developing an outgoing mindset like she had. It did not come naturally, and it would be something I would have to deliberately concentrate on doing it. After 52 plus years of marriage, I am still impressed with her outgoing concern of others, but how she still loves the outdoors as well. She can somehow balance out the love of the outdoors with visiting the sick, encouraging someone on the phone or making a meal for someone in need. That is not me, but I wish it were. I am so proud to have her represent the Cressman family in that way.

BIBLICAL ADVENTURES

We attended a local church, and we became Sunday school teachers, working with the youth, and I was an organist in a matter of weeks or days. My parents were so happy about that. We visited nursing homes, hospitals and walked around the neighborhood inviting people to church. We drove around Topsail Island loading up my convertible with teens for a Sunday night youth meeting. It was a small church, but we felt like we were doing God's work and we were excited to do it together.

I read in the Bible about Jesus healing people and later the Apostles healed the sick by laying their hands on their heads, or by their shadow passing by or a piece of cloth that was prayed over. While growing up, I never heard of an individual being healed or asking for healing nor my family talking about healing. If I remember correctly, I was skipping Wednesday night prayer meetings to be a Little Devil, so I am not sure what happened there. I never heard of anyone asking for prayers for healing. Only in Sunday School did I hear about healings back in Bible times and that was from Jesus. I wondered if God still healed today but we still prayed that Diane would be healed of her problems.

As Diane and I went out to visit the sick and elderly at nursing homes, we prayed for God to heal them. When we came back to visit them again, we were expecting them to be healed, most were not. Paul was not healed of his infirmity. I figured for the time being God no longer healed. As my life progressed, I would see many healings. Healing to me is not a proof one way or the other that God loves us or that He exists. I think there is more to a healing than just praying for someone or having faith that God will heal them. I learned later in life that even though I asked for prayers, I had faith, I did everything I could including being anointed with oil, I was not healed for two years because I think God wanted me to learn something. That is how rebellious brats and little devils learn when they grow up in the '50s.

When teaching Sunday School, there was no information to teach from. The pastor said, read the book, the Bible, and teach it. That reminded me of when I was teaching in the Marines. My background was mechanics and now I was teaching infantry subjects. I did not have experience in some of the subjects and did not feel comfortable. The Marine in charge gave me the Marine Corps manual and said read it and teach it.

I do not think it was a good idea to have us, as new Christians, teaching others, regardless of our zeal. A teacher should be a well-seasoned, experienced person, not a new person. I was not old enough for Catechism in my mother's church. Basically, all I knew was Jesus stories from Sunday School and now I knew repentance. After teaching what I read in the Bible, everything was going well. While reading the gospels and on into the New Testament, I saw that Jesus and disciples went into the temple or synagogue on the seventh day Sabbath. I remembered on the radio traveling to PA, a preacher talking about a Saturday Sabbath, but I had no idea what he was talking about. It all was confusing to me because I heard deacons pray and give thanks for the Sunday Sabbath.

As a kid I remember nothing being open on a Sunday and nobody worked. I heard it was a day of rest. I thought, what in the world is a Saturday Sabbath. I always heard the Jews that rejected Jesus kept a 7th day Sabbath. One Sunday, as I taught Sunday School, and I read the scriptures about Jesus and the disciples keeping the Sabbath. At creation, God rested on the 7th day Sabbath. He wrote with His finger in stone the fourth commandment which is keep the seventh day Sabbath. It appears to me that the Sabbath will be kept on the new earth and heaven according to Isa.66:22-24. I then asked why we do not keep it since Jesus did? I asked others at church and no one knew. I did not know either, no one ever told me why we go to church on Sunday. There seemed to be many things I was not told. One Sunday, I taught what I knew about the Sabbath and asked questions to the class. I always like people to think about what they do.

It did not take long for the pastor to come to me and say the church did not believe what I was teaching. I asked why not; the Bible said it. He said the Biblical Sabbath was changed to Sunday to honor Jesus resurrection and, once again he said I should go read about it, so I did. It was off to the library on Camp Lejeune. At the library I Googled it and watched the Sabbath debate on You Tube. Just kidding, no You Tube yet or Google yet. I did not find much at the library other than Sunday was legalized by the Council of Nicaea in 325AD. When I asked people at church more about it, some said they trusted the pastor, some said the apostles changed it to Sunday, others said it did not matter which day you went to church on, some said Jesus was the Lord of the Sabbath and some said the Bible calls it the Lord's Day now. None offered any scriptures.

This bothered me just like when I was told God lived in a church, kissing, card playing, movies, alcohol were all sins. I wondered where all this came from. Was it from the Bible? My inquiring mind wanted to know. I wondered if this was Johnny Angel seeking truth and to know God better or my Little Devil side wanting to be mischievous. It did not take long in a small church for people to know there was a Little Devil questioning the beliefs of their church.

A BRAND-NEW ADVENTURE....THE BIBLE?

This would be the beginning of an adventure like I had never been on before. It would lead to a lifetime of searching the Bible and other sources for the truth. I would ask myself many a time like Pilot asked Jesus, "what is truth". One definition I found was that "what you say corresponds to reality". So, I would start searching for the reality of their sayings or assertions about the Sabbath. I never found the reality of why the Sabbath, a day of rest and a meeting at the Temple, was changed to a day of rest on Sunday. Some religious groups kept a strict day of rest on Sunday. Where did that come from? They came to America to have religious freedom and worship the way they thought was right. Then they forced their beliefs on others and persecuted others, like the Ana-Baptists and Sabbath keepers that did not agree with them. That was strange for people seeking freedom to do.

We felt convicted by what we read but did not have complete knowledge yet. We started resting on the seventh day Sabbath and went to church on Sunday. If the Sabbath was changed from Saturday to Sunday, should there not have been like a vote, a doctrine statement, anything in the Bible? How could I find out?

To find out the truth, I would have to put myself back in time just like Sam and I put ourselves back into the good old western days of the 1800's. I needed a time machine to go back to the good old days of Jesus and the Apostles to get an answer and see what was happening. I was not interested in knowing what happened to Christians like in the book "Foxes Book of Martyrs". I just wanted to see who changed the Sabbath to Sunday. I modified my '63 Chevy with a flux capacitor and I had a time machine. I added 2 Holley four-barrel 650 CFM carburetors to achieve the needed speed and I was ready.

What do you think happened when I went back in time to the beginning of the church age and asked who changed the Sabbath to Sunday?

A. The Jews gave me a Jewish flogging for even mentioning the idea.

B. The Gentiles stoned me for mentioning the Sabbath.

C. They took me to Herod, and he gave me a temporary doctorate in theology to find the answer. He said if I find out to let him know so he could take credit.

D. I asked a Christian and he said he sold everything, quit his job and moved to Jerusalem to await the return of Jesus, the son of God, in the clouds, every day was a sabbath, every day is the same now.

E. I met a man named Saul on the Damascus Road and asked him. He said it was blasphemy and threatened to arrest me for blasphemy or if I was a Christian. He said if I found out who changed the Sabbath to Sunday to let him know so he could arrest him. As I drove off, I saw a bright light and Saul fell to the ground. Wow.

F. All, any or none

It was F. But I think D sounds good.

Then I set my time machine for 325AD around the time of the Council of Nicaea. When I arrived, I was met head on by men on horseback and men in chariots. They were wearing a cross on their uniforms, chariots and helmets and were headed to war in the name of Christ. Wow, I thought.

Fortunately, I was able to hide the time machine in a cave and went to Rome to ask who changed the Sabbath to Sunday and what do you think they said?

A. Some did not know but things were better now because before there was so much confusion, some kept Sabbath, some kept Sunday, there was eastern Christianity and Western Christianity. Now Rome was united.

B. Some said The Council of Nicaea decided it to be Sunday for the sake of unity.

C. Some said Constantine ordered it since he wanted to have Rome a united Christian nation

D. Some said Constantine allowed Christian worship now, baptized all his soldiers and everyone was happy to worship on Sunday

E. I found a Sabbath keeping Christian and his group believed they kept the right day but had to go into hiding now because of persecution.

F. None

It was F, I realized I fell asleep and dreamed the entire time machine adventure, it never happened or did it? Sometimes my imagination gets the best of me, but those are some of the answers I have found that are said about the controversy. If the time machine were true, I would still choose to go by the Bible.

This Bible adventure would be better than when Sam and I went looking for adventures and explorations like Frontiersman Davey Crocket and explorers like Lewis and Clark. It would be more exciting than climbing rocks, swinging on vines, riding trains, canoe tipping and everything else we did in search for adventure. The early frontiersmen and explorers had opposition and tests of their endurance as they went along, just like Sam and I encountered. Diane and I would face similar opposition, but this opposition would come from friends, family, and the church.

So back to our first church. Our pastor asked us to have the youth put on a play about the meaning of Christmas. Other than Jesus' birth, I did not know much about Christmas, I just followed traditions every year, like most people. Christmas was the best day of the year. I got many gifts, ate a lot of delicious food, helped my dad on the roof putting up Christmas decorations, drove around looking at Christmas lights with Sylvia, went Caroling with other church youth and kiss the girls under the mistletoe and keep on kissing on the way to the next house to celebrate Christmas. That is how the Little Devil in me looked at it.

The Johnny Angel side wanted to go to church to hear about baby Jesus and celebrate with the girls at a Christmas party. Was there something more to Christmas? The pastor said, once again, to go research it. I did. I think the pastor was looking for what the different symbols of Christmas meant and how people around the world celebrate the birth of Christ. As I went to the library and asked the librarian where the books on Christmas were, she pointed them out to me. She was happy to help me because of my good looks and big muscles and superior intellect. She helped me join and get my library card. She probably thought I would be an excellent librarian. I eventually learned how to use a card catalog to find books on certain subjects. No computers back then. That took superior intellect and I had it. Diane was supportive and believing in me to find out the answers we were looking for.

As I read books, they all seemed to have a common thread and that was that, most likely, Jesus was not born on Christmas Day and no one knew of Jesus actual birth date. My guardian angel probably stood behind me in case I fainted. Oh no, you mean 21 years of keeping Christmas to honor Jesus and we had the wrong day. Well sometimes I was out of town so we celebrated my birthday another day so everyone could be there. I figured that was OK. We the people had the right intentions.

As I read on, I read that close to the end of December is the shortest day of the year. A long time ago, people had a day to celebrate the days getting longer. They did not believe in the creator God, they believed in many gods and one was the sun god. The festival was called Saturnalia and they gave gifts to each other and lit candles to help celebrate the birth of the sun god. Later as these sun god believers came into the Christian church, they changed the meaning from the birthday of the sun god to the birthday of the Son of God. Wow, I never heard that, why did not someone tell me? I was angry at first because once again I was not told anything. I went to church on Sunday and did not know why; I kept Christmas thinking it was Jesus birthday and did not where it came from and what all the traditions meant. I could not help but wonder how much of what I heard in church was true. Some examples were: thinking kissing makes a girl pregnant, storks bring babies, young girls fall off the roof, playing cards and I was going to hell because I went to see the Ten Commandment movie.

I figured most people were as ignorant about Christmas as I was, so we put a play together to tell the history and meaning of Christmas. I figured as Johnny Angel; people would be so happy to hear the truth.

When I presented the proposed play about the history of Christmas to the pastor, what do you think he said?

A. He congratulated me on my research and the play was a success.

B. He looked at me like I was two nuts short of a fruitcake.

C. He told me to nail my thesis on the church door.

D. He explained how Christians want to honor Jesus' birthday through these practices. It might not be a good idea to do this play. It could cause confusion and offense.

198

It was D, and we did not do the play

I know there is no command to keep Christmas nor is there a command to not keep Christmas. I read where there was a time in 1659 when Christmas was illegal to keep in America. Groups like the Puritans did not like the idea of festivals from pagans being observed in the church but at the same time they put strict laws in place to keep Sunday like the Sabbath. That is strange. That is how Sunday was when I was young. I did not understand why Christians wanting to get to know the true God, would not want to be taught truth and decide how they want to keep it.

Unfortunately, Christmas had become almost totally commercialized. I was rather bitter about all this and our relationship at the church was never the same. I think people thought I was more of a Little Devil than a Johnny Angel, so eventually we were asked to leave, maybe to find a church with teachings we believed in. There always seems to be conflict when each person believes he is right and will not listen to the other person. I would have to learn that my ideas are not always right just because I have a relationship with God.

WE SAID WE WERE NEVER GOING BACK TO THAT CHURCH / GOD SAID YOU WILL BE GOING BACK (IN 45 YEARS)

We never went back for 45 years. It is amazing how God brought us back and what miracles happened when we returned. Keep reading. Were we welcomed or stoned? No wander God told Israel, when your children ask why we are keeping all these traditions, God said to tell them. Deut. 11:19, Deut. 6:20.

During our stay at the church, I was the organist and really enjoyed playing the organ. It made my parents happy to have me following in their footsteps. There was only one thing that bothered me, and that was the last song the pastor did. Week after we ended the service with "Just As I Am". If I adjusted the organ's sound and played the song slow and draggy, coupled with what the pastor was saying, it produced an emotional response in people. I saw people come up to the alter to give their lives to Jesus every week. I cannot judge what goes on in a person's life, but it seemed like after church, the person reconsidered.

It reminded me of me growing up and hearing an emotional message or song and feeling like I wanted to change, but it never happened or like when in Washington, DC where I was given an emotional message to cause me to give my heart to the Lord before eating their food. I felt kind of guilty about playing a song to cause an emotional response and talked to the pastor about it. He said when I gave my testimony that it also created an emotional response, did I want to quit giving it if people did not respond the way I thought they should. He made a good point, but he began to vary the last song more often.

That would be something I would have to learn as I went through my Christian life that what I thought was the only right way, or God's way as I would come to call it. I know God can use emotion to see our sins and what we have done and who we are inside that we need a savior.

EXTENDING MY TIME IN THE MARINES

They scheduled me to get out of the Marines in September 1968, but I was happy teaching at the Infantry School and would have stayed in the Marines if I could have continued there. When the recruiting person asked if I would like to stay in the Marines with many incentives, like a promotion to Staff Sgt., pay raises and a guarantee to stay in the instructor position. I wanted to think about it, so I extended for three months to give me time to check out the job market in the area. During that time, they transferred me back to the mechanic job because they were short of mechanics, so I left the Marines in December 1968.

Before getting out of the Marines, I knew we would move away from Surf City to be closer to a job. I went to visit a church in the area we were moving to, and I was not happy with what I heard. Whoever was speaking or praying spoke a lot of thee and thou words from the King James language there and I did not hear much about the Bib le. I guess back in the old days, a person may think he is pleasing God by speaking KJV Bible language or having a certain religious tone to your voice. Through the years, I have heard many people tell me what I would have to do to please God. The list included a blue or gray suit, a red power tie, knee high black socks, wing tip shoes, speaking God's language, use thee and thou, slur my voice a certain way to get that perfect religious tone and many other suggestions. Little Devils from the '50s do not do that. I believe everything should be true and honest not putting on an act or making believe.

I wonder what my guardian angel thought about all my questions and not accepting traditions of the church or my parents. (I think in the '50s and '60s there was a general rebellion against our parent's traditions and society's standards. Some rebelled totally, but as a Christian, I wanted to find the truth and decide which to do and which to stop.) He probably thought he had protected this Little Devil of a kid so he would read the Bible and go to church, and now this guy questions everything. This Little Devil was still going to be a troublemaker, even as a Christian. A guardian angel's job is never ending.

Since Diane was only 17 and a senior in high school, she went back to school in September. I became her husband and parent since I had to sign her report cards, go to-parent-teacher meetings, and joined the PTA. That was an adventure with many challenges. I expected "A's" on her report card, and she was sometimes not getting them, so I had to motivate her by limiting her cell phone use, her listening to I-tunes and watching cable TV. Oops, not invented yet. So, I had to do the old method of encouraging her and helping her with her homework instead. That was the best part of marriage, helping a mate to be a better person.

I was also trying to help with her low blood iron. My mother said liver was good for the blood, so I cooked her some. She said she ate it all, and I was so happy because I knew she did not like it. The dog was smelling a bottle and when I looked, I saw the liver was in the bottle. I gave her a mean look and she took off running. I chased her just like my dad chased me. She ran outside, all around the yard and then climbed up on the roof. When I climbed up on the roof, she had no choice but to grab a rope we had attached to tree and swing. The rope was just like when I was a kid. She swung way out and when she came back, I dove off the roof and grabbed the rope and landed aside of her. We just laughed and laughed. When the rope stopped, I was too tired to do anything but say, the liver would have been good for you. She loved me so she tried it. I do not know if the liver helped or God just healed her, but she really became a healthy girl.

The photos below are our rope swing that our neighbor boy, Diane, and I enjoyed.

She had a beautiful singing voice, so at her high school talent shows, I played the piano for her. Her favorite song was "Tammy" and she sang it so well. We named our first puppy Tammy and our first daughter Tammy. Our daughter Tammy accused us of naming her after a dog, but we loved the name and the song so much, it meant a lot to us. Before Tammy was born, we took our dog Tammy to PA to visit my parents. She often peed on the carpet, so my parents wrote us a letter saying to not bring Tammy with us anymore because she peed on the carpet. Years later, our daughter Tammy found the letter and was hurt. She thought it was her.

After getting out of the Marines in December 1968, I started looking for a job. I could not find a job doing heavy equipment because the Marines used older equipment than civilian industry. Auto mechanic jobs were at least 30 miles away, so it would mean moving. A Christian girl at Diane's school said she used a Ouija Board to talk to God and maybe we could use it to find out where God wanted me to work. I never heard of a Ouija Board, so we tried it. I was amazed, we could ask a question, and this little thing spelled out answers. We asked a few test questions and then asked where God wanted me to get a job.

It told me a Ford Dealer near us and gave us a name of a man to ask for. I drove up there the next day and found no one by that name worked there, and they were not looking for any mechanics. I was devastated, but while there, I went to the Chevrolet Dealer and they needed a front-end alignment specialist able to do mechanic work in about a month. The dealership was old but unique.

202

They had photos of when new Chevrolet cars came to them in a box and they would assemble them there. They had a lot of old equipment there, but still worked. I accepted the job and used that months' time to study and pray, wanting to know more about this God of the Bible. We gave the Ouija Board back to the girl and never touched one again. No one told me it was not good. I was never taught anything about how God communicates with us. I would have to learn.

My experience is that I would love to get an answer from God right away, but it seldom works that way. Getting into my seventies now, I look back and see how God was working in our lives and answering prayers, but we did not understand it was happening at the time. We just went along praying like it all depended on God and working like it all depended on us. I just do not feel comfortable looking to hear a voice or looking to see a sign every minute of the day.

For the last 52 years, I have seen people in search of God's will or to get a "word" from the Lord or to hear "God's voice". Like me, I think people want to please God and sometimes feel the Bible is not real clear on certain things and they want God to speak them of which way to go or what to believe in.

The Ouija Board does give access to a power, but where is the power from. What if it is from the demonic world? Some believe using it could lead to demon possession, or worse. I will not downplay anything that God can or cannot do, but I think seeking to hear God speak to me or seeking anything supernatural can be dangerous. I have found that God does not reveal everything we would like answered or would like to know.

THE BIBLICAL MYSTERIES AND SECRETS - A PERFECT ADVENTURE AWAITS

I found Jesus sometimes hid the meanings of his message from his followers and his disciples. Luke 18:34. Matthew 13:11-15 says Jesus hid the meaning of parables, otherwise they would understand, repent and be forgiven. I was always taught that repentance and forgiveness was a good thing, why would Jesus hide it? I thought the job of a preacher was to encourage understanding, repentance, and forgiveness. I had to wonder if those things were hidden from a person or people and they went to hell because of not knowing, is that fair from the loving God I was beginning to know. In researching the subject of what happens to people that never heard the name of Jesus Christ when they die, I found many people and religious leaders do not have an answer, including Billy Graham. I recently read that he believed that people will be judged on what they did with what they knew. I think that is speculation and not from the Bible. I will also speculate later but cannot prove it from the Bible either. Maybe the answer to that question is hidden from us right now.

Those kinds of questions have given me a great desire to search the Bible for answers. The Bible is full of mysteries and so interesting to see what these mysteries reveal. It is like riding a bike, or hiking, on a mountain trail and wondering what is over the next mountain and then what is over the next, etc. It is an endless adventure. Paul said we are saved by his gospel. I Corinthians 15:1-3. What about Jesus gospel when he preached the kingdom of God, is there a difference. Paul revealed the mysteries of God. Daniel was seeking to know about a prophecy given to him, but God told him to seal it until the time of the end. Dan. 12:4. I have spent 52 plus years trying to find answers and still do not have them all as you will see, but it has been a glorious adventure but has worn my guardian angel out. I do not know how many times he has called for one of those flaming chariots to take him away for some R&R. (Rest and relaxation)

Anyway, back to getting out of the Marines. I took a month off to study and pray, wanting to learn more about this God. I spent most of the day reading the Bible, trying to understand it. On the property we were renting, there was a small one room, up on stilts overlooking the Intra-coastal Canal where I did my study and prayer. Soon it was deer hunting season in PA. so I went back to PA. by myself to provide meat on the table like a true wilderness mountain man would do. I wanted to get back in the woods to enjoy the outdoors. I got my first buck on the first day from the top of a pine tree while reading the Bible.

Still loving to climb trees, I was at the top, probably pretending to be a sniper. I carried the deer out of the woods on my shoulders like they trained me to carry a wounded person. I was glad no one took a shot at the deer on my back. I am sure my guardian angel held up his wings over me like a fluorescent orange cover, which was only visible to hunters. The Bible says in Ps. 91:4, He will cover you with his feathers, and under his wings you will find refuge; his faithfulness will be your shield and rampart.(wall)

After having my uncle cut up and butcher the deer, I headed home to Diane, who was in NC going to school. We must have been happy to see each other because nine months later, we had our first son John Elijah meaning "God is love" and "The Lord is God". That was very appropriate since the doctors said she could not have children.

It was a profitable month off studying the Bible. I made many trips to the library on base and learned how to use a Bible dictionary and commentary. Eventually, I bought my own. I bought a new Bible and started to mark it with what I learned from the library. People from the church we had just left stopped over to talk and occasionally brought us food since they knew I was not working. That was a real Christian attitude. I wish we could have had an intelligent discussion about it but both of us were too hardheaded.

One thing about my personality is that I have a deep craving to know how things work, how things got the way they are and what was it like to be a cowboy, a pioneer and an explorer, or an early Christian knowing exactly what Paul and the Apostles taught and did their teachings survive until today?

During that month, I tried to get understanding. When I am taught something or read something, it must make sense in my brain for all those little wires in there to connect. I have an example of seeking understanding and knowledge in a quick story from my auto mechanic classroom days in high school. In class one day, the instructor was teaching us about how the carburetor works. He said air passes through the throat of the carburetor into the engine. There is a bowl in the carburetor with fuel in it, and then there is a tube going into the throat to mix fuel with the air. The only problem I had was that the tube was higher than the fuel bowl, so what made the fuel go uphill into the throat of the carburetor? I could investigate the throat as the engine ran and see the gas coming out the tube, but what made it do that.

The instructor said the gas is sucked up the tube like I would suck a delicious chocolate malt up through a straw. I took a look into the carburetor, but I saw no one sucking up the gasoline so what made it come up the tube. He never could give me an answer, so he said go to the library and read the book. People telling me to go read the book would be repeated often in my life. Finally, after researching many older textbooks, I found the answer. As the pistons go down, they create a low-pressure area or a partial vacuum in the cylinder. Gravity pushes air into the cylinder through the throat of the carburetor. They designed the throat to create more of a low pressure or vacuum in the throat and thus gravity pushes gasoline in the bowl up the tube and into the air flowing through the carburetor. The faster the engine turns, the more air, the more vacuum and thus more gasoline.

Finally, I understood how it worked. Seeking answers has been my life. Many in my class never wanted to know how things worked like I did. With this understanding, it helped me trouble shoot engine problems later, especially in Vietnam. While I was living in a village in Vietnam, a shortage of mechanics occurred, and they transferred me back to a service battalion. My job would be to drive around in a service truck and repair broken down equipment and generators, mostly at field hospitals, mess halls, officer's club, and lights around the perimeter of airfields in Danang and Chu Lai. Fixing a generator at an officer's club was rewarding since they thought I was General Johnny Angel, sent from heaven to fix their generator and invited me in for a drink.

If I could not fix the generator as fast as they wanted, I was soon to be Private Little Devil on my way back to where I came from. Fixing a generator on a security perimeter was dangerous since occasionally, I had to keep a generator running during a fire fight or sniper fire. I knew if I stayed in the shadows, I could not be seen, just like when I played hide and go seek or tag as a child. My search to understand Christianity would be the same, sometimes rewarding and sometimes dangerous.

I went to work about January of 1969 and found a library close to the dealer, so I often stopped there after work. I worked there about 6 months. until offered a job from a member of the church we started to attend. We researched different churches and attended a few but did not find what we were looking for. We finally found a church that we liked, and they also observed the seventh day Sabbath, so we wanted to try it there.

WOW - HAVING BABIES, NOW THAT IS AN ADVENTURE - MORE LITTLE DEVILS

In September of 1969, Diane was ready to have the baby. In the hospital, Diane had an unpleasant experience with childbirth. Once labor started, I had to leave, and I was not allowed in the delivery room. The baby started coming before the doctor arrived, so the nurses had her restrained and held her legs together to prevent the birth. The doctor later came, and the delivery was hard, but everyone was healthy. I knew just how she felt being restrained at the dentist, as a child, and in Vietnam, so we both agreed to look for alternatives to prevent that from that happening again. Despite everything that happened to her, no adventure I was ever on produced such excitement as having a baby produced by two people sharing their love. It would only get better.

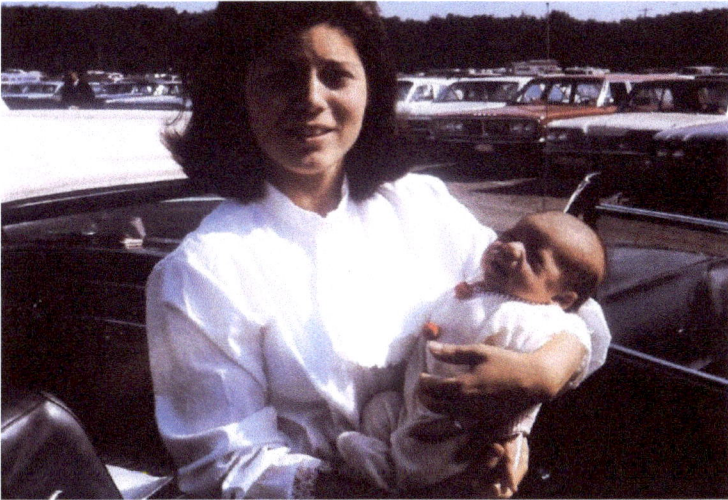

During the birth, I was working at a gas station doing mechanic work. Diane and I started attending a Sabbath keeping church that did not keep Christmas. A family kind of took us under their wing and offered me a job at their gas station. He wanted to train me to take over the business so hc could concentrate on selling cars. Diane and I grew close to my boss's family during her pregnancy and delivery in September. We felt like we had found a church that had the teachings of the Bible. I particularly enjoyed working with the youth, especially since they had close order drill competitions. I thoroughly enjoyed marching the youth around the parking lot, yelling out a cadence and orders for changes of directions just like back in the Marines.

I am not sure why we derive pleasure from executing power and control over someone else, but that desire is real, like any other human desire.

During our stay in this church, we studied into the church more. We noticed that many of their beliefs had their roots in the Millerites in the early 1800s. After the Second Great Awakening, a woman started the church, and they highly regarded her writings. If the Bible was not clear, they went to her writings. Once again, we started having a problem with some traditions and teachings not being found in the Bible. They claimed to not keep Christmas, since no one knows Jesus' birth date, but many celebrated it anyway. Maybe because of the Marine Corps, I expected people to do what they believed. Maybe I had PTSD or something else, but I started to feel uncomfortable there, so we looked at other churches. By December, we were not attending that church anymore because we had found a new church. The owner's attitude seemed to change, as he started finding fault with my work.

Even though we had been so close while on the job and at church, it was not long before he did what? Another question:

A. He fired me.

B. Attended our new church with us and told other members to attend

C. Accepted my ideas and gave me a bonus

D. Made me manager so he could sell cars and not see me

It was A. My first time being fired. This was the beginning of finding out hateful a person can be if you do not believe the same way they do. There was no discussion about where we disagreed just fired.

I am sure my guardian angel was thinking, how will I keep this guy safe and in a church.

I had requested literature from a church I heard while traveling back and forth from Camp Lejeune to home and found many answers to my questions. They presented much research and answers into areas I had questions about. They stirred up my curiosity to research and study more. I found they had a structure much like the authority top down that I was used to in the Marines. In a way they encouraged us to study but they also told us what the answer was going to be. I found that helpful at the time but eventually I saw that I was putting my trust in another's man's study and in the books and commentaries other people wrote when I knew little about those men.

They had the title Church of God, kept the Sabbath, and did not keep Christmas. We attended there for the next 25 years and did not celebrate Christmas for about 40 years. In our new church, a member who was a manager at a steel plant on the Wilmington ports gave me a job as maintenance man. I learned how to weld, pour, and work concrete and do electrical work. This came in handy when we built our first house. We did our own carpentry, electrical, plumbing and concrete for our septic tank. We put down our own well also, but that I learned in Vietnam.

Before attending this new church, we researched its doctrines and beliefs and compared them to the Bible. After considerable prayer, we believed this new church to have its teachings and doctrines from the Bible. They answered all our questions, and the church was comprised mostly of country people and farmers. They were so friendly and hospitable; it overwhelmed us. We learned a lot from them including gardening, food preservation, eating healthy organic food, child-rearing techniques and mostly how to love God and how the holy spirit lives in us to make us more like Jesus. It impressed us with how families worked together on a farm. We wanted to be like that. Eventually, we would see the Osmond family entertaining on TV, and we wanted to be just like them. We wanted a family that would enjoy each other and work and laugh together. I believe God blessed us to be able to experience that and pass it on to our grandkids.

Diane sang, and I played the piano sometimes in church, but could we someday entertain people as a family? We prayed we could, but first would need a family. God allowed us to do it much later in PA as God opened doors for us and we went through some training first. God is like a shepherd; he leads us where we need to go. The message they preached, the doctrines, and the way they lived seemed to all come from the Bible, plus they traced their history back to the Apostles. Later, I would find out that if they traced their history back to the Apostles, it was the Jerusalem Church which remained more like Jews but believed Jesus was the son of God and Messiah but they did not completely understand grace and salvation.

This church not only went to church on Saturday, the Sabbath, but obeyed many of the other commands given to Israel. It was like a Messianic Church which kept the Sabbath and the Holy Days of Lev. 23. Instead of keeping Christmas and Easter, we kept the Passover, Pentecost, and Feast of Tabernacles. It was cool for Sam and me to experience what the frontiersmen experienced but now Diane and I would experience what it was like in the days of Moses with all the laws to obey.

This new church was made up of many NC country people and farmers. Many of these farmers had their children at home by a mid-wife. We met several young couples that had their babies at home with a mid-wife or in a clinic, some at home that the husband delivered but all were natural childbirths. It sounded thrilling to have children that way and, in all cases, there were no problems. We did some research and had our second child naturally at a country clinic instead of a hospital. That meant I could be there with Diane during the delivery. Now that sounded like a real adventure to me. After much false labor and driving 45 miles one way each time to the clinic only to be sent home, Diane finally went into real labor. After about 8 hours of labor, the pains got worse but no signs of delivery. It appeared there was a problem with the baby being turned wrong for delivery, so we said a quick prayer for things to change and I went outside to a pay phone and asked the church to pray for us.

When I returned inside, Diane felt the baby turn and the delivery started. Just as the baby was crowning, the doctor said he needed to do an episiotomy. We specifically asked the doctor to not do that and allow her to go slow and have it without the surgery. He said he did not have time to wait and was going to do it. The doctor told the nurse to give her some gas before the surgery as he numbed the area. It looked like a mask fastened to a little camping propane bottle. I suppose it was ether gas again, like I had the trauma with as a child. It was supposed to be a natural childbirth, so my wife said she did not want any gas, but they put the mask over her face, anyway. Watching as the nurse tried to force her to breathe the gas brought back terrible memories of me being forced to breathe in that gas.

I was right over her face and got a taste of that unforgettable gas odor which really brought back unpleasant memories. Anxiety built in me, and I wanted to grab that nurse, throw her down and hold that mask over her face, but I restrained myself because I was not sure if my wife needed it or not. My wife fought the gas and would not breathe it in and finally reached up and knocked the mask off her face. She wanted to have this baby naturally. When she did that, the mask turned upside down and before I knew it; I had breathed in a big gulp of the gas and fell to the floor. Fortunately, it was not much, but I still got up in a fog and stumbled out of the delivery room and into the waiting room.

This was 1972 but, unfortunately, in this NC country doctor's office, it was segregated. There was a waiting room marked colored and one marked white. This was the first time I experienced segregation and I wondered why is there still segregation? Anyway, in my fogginess, I walked out the delivery room and into the colored waiting room. I flopped down in a chair to gain my composure and I remember other people in there looking at me and one asked if I was all right. I tried to gather my thoughts and I said, "I am having a baby" and that caused them to gasp with their mouth open and tongues falling on the sterile floor. When my head was clear, I got up and said, "I have to finish having the baby," and then walked out.

I can only imagine what those people thought. Maybe they figured in the other waiting room, men have babies instead of women. This was just a simple country clinic in North Carolina where I just walked back in the delivery room like nothing had happened and watched as the doctor pulled out my new son. My wife, son and I would all be fine now. After a few hours of rest, my wife, and our new baby boy, we named David, were ready to leave so we all went home thanking God and feeling very blessed. After watching the forcing of the mask on my wife, I added a mask to my list of bad memories. From then on, masks were a big NO-NO for me and her.

Again, I wondered when we pray does God do the actual answering or does the guardian angel have that authority. Who reached in there and turned the baby when we prayed? When God created Eve, it says the Lord caused Adam to sleep and took a rib and closed the area with flesh. That sounds just like surgery to me. So, I wonder did God stop time, come down and do surgery to turn the baby and then close her up and start time again? Maybe the Lord just spoke it from Heaven in His booming voice and the baby obeyed by doing a flip flop. I like to know but it does not matter as both were fine.

I always wanted to teach auto mechanics but was told I needed experience in a shop and teaching first. I received some experience at Cape Fear Technical Institute (As called in 1969) since the person in charge was a former Marine, he saw my perseverance and gave me a chance. I taught small engine repair and diesel engine repair at a night school and now was able to list it as experience teaching at a reputable school.

In 1970, I was offered a job teaching auto mechanics at a high school. I accepted and taught there for 4 years. I loved teaching to high school students. Beginning class was for 10th graders and advanced auto mechanics was for 11th and 12th graders. I have many enjoyable memories from there. I was still a fit Marine, so every Friday we had a push-up challenge to see if anyone could do more push-ups than me. I always won. I was also still a fast runner if I did not take sugar tablets, so occasionally I would race the students across the ball diamond and back. I usually won there as well. I did not care for vulgar language in class, plus it was against school rules. If a student used vulgarity, they had a choice of going to the office, putting a quarter in a baby bottle, or sucking on the nipple of the baby bottle. The baby bottle usually was full by Friday, but the nipple was untouched. I took the money and bought snacks and sodas every Friday for the students.

ROASTING MOTORS IN AUTO MECHANICS

Mr. Cressman, Auto-Mechanics

Roasting motors in auto mechanics was the title of a school newspaper article after a test engine caught fire in the classroom. The students rebuilt an old test engine, and I wanted to see if it would start. It was on an engine stand, so when we cranked it, it started right up and purred like a kitten. Everyone was happy as we celebrated the student's success. We only had a little gasoline and it started to run out, but it backfired and caught some leaky gas on fire, which was on the engine, stand and floor. We tried the powder fire extinguishers in our shop, but they did not work, so the students ran

212

into the main building to get more. The fire extinguishers were the water type with a handle on the bottom. The problem was that when you turned it upside down to grab the handle, they shot water out immediately until empty. The students grabbed the fire extinguishers and turned them upside down like they saw me do.

Then what do you think happened?

A. They ran back to auto mechanics and put the fire out

B. The water started shooting out in the hallway and into classrooms

C. The fire extinguishers were empty by the time they got back to our classroom

D   Some students panicked because they thought the school was on fire

E. All the above

Once again, unfortunately, it was B, C, and D. That was a day to remember but we finally got the fire out by using sand. At a class reunion, I probably will not be remembered for my push-ups nor fast running skills but for the Little Devil that tried to burn the school down. We never needed the fire dept. Another time a student was welding on a practice car outside before going to the junk yard and the car caught fire and burned up rather quickly. It put out a thick black smoke that went into the high school through the open windows since that was before A/C.

I am sure my guardian angel was pulling out his angel hair and wondering if there was a recall on my brain model. I am thinking at a class reunion, I will not be remembered for my you know what. No wander the next section may make sense. No one was injured during the ordeal. We did order the correct fire extinguishers for liquid fuels for our shop and made sure they were up to date. Most schools and businesses now have a company that does that for them.

Before accepting the job, I informed them I needed about five-8 days off a year for religious reasons and never had a problem. We believed like many Messianic Jews believe that we should seek fellowship with God on the Sabbath, and Holy Days He ordained in Lev 23. Since I saw in the Bible that Jesus, the Apostles and Jerusalem Church were also keeping these days, we did as well. I did not see any changes to keeping these days in the Bible. It took almost 50 years for me to see a different side about keeping those days. So even while I was seeking truth, there were things I did not understand.

But more importantly, I believed if you believe it, live it. I eventually came to see that a person could prove anything he wants from the Bible. You pick out scriptures to agree with your idea, let people read the scriptures and then say the Bible is clear that my idea is right. I needed to see the whole Bible and what is says. Then I had to be careful about who I seek answers from and whether I can trust them to tell me what it says. Back to school. Every year I requested the time off, the superintendent and the School Board approved it.

THE ADVENTURE OF EXPERIENCING: RELIGIOUS DISCRIMINATION & PERSECUTION

After 4 years, the state board of education passed a law that teachers could only take off 2 days a year for personal reasons and 2 days for sickness. A new superintendent sent me a letter stating I could no longer take off more than the 2 days for personal reasons and sent an agreement for me to sign that I would agree to or my contract would not be renewed. Since I needed to take college classes every year to keep my certification, the letter also required an agreement to stay certified. I could agree to that with no problem. This was more than a church convention, going to church on Sunday or just wanting to take off for religious reasons, these days I believed were holy to God and we were commanded to keep them like Israel did. I read in the Bible that Jesus and the Apostles kept these days and even Paul in Acts 20:6 and I Cor. 5:8 kept the Holy Days commanded to Israel in Lev. 23 so I believed at the time that I should also. Teachers across the state with similar beliefs received the same letter. I responded to the letter explaining my beliefs and said I could not sign the letter. They responded with a letter saying they were sticking to the state policy, but I could appeal to the school board, so I did.

At the school board, I explained my good evaluations for 4 years and my love for teaching. I also explained my beliefs and why I could not agree to the terms of the contract to not take off over 2 days. I was not tenured, so I was on a yearly contract and the school board could decide to not renew the contract for any reason. However, they put in writing that it was for not agreeing to take off over two days for any reason including religious reasons.

At first, I had questions about my beliefs but it soon very hostile if not hateful. These men, I am sure the way they talked, were all church going men, maybe even deacons in their church, but once again it reminded me of my childhood when I heard my parents believe all other religions were wrong except for their own.

They accused me of not loving my family, my job, my students and being a poor example of Christianity. They wondered how a man with a family could give up a job for his beliefs. They said God expected no one to give up a job for such days, and such a belief was ignorant. I think it also angered them I, a young 24-year-old, new teacher, Yankee, and Vietnam vet would go against their authority. I was hurt, angered, and overwhelmed at their response as they continued to attack me and my beliefs. I also needed one more college class to get my certification and when I showed up for it, the superintendent met me there and said it was only for teachers under contract for the following year and I was going to be fired, so they refused me entrance. I became uncertified. The federal law required employers to make reasonable accommodations for religious beliefs if it did not produce a hardship on the employer. The local school board claimed it did.

My contract was not renewed, many Messianic Jews, Jewish teachers and others were fired in the state that year. We all applied for help from various organizations, like the EEOC, because we thought it was religious discrimination. Eventually everyone, that I know of, was hired back, and allowed to take the time off for religious reasons. I was not hired back and had to go to court. I did not have enough money to hire a talented lawyer, so the EEOC helped me find one at low cost. No one else wanted to represent me, because now there was the certification issue. Because I never became certified and was not a tenured teacher, the court found for the school board. Somehow my lawyer could not convince the jury I was not certified because the superintendent refused my being able to take the course because I would not sign the contract. It also devastated me to see our court system, that a court is not there to find out the truth but to see who puts the best scenario together with collaborating witnesses. I was asked simple questions, but then later used those answers were used against me. I felt a bit disillusioned that the country that I was willing to die for allowed this. My thoughts were shattered thinking courts were seeking truth and justice. To receive justice, it would take a high price lawyer. I may have also wondered why God allowed this to happen. I wondered where my guardian angel was. After all, He protected me from dangerous circumstances during my entire life. Unknown to me, but this was the beginning of what my wife calls the tribulation years. It may have meant a little something to me when their lawyer said he was sorry he had to do that to me, but he was told he had to win. That is the world we are in. I did not have the money to appeal, so it was finished. No more teaching in the state of NC.

I then applied and was hired at a car dealer as a service writer, a person who greets people and writes up what service they need. I told the service manager what days I needed off, and he was agreeable since he said he was a Christian also and he believed a Christian should live his beliefs. That sounded good to me. We would often have some excellent discussions about God, and I enjoyed that. He belonged to a church that we had researched, and I knew what they believed.

We seemed to develop a friendship, even though I saw his religion took a hard stand on some non-Biblical beliefs that forbade him from eating chocolate, drinking coffee, tea and anything with caffeine in it. During the 1974 oil embargo, it hit the auto industry hard, and our dealer was hurting for business. As I did my work, I would occasionally overhear conversations about charging for warranty work that was never done to keep money flowing into the service department. It saddened me to hear that it took cheating to keep afloat. That put a damper on my relationship with the service manager and dealer.

Then one day the service manager came to me and wanted me to forge a woman's signature of a car owner to say they had done work on her car. He said he felt a need to keep the mechanics employed during this time of hardship and everyone in the service dept. had, at one time or another, forged a signature of a car owner saying they had warranty work done on their car and it was now my turn. He said God would understand and I should not feel bad because I was helping my fellow employees. I knew God would not approve even though I could have used the excuse that I was like Robin Hood, a person I had never imitated, robbing the rich to feed the poor. I said I could not do that; it was illegal and a sin. He said without it they would have to eliminate someone's job.

I had to refuse anyway, and can you guess what happened?

A. Everyone repented, and we had a prayer meeting

B. They said I was right and made me finance manager

C. Diane and the kids came down, and they stood by the street in Elmo costumes while Diane sang country music to bring in business. (That is what we did for our family businesses)

D. My job was eliminated, meaning they fired me.

It was D. of course

I then went across the street to another dealer where I was hired as a front-end alignment mechanic. Even though work was slow, I kept busy with work. I often did front end work on cars that were involved in a collision and saw the work orders and what body repair men were being paid. We were all on commission and worked 40 hours a week. However, the body men were making double of what I was making, so I ended up quitting and using my GI Bill to get my Associate Degree in Collision Repair Technology.

During this time, to bring in money, I cut grass at rich people's homes and Diane worked as a waitress to give us income. I learned while cutting grass for rich people that I never wanted a fancy yard since it was so much work. I also learned what it was like to be sweating, dust and grass covered and thirsty, and watch the owners sipping iced tea on their screened-in porches or sitting by their pools. I just hoped God had a plan for all this. I believe He did. The best thing was that I took my sons, Johnny, and David to help me and after a long hard day's work we went to Krispy Kreme donuts, still a tradition today. That was their training in a work ethic which they still remember or at least the donut.

I heard what happened after the Great Depression in1929-1933 was that parents like mine did not want us kids to experience what they went through and made our lives easy and gave us many things. Amen. Many kids like myself did not know what hard work was until, like me, joining the Marines and later God brought me a hard-working farmer's daughter that taught me what work was. Then the friendly NC people in our church had us work on their farm if we went to visit or spend the night. My lovely NC wife used to make our kids' friends work in our garden when they came to visit. Some loved it and some never came back. Some still remember and comment about those days when we see them all grown up now. Like me, remembered for climbing trees, Diane is remembered for making visitors work in the garden.

After I graduated, I came back to the same shop and got a job in the body shop and was making good money. Months later, as I worked on a new car doing warranty work, I ended up seeing the completed work order and that more work than what I had done was being charged and those charges were going to the service manager and his son who worked there, as if they had done some work to the car. His son also got all the gravy jobs, we called them, but was not a good body man so we had to fix his mistakes for an hourly wage instead of the commission which lowered our paychecks. I was once again disillusioned and asking if there was not an honest person on earth? I prayed about it because I really enjoying doing body work but felt I should tell someone.

Seeing corruption really bothers me. The manufacturer and us employees were being cheated. I guess I was going to become a whistleblower. I thrilled the owner of the dealer with my work and often talked to me. I told him what was going on. That was a big mistake because a few days later, the body shop manager called me in to his office.

What do you think he wanted?

A. To give me a pay raise for doing excellent work

B. To make me manager since they fired him

C. To fire me for squealing

D. To ask my forgiveness and pray for him

It was C. Turns out the owner told him I squealed on him but did not tell him to stop. I will not speculate on the reason. Can you get an idea what it was like to go home and tell my wife I was fired again? She has always been from day one when I first met her very encouraging, understanding and not a judgmental person. Plus, she loves me. I know what you are thinking. Who would love a little devil like me? Through it all, I never turned to alcohol to forget my misfortunes or stupidity like I did while in the Marines. I did however have more questions for God, but I still believed I did what I had to do, and that God would provide. The photo below is Diane's book she wrote: A Family's Journey Through prayer.

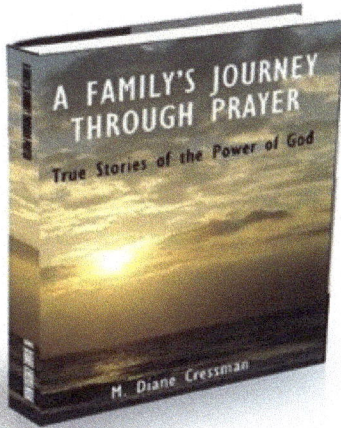

My social security records show that for the 10 years following my Marine discharge, that I had 10 jobs. My teaching job lasted for 4 years so I went through 9 jobs in 6 years and most of them, they fired me because of something to do with my beliefs. That is an average of about a job every 4 months. The VA said it was because of PTSD. I will not rule that out since many vets had trouble finding and keeping a job after the Vietnam War. I think vets had trouble staying in a church also. They felt everyone was against them. I was also a Yankee and possibly smart-mouthed, or so I heard from some family members.

For the next few years, I built a garage at home and did body repair and painting at home. I think it was about 1978 when a fellow body man where I worked was also fired. They hired him as a body shop manager at another dealer. He said I could have off all the days I wanted and that he would run an honest business. I accepted, and we got along very well, and I was earning a lot of money.

I had been waiting years for a vocational School to open in PA near my hometown. Later in 1978, I was offered a job in PA teaching Auto Repair Technology, but at the last minute they found someone with more experience. We were disappointed but had faith I could get back into teaching someday. Diane was pregnant with our fourth child, so we needed a bigger house. We put a down payment on a little farmhouse with an enormous garden and lots of land to enjoy with the kids.

A few later we received a call offering me a teaching job in Collision Repair Technology, making double of what I was, so I accepted. We loaded up the truck, and we moved to Beverly, oops I mean PA., close to my hometown. You might say wonderful, that was the end of your tribulation years. Or was it? I had no more problems with employment discrimination. It took a while, but I felt my prayers were answered.

During our years in NC, we had become much involved in the church and made many friends. Diane was involved with children programs and I used my musical experience in being a song leader, piano player and gave what we called sermonettes, which was a short 10-15-minute teaching before the longer 90-minute sermon. The church was small but very united in beliefs and friendship, plus we had a terrific pastor. Him and my current pastor were the best pastors I have ever had. They were down to earth, common sense, non-judgmental men.

For our next child, we were going to the same doctor for checkups and as time got close; we were at the clinic quite a bit but sent home because of false labor. Since she liked to have this false labor in the middle of the night, both the doctor and I were growing weary. It was also about 40 miles away, so everyone was getting frustrated. Because she already had two episiotomies, the doctor said he would have to do another one or she would tear, so we accepted that, which meant the possibility of more gas.

CALLING DOCTOR JOHN - A DELIVERY FOR DOCTOR JOHN

On the day before Thanksgiving, Diane called me in from outside and said she was having labor pains. We both agreed that we would wait until we were sure it was the real thing. I went back outside to finish my work and shortly after I heard Diane screaming my name. I ran in the house to see her gripping the headboard and yelling out that the baby is coming; the baby is coming. At that point, there was no use of trying to leave for the clinic or even trying to get to a hospital.

Fortunately, we had read natural childbirth books and there was a section in there about emergency delivering of a baby at home which we had read several times, especially with all the false labor she had. We had several new towels boiled and in plastic bags, a scissor and a new shoestring ready to go just in case. I quickly washed my hands, put some water on the stove to boil and made her comfortable. My two boys gathered around wandering what was going on. When I saw the baby crowning, I coached Diane to breathe and not push which she did. It scared me because what I saw was wet and black.

Then as the baby's head slid slowly out without tearing her and I realized it was the long hair of a beautiful baby. I held the baby as it finished coming out and saw it was a girl. I wiped it off with the sterile, new towel and handed her to Diane. She was so happy. I had the shoestring and scissors ready and after the cord turned white and shriveled up, which meant the extra blood in it had gone into the baby; I tied and cut the cord. I had boiled a washcloth that Diane used to clean up the baby. Eventually the after birth came out, and we saved it to show the doctor. After resting, we called the doctor and then went to the clinic to get checked out. He seemed to be annoyed that Diane was doing so well and had the baby without an episiotomy. After a quick check up, he sent us home. We praised God that the baby and Diane were both fine. We named the baby Tammy Diane.

It was such a wonderful experience, better than any adventure. My two boys were there and now knowing where babies came from. For our family, we wanted to be sure we taught the truth. We wanted to put an end to old wives' tales, stories about storks delivering babies, no more girls falling off the roof or any other misinformation. I eventually found out that it sometimes is not wise to give all the truth at one time or a certain time. Sometimes truth is given a little at a time especially to younger children.

I would find out later that God also does not give us all the truth at once. The Bible says truth is hidden from some until later when they are ready. It was so exhilarating to see Diane and the baby in good health and everything happening so naturally. This just went along with everything I ever felt about God, nature, and His creation. His creation is beautiful, and nature takes care of its own, but there are rules which make nature work, and it makes things go smoother if you get in line with them. Here is a familiar poem that I changed some words around to fit the experience:

'Twas the night before Thanksgiving, when all through the house.
Everyone was stirring, especially my spouse. Her clothes were packed by the door with care, In hopes that Tammy Diane soon would be there; The children were not nestled all snug in their beds; Because visions of a baby sister danced in their heads; With mamma in her pj's, as I looked for my cap, She just finished false labor for a long due nap, When out on

the bedroom there arose such a clatter, I sprang from the garage to see what was the matter. Away to the bedroom I flew like a flash, I saw Diane screaming and gripping the sash. Now to the doctor was no time to run, because the coming of the baby had already begun, Emergency childbirth, I had to be cool, but all I had, was my mechanic's tools. As I grabbed some towels, and was turning around, down from her belly, Tammy came with a bound. When what to my wondering eyes did appear, but a small baby girl so sweet and dear. More rapid than eagles this baby had come, we screamed, and shouted, and called her by name. Up to the housetop Johnny and David they flew, they yelled out her name so all would know too. Her cheeks were like roses, her nose like a cherry! Her eyes, how they twinkled, her dimples, how merry! Diane's mouth smiled big, like a fully drawn bow, while my pale shocked face was as white as snow. She had a broad face and a little round belly, that looked to me, like a bowl full of jelly. To the top of the porch, to the top of the wall, I delivered my daughter, don't that beat all! We all thanked God that nothing went wrong, as we all gathered together in praise and song.

MORE BABIES AT HOME

We continued our research and had the next baby at home with me delivering them. Diane went to a doctor to be sure everything was ok. Our next baby girl, we named Melody. A lady from church assisted and was there at birth.

The next baby was born in PA, two months after moving there. We had Carl at home also with my mother being there to assist. She was familiar with babies being born at home since that is what happened when she was young.

The last boy, named Sam Adam we had in a birthing room in a hospital with the doctor allowing me to deliver it one last time. After all, I was an experienced midwife or husband. Honestly, the woman does all the work, I just coached and caught. We went to the doctor for regular checkups as she was pregnant and had found a doctor to work with us. The doctors were usually older ones that were used to having babies at home as they did in the early 1900s. After delivering a baby, any other adventure is insignificant. But there will be more.

Being a father, I sort of calmed down on my wild and crazy adventures for a while. My Johnny Angel side came out. I was content to just do some normal camping in the Pocono Mts. of PA, the Appalachian's in NC and at the beach in Jekyll Island, GA. Working with teens in the church we were attending, we went camping with them and showed them how to enjoy God's creation.

I also helped fix up an old school bus and took a group of teens to Disney World in Florida. Now that was an adventure to remember. I had a whole busload of Little Devils to control, plus our three little angels along. They paid me back for causing adults anxiety.

We eventually bought our own mobile home and a lot in the woods and had it moved there. The man we bought the lot from had put in a road through the woods, put down a well and cleared the land only to find out it was not his lot. His lot was the one next to it.

We cleared enough of a spot to put in a mobile home and worked on the lot as we lived there. We were like real pioneers, working and clearing our own land. We had a hand pump on the well and would carry water to the mobile home as needed. We had a barrel of water at the well that heated during the day (like in Vietnam) so we washed outside the barrel using the warm water and then got into the barrel to relax just like in Japan. Later, someone gave us a well pump so we could have running water in the home.

We always involved the kids in the work as we did it in whatever way they could. They had their own hammers, shovels, wheel barrels, tractors, etc. We cleared the land ourselves, dig and put in our own septic tank, drove down a well by hand, built an edition and did all the electric and plumbing ourselves. It was a lot of work, but Diane and I always took time to play with the kids, take them to the beach, teach them how to swim, build fires and various things involved with camping. We bought play tools like we were using so they could pretend they were helping. We built a tree house out back, and the kids played a lot in there and pretended to be

Daniel Boones with their stick rifles.

We even slept in it several times with the kids. We did not want them to pretend to kill people, just could pretend to hunt for food. My desire to end wars and not teach hate of a people we called the enemy continued. I wanted to teach the proper use of firearms. The kids were not allowed to point their play guns at people until NERF guns and water blasters came along. All the kids went through a hunter safety program to learn about the safe handling of a firearm and hunter safety.

KIDS & LOAN OFFICER NEGOTIATE A LOAN IN THEIR TREE HOUSE

At one point I had applied for a loan to build an addition as more children came along. The loan officer, who was also the bank manager, said he may stop by some time to see our property, but I forgot to mention it to Diane. One day when she was in the tree house with the kids playing house and serving tea in a plastic tea set, a man came in the yard in a suit. He just asked for me and did not identify himself, so Diane said I would be back shortly and invited him up in the tree house. He went up and had some tea and asked a few questions about what we were doing. The kids told him about our plans to build their extra rooms and how they were going to help us build it with their tools.

Later, when I came home Diane told me about this man that came and had tea in the tree house. I almost fell backwards out of the tree house knowing it was the bank loan officer. Fortunately, my guardian angel caught me. Thinking he would say we were crazy people and would surely disapprove us, I became discouraged. He later called and said I had a lovely family and they approved me. Imagine that. I learned that my way is not the only way that works. Could I remember that and for how long? Diane came through with her down to earth approach. I would have tried to impress him with my 3-piece polyester suit, power tie and wing-tip shoes. God made sure I was gone when the loan officer came. I love that woman.

We lived ten years in NC and had four children there. During our stay there we often shared our love of the outdoors by inviting others to share picnics with us at the beach, at a park on the way home from church and any location that we could turn it into a fun spot. We also found a roller-skating rink and taught the kids how to skate and organized several church skating parties. After bending over to hold up 6 kids while they learned to skate, it is no wonder I have back problems.

I think some of our scariest adventures were going out during the night flounder gigging. At low tide we would go out in our aluminum boat with a light and a spear to look for flounder laying on the bottom. When a tugboat pushing a barge came along the Intra-Coastal Canal, the water level would change quickly with large waves coming at us. Then after the barge passed, the water would rush out trying to pull us out into the middle of the waterway. When the water got higher, I had to be careful to not let it wash us up on what would become dry land after the water receded quickly. It always took careful maneuvering to avoid danger. The whole time it would terrify the kids, plus they did not like bloody flounder jumping around inside the boat.

Chapter 20: MOVING TO PA - WHAT'S IN STORE FOR US AND PA?

During our years in NC, we had become much involved in the church and made many friends. Diane was involved with children programs and I used my musical experience in being a song leader, piano player and gave what we called sermonettes, which was a short 10-15-minute sermon before the longer sermon. The church was small but was very united in beliefs and friendship, plus we had a terrific pastor. He was one of the best pastors we ever had. He loved God and Jesus. He had an excellent balanced approach to Christian living and was a real down to earth man. One time he was having his car worked on and asked me to pick him up at the dealer, since I was working from home. He also asked if he could borrow my car to go visit some new people interested in our church. I had a '64 Chevy with a custom paint job, mag wheels and wide tires, performance loud mufflers, a high performance cam that rocked the car at idle, stick shift with a floor shift and bucket seats I had welded in place with no adjustment to fit me. As he drove off with his knees high in the air and slipping the clutch with the engine racing away and the mufflers just purring that great sound, I wondered what people would think of this pastor coming to visit them in a hot rod. He never did comment. Our present pastor is much like that.

I had applied and hoped to get a teaching job in PA at a new vocational school opening. When the school was complete and hiring people, I did not get the Auto Technology instructor position but in a few weeks the school called to see if I wanted the Collision Repair Technology instructor position since I had an Associate Degree in Collision Repair Technology. We loaded up our truck and sold our house and moved to a farmhouse about one half mile from the school in Schnecksville, PA. Since Diane was ten months pregnant, we quickly found a country doctor to deliver the baby at home. After finding a doctor, that would come to the house as back up, we had another son at home with my mother assisting in the birth. In her day, doctors came to the house and delivered babies at home, so she was familiar with it. The doctor lived two blocks away and came to our house to

227

check out the baby and he was fine. We named him Carl after my dad.

Four years later Diane was pregnant one last time to make it a half dozen. During the doctor's visits and examinations, the doctor alerted us to some possible complications. We did some research and found that the world was catching up to our way of thinking. There were now birthing rooms at the hospital set up to resemble a home bedroom, but with all the protections of a hospital. We went that route and at delivery; the doctor allowed me to deliver it since I was an experienced mid-wife doctor or whatever they would call me. It turned out that there were no complications, and everything went well. We named him Samuel Adam after my long-term friend and blood brother, Sam Wilcox. This was the first time we had health insurance.

I think being with Diane during the delivery each time and seeing the pain and work she went through was just one more step in the adventure of learning about her and being involved in such an intimate act.

Once again, we got involved with the PA church and went on several camping trips with the teens. We also joined a church band, which played a mixture of country and oldies. Diane sang with them and I stayed home with the kids. That was her night out. Later I joined the band and played the trumpet. We mostly played at church events, nursing homes and hospitals. Several years later the band broke up, and we were asked to put something together for a wedding. We did, with me playing the keyboard, David played the drums and Diane sang with two friends playing the guitars. We loved watching Donnie and Marie Osmond and the whole Osmond family on TV, and this would be the beginning of a family band.

A WHISTLE BLOWER NEEDED IN CHURCH - WHY ME?

We still attended the same denomination church just in PA. Originally, we chose it because we believed they taught and lived by the Bible, showed love for one another, visitors, and new people. They also answered all our questions. When we moved to PA, we expected everything to remain the same. However, as we got more involved, we realized something was different. To make a long story short, the pastor had allowed his own ideas and speculation of some members to take precedent over the church's teachings.

228

This was a top-down church with all churches supposed to be teaching the same thing. New people were being taught things that the church did not teach. We became genuinely concerned about this. Many people like me, enjoyed researching subjects and looking for truth. The problem I faced as well as others was that it is easy to get too involved and out of balance with the new knowledge. Sometimes it is hard to know what to do with this new knowledge. I think that was the problem at that church, they got out of balance with new knowledge and effected the doctrines of the church.

When Diane and I talked to the elders of the church, they knew about it but said if they did anything, they would be removed from their position. They thought they were more useful in a position to help others. God will have to judge that.

We eventually, after at least a year of prayer and counsel from pastors in other churches, wrote a letter to headquarters expressing our concerns. It was a tough decision to make but once again; we felt we had to do it knowing we could be wrong, but maybe we were right. We wondered what the consequences of this letter would be since my whistle blowing had not had very favorable results in the past. It was in God's hands now. It was an extremely stressful, discouraging, frustrating time in our life. One night, totally discouraged, talking to God, I sat in the road wishing a car would come around the curve and kill me. I was tired of this. It seemed my entire life; I did nothing but get into trouble. I thought, even my guardian angel cannot help me this time. Time for another question:

What happened next?

A. Sam had driven up from Lancaster to apologize for sitting under an umbrella with Marta at the lake and ended up sitting with me talking under an umbrella.

B. Diane saw me and came out and beat me with a broom, like her mother did her.

C. My guardian angel played like the Allstate mayhem man and caused an accident down the road, so no traffic came my way.

D. God took away my concerns and gave me peace.

It was D. A car never came even though it was Friday night and people should have been on the road after a football game, but after praying, I felt a peace come over me and a positive attitude that everything would work out so I got up and went back home. The next day, I found out that there was an accident down the road, and they detoured traffic. How did that happen? Did my guardian angel do it like the mayhem man?

I was exciting to see the chief leaders of the church come out and visit the church area. The pastor was eventually transferred but before going he announced that someone in the church had written a letter about him and that is the reason he was being transferred. He hinted around that the letter caused division in the church, and just like in the Marines, should be dealt with. It appears we were the ones in the wrong. Eventually, it got out that it was us that had written the letter, and some said they were happy someone wrote a letter, and others shunned us. That remained for many years. Sometimes I would ask myself, why could not I just be a normal guy, whatever that is, and just enjoy serving in a church and staying in one church my whole life? Why did I always want to experience things? Why did I get upset when I saw people cheating or not doing what I expected them to do?

Headquarters sent pastors to a local church, not by a local church committee hiring them, so for the next several years, we had several pastors come and go. We noticed that each pastor had his own interpretation of the Bible, and things were just not the same as the church we first went to in NC. The NC church had the best pastor that we have ever had. We were new Christians, and the church set such a high standard in our minds; we have not found one like it since. For the next 12 years, everything went fine mostly. When a liberal pastor came in, the liberal members got involved. When a conservative pastor came in, the conservative members served. Like politics, a complete change of administration took place. I do not think it is supposed to be like that.

However, even in Paul's day, there were some that said they followed Paul, and others followed Jesus. I Cor. 1:11-13. Paul asked if Christ was divided, he said they were human to prefer different pastors. I might have to answer yes to that question as far as the church being divided. I read where during the Civil War, many churches split over whether slavery was right or wrong. It appears people would rather split, tear apart relationships, tear apart families, go to war than give up what they believe, even if the Bible did not support their belief.

When the Bible is not clear on a particular question or we read different meanings in a particular scripture, what are we to do?

A.   Fast and pray

B.   Ask the pastor to decide it

C.   Take a poll to see what most people would like it to mean

D.   Do not decide until God makes it clear

E.   Seek God's voice to speak the meaning to you and then tell others God spoke to you

F.   Tell people the Bible is not clear but based on other scriptures or principles of the Bible, the church has no standing, so decide for yourself.

G.   Clear your mind of all thoughts and allow God to speak to you.

H.   Use a Ouija Board

There are some on the list I hope no one uses. There are some unfortunately, I know people used. It is something we all face as we search for help to understand a scripture. There lies the reason that there are so many churches. I always assumed that if I prayed and fasted that I was close to God and what He revealed to me was His will or His truth.

Then I found out that others had fasted and prayed and still came up with a different answer. How can that be? I always was asking myself; how did the modern-day Christian church develop from Jesus and the twelve Apostles who were keeping all the Jewish laws and traditions? Was there a new set of stone tablets written with Jesus finger telling the disciples what to change. I did not see any.

Jesus said when he sent out the twelve to NOT go to the Gentiles. Matthew 10:5. Peter experienced looking at Gentiles in a new way when God showed him not to call any man unclean. God showing Peter was a mixture of a dream, circumstances, and opportunity. Is that how it happened?

I also asked if I were a Jewish person in Jesus' time, where is it in the Bible that would make me change to "the way", as they called Christianity. Since I believed in the God that protected me and changed me, I wanted to please Him and learn more about Him from the Bible. By keeping the

Sabbath, Holy Days, and food laws, I thought this was God's will for us. We were not observing any traditional days that were not commanded in the Bible.

A FAMILY BAND

I remember at my mother's church when they had a social; they put together a kitchen band. They got items out of the kitchen and made them look like instruments and then hummed through a Gazoo. That was a fun tradition. Too bad there were so many so-called church traditions, otherwise it would have been an enjoyable place to learn about God. The Osmond's set aside a family night to enjoy each other, so we desired a time to enjoy each other as well. Friday night was our family night since it was the beginning of the Sabbath. Unfortunately, or fortunately, depending how you look on it, our kids could not take part in any school sports or activities that were on Friday night or Saturday. Our church had its own sport program with competitions along the east coast.

So, on Friday nights we had a Bible study and prayer and then some fun times. It may have been hide and go seek, a picnic, other games and attempts at a family kitchen band. I bought Gazoo's, and the kids picked something from the kitchen to pretend to play. We had a lot of fun and laughs doing that. The kids made instruments and hummed through a Gazoo. As Diane and I progressed along with our band, the kids gradually joined in with instruments they started to play.

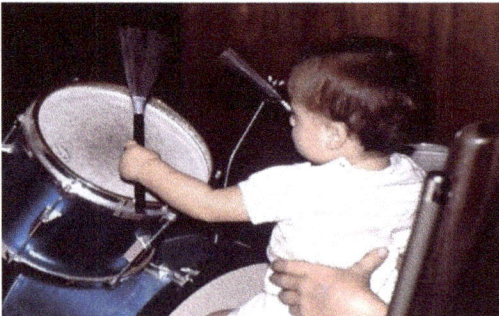

Diane and I put together a duo with her singing and me playing the keyboard. We started entertaining at state parks, nursing homes, hospitals, and Veteran Hospitals. Diane composed a song "Salute to The Troops of Vietnam", and I wrote the music. We started playing our song at more

Veterans Hospital from Florida to Vermont, including Washington DC. She sang country, and I played the keyboard. The vets loved the way she sang and related to them, so we kept getting invited to more hospitals and veteran organizations. We continued to get more requests to perform at various places like fairs, festivals, carnivals, and state parks. Gradually David, Tammy, Melody, Carl, and Adam began singing with us. David also played the drums, Tammy played the saxophone, Melody played the keyboard, and Carl and Adam played the guitars. Johnny sang some, but mostly entertained with magic before the show. When Adam was four, he just sat on stage and looked cute and people loved him.

One time at a State Park after a week of rain, a room full of weary, discouraged campers came out to see us. Suddenly, the Little Devil in me sprung to life, and I ran around trying to make people laugh. We started using the Cressman sense of humor passed down from my mom and dad along with audience participation. We got the people involved in the music and they exploded into a bundle of laughter and clapping. I quickly made some paper signs to hold up for people to know when to clap, yell, scream, etc. We started doing more audience participation at our shows, and the kids fell right into anything that got a laugh or some good screaming. We had professional signs made up by my buddy Sam, to carry to our shows and people loved it. For over 20 years, we performed from Florida to Vermont at fairs, festivals, carnivals, hospitals, and amusement parks with our signs. I was the Little Devil for people to laugh at, but soon to be replaced by other cuter Little Devils in the family.

Center Stage: Entertainment Excels at Sullivan Co. Fair

233

Below are some photos of our family as we progressed and changed through the years with a band and then an entertainment group.

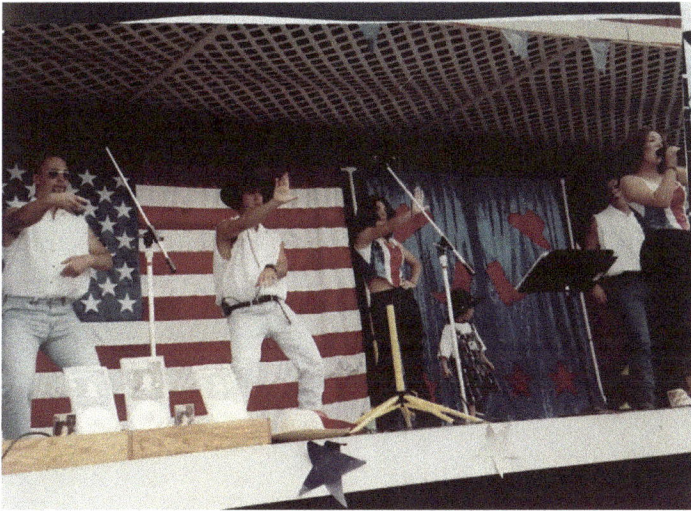

DeeDeeLee's HOT COUNTRY
COMEDY-MUSICAL SHOW

One song I sang was Honky Tonk Superman, so I had this shirt with the superman "S" on it. I put a parka over it and got a pair of black eyeglass frames. While singing, I would lift the parka and show my shirt and take it off like I was turning into superman.

One time I forgot to open the zipper, and the parka got caught on my head as I pulled it up. I could not see and ended up falling off the stage. I am sure my guardian angel caught me. I recovered quickly and kept on singing. The people loved it, so I made a habit of getting the parka caught and falling off the stage in every show. We did that at a church social one time and still today some people remember that instead of my good looks, muscles, and superior intellect. Such a Little Devil, I still am.

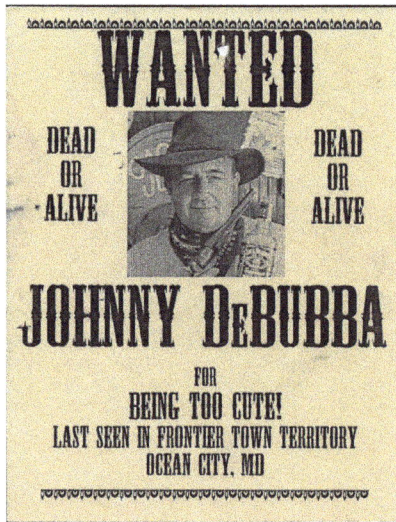

WANTED

DEAD OR ALIVE

DEAD OR ALIVE

JOHNNY DeBUBBA

FOR BEING TOO CUTE!
LAST SEEN IN FRONTIER TOWN TERRITORY
OCEAN CITY, MD

BECOMING A REAL CLOWN

At one point I took a clown course at a community college from a real clown and after that I would paint my face to entertain people. Now I could act crazy like I wanted to do, and no one would know it was me. As part of the class, they taught me juggling and some magical tricks. I never learned how to juggle, but while watching me practice at home, my son David became an excellent juggler, and we added a juggling act into our show. Johnny learned magical tricks, and we added magic as an opening act. Because of joining a clowning organization, I was able to get Liability Insurance to cover our entertainment, band, and DJ businesses.

236

During my clown class, my son David went with me. Our teacher covered a wall with plastic and had us throw plates full of whip cream at a person standing there. That was my favorite class. It reminded me of the three stooges and I could be Curly. While the teacher went out to get some more hand towels, guess what happened?

A. We all sat down quietly at our desks with our hands on our laps.

B. David and I ate all the whipped cream.

C. Two little devils started throwing pies around like the 3 stooges, and soon everyone joined in and the classroom got covered with whipped cream.

D. Same as C

It was C & D and was it a mess. The teacher did not think it was funny, maybe we should have thrown one at him. I am sure it did not smell good in there after a few days. I do not recall going back to the class or else that was the last one.

Diane and Tammy opened a consignment store and we all dressed up in various costumes to attract business in front of the store. All six kids, plus one of their mates, still work for an entertainment company where they might be costume characters, singers, do karaoke or DJ. I got to be a clown and rode an ostrich with a limo tour sponsored by a radio station in Allentown, PA to visit businesses. John makes a good pirate, Sam Adam looks like a bat and his wife Katie, Carl looks like a spider, David looks like an America hero, I rode an Ostrich, dressed up like a bird and John was a hobo and pirate.

The photos below show some of the costume characters the kids dress up as.

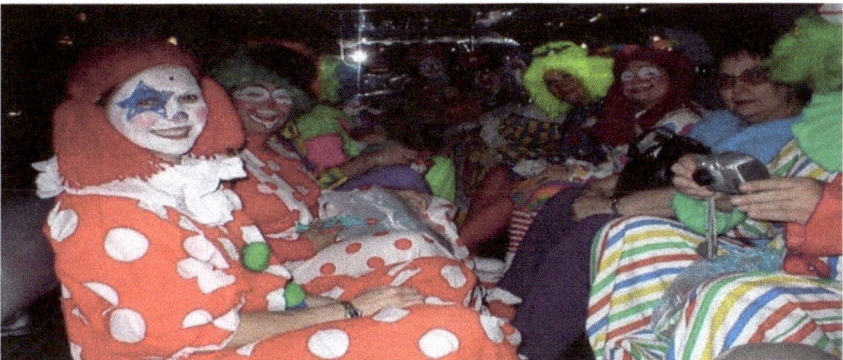

A CLEANING WOMAN GETS TO RECORDING CONTRACT AND TOUR WITH OUR FAMILY BAND

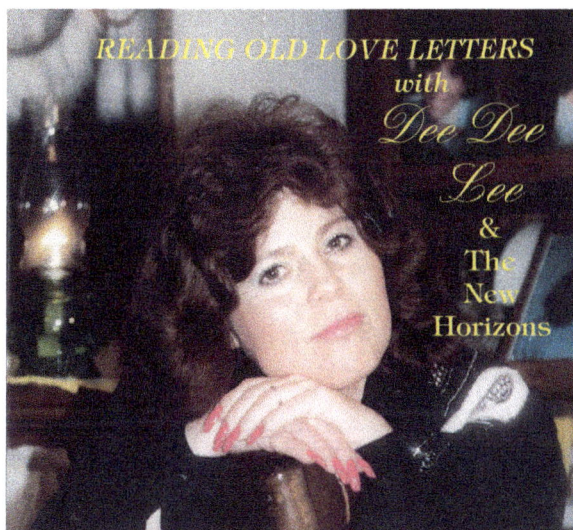

Now let us get back to the band. Being a vocational instructor meant I could teach with just experience but would have to work toward getting a degree from a college. On one of our leaner years, Diane worked part time with a friend cleaning houses. She was doing some cleaning one day at a millionaire's house and he heard her singing. She does a terrific imitation of Patsy Cline and Loretta Lynn. The owner, after talking to her about her singing and her goals, offered to pay for a recording of the songs she wrote, buy us better equipment and pay for a tour to promote the album using his motor home. She used the name Dee Dee Lee on her album. It sounded more country than Diane Cressman.

FARM GIRL GOES TO WHITEHOUSE

I took a sabbatical year off from school, and we went on a tour from South Carolina to Pennsylvania. During the year of the tour, the Gulf War took place, and we quickly put together a song to support the troops. We had already made a song to support the Vietnam troops, which one time they invited her to sing it at the Vietnam Memorial in Washington, DC. The local press, TV, radio stations and various veteran organizations worked with us to promote it. They invited her to various veteran support rallies and met many of the local politicians. A congressman invited her to sing it at the Reflecting Pool in Washington DC and meet with various high-ranking military leaders and politicians at the Whitehouse.

With the help of our local cable company, Blue Ridge Cable, and the Defense Department, we produced a musical video to her song with scenes from Kuwait and Iraq with local Marines giving a 21-gun salute. It amazed me that this country girl from NC could have intelligent conversations with Army Generals, Congressmen and even the Defense Dept. about the war and to get permission to use war videos for a music video. I thought that touring and the music video production was an exceptional adventure for all of us. I felt out of place with dignitaries and groups of people, so I was happy to stay behind with the kids and let her do her magic.

On the tour we got to meet Loretta Lynn and toured her bus, Barbara Mandrell, Lori Morgan, Brad Paisley, Tracy Lawrence, Sha Na Na and quite a few country and oldie bands. We never made it big, but Diane sold quite a few CD's, we met many amazing people who loved family groups and most important we could spend time as a family enjoying each other. The kids and I cut up and chose songs to make people laugh, forget their problems and feel good while Diane chose songs that related to what was on people's minds, their sorrow, their pain and brought out how faith in God was the answer. Diane and I never got to an overseas mission field like I hoped we would, but I think in our own way, we did it at home.

We had two mottos, one was a family that prays together stays together and the other was a family that plays together stays together. Our church did not particularly care for country music, but we only did clean, up-lifting, fun songs that any age could enjoy. We hired a company to promote her CD and they ended up extremely popular in Europe.

She was offered a tour in Europe, but we did not go because of all of us being away from school and work and were not sure we would have control over keeping the Sabbath and Holy Days.

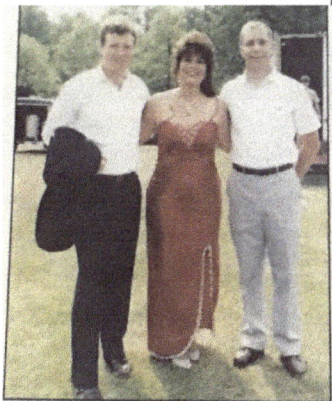

Left, PA Congressman Charlie Dent and former PA Representative Bob Nyce posed with Dee Dee Lee, whom performed at the 2nd annual "You Are Not Forgotten" benefit held at Becky's Drive-In Theatre on May 26, 1991.   -Photo by Cindy Beck Deppe

ne to my late dear friend Lehigh County Veterans Affairs Director Gene Salay, who encouraged me

Ten years later our church made some changes, and a highlight of our career was performing at Myrtle Beach Convention Center for our church convention in front of thousands of people. When Diane got cancer, we basically slowed down to just a few performances a year at Knoebels Amusement Park in PA and two local Firemen Carnivals. As grandkids came along, we involved them in the show as well. Eventually, Diane was healed but as everyone became more involved in their jobs and family. Diane and I became the roadies and we had to stop the family group but that was not the end.

Carl sang with several bands, recorded an album in Nashville TN and was a finalist in Nashville Star. He now has 6 children. Sam Adam sang with several other bands, recorded his own album in Nashville TN. He also sang and entertained on a cruise ship for about two years and now has 2 children.

Tammy has sung with the Young Ambassadors at college and performed with several theatrical performances with her 3 children. Jade, her daughter has also performed, played piano, and sung in various theatrical performances. Johnny who did magic shows during our shows has continued with magic, hypnotism, mentalism, costume characters and DJ work with an Entertainment Agency.

David works for an entertainment company and costume characters, DJ, and juggling acts. He has two children. Melody sang with us but uses her entertainment skills as an aqua physical therapy assistant. When people are hurting and go to the pool for therapy, she makes the pain go away with laughter and a smile and encouragement. It was and is such an outstanding experience to watch them perform on stage and live very balanced lives, taking time for their families. The cousins are best friends and are always hanging out.

The photos below show Tammy with Young Ambassadors, Carl with Nashville Star, Sam Adam recorded in Nashville.

YOUNG AMBASSADORS
1994-95

The next country star?

Demetra Stamus Special to The Morning Call
CARL CRESSMAN of Slatington opened the Nashville Star concert July 16 at the State Theatre. He beat 15 others vying for the opportunity.

ROCKSTAR

Adam in Nashville

I don't want to give away the rest of the book, but whatever job problems I had, whatever religious questions went unanswered, whatever negative experiences I may have had in life are all worth it to see the family enjoy each other and play together. Here now in 2020, almost all of us went whitewater tubing, and I went in a pontoon kayak to help me stay upright, which did not happen, and we all had a ball with each other. So, from ages 5 to 73, we did it. I think family is important to God. First there was Adam and Eve. Fortunately, God said it was not good for a man to be alone and made Miss Eve to be his beautiful bride. God told them to "replenish" the earth. Then there was Adam, Eve, and children. He also is making the Christian Church to be Jesus' beautiful bride. Will they do any replenishing and how would they do it, I wonder? There is a big universe to fill, is all I know.

Okay! Back to the story.

AT CAMP, TEACHING OTHERS TO LOVE GOD, JESUS, AND THE OUTDOORS

Our church wanted to take the younger children, ages 6-12, to a camp during the summer to enjoy the outdoors. They found a university camp in the Pocono Mountains that had a lake, trails through the woods, cabins, mess hall, campfire areas and a huge grassy play area. Diane and I were asked to help organize and be Directors of the camp. We would oversee the teaching of camping skills, outdoor skills, Christian living principles and most of all enjoy each other and God's creation. I jumped at the opportunity and put together everything I could remember from Boy Scout Camp, our church camp at Mt. Gretna, Marine Corps training and wilderness survival skills.

We had to staff the Camp, so asked Church members and teens to help teach many of the skills. Our goal was to seek volunteers that loved God and Jesus and lived by His principles and were fun people good with children. I remembered from Vietnam that a good marine was not always good with people. We knew that just because a person was a Christian, did not make them good with kids. Three of our kids were teens and were good at all the skills taught, so they helped teach. They taught canoeing plus how to survive a tipped canoe. we taught archery, fire building skills, hiking, fishing, knot-tying and even for the older ones we taught survival skills allowing them to build a shelter in the forest from branches and leaves and then sleep in them overnight.

I played bugle calls to wake them up, put them to sleep and when to eat. We went around in the mornings to inspect the cabins and to be sure they cleaned up. That was a lot of fun since I went out and bought a drill instructor hat and inspected like they did in the Marine Corps, except with no obscenities, just fun. We gave awards for the cleanest, most creative etc. cabins. We had terrific counselors and staff that worked with us to make the experience fun as well as educational for the young people. Diane had coached softball, cheer leading and soccer during the year in church so many of the kids there were familiar with us.

Recalling some of my Little Devil tactics, we had the teen helpers along hiking trails pretend to be Indians and throw water balloons at the campers from the rocks. I put up a rope to swing on across a small creek. It represented faith to cross the Red Sea. If they fell or did not make it across, they landed in the creek. Lack of faith. We even had a person teach swimming to those that did not know how to swim. We also taught fishing in the lake, and the kids got a thrill when they caught a fish. Unfortunately, we could not teach tree climbing or cave exploring.

We sang many of the songs I had learned at church camp and some from Boy Scouts. Our family still sings them around a campfire when camping.

The photos below show activities we did at camp, archery, team skills and canoe tipping and recovery. While teaching knot tying and fire building, we decided to pretend to burn the assistant director at the stake. The Little Devil had the idea. Also taught was survival skills like shelter building and sleeping in the one you build.

ADVENTURES WITH THE FAMILY

During our first 20 years of marriage we were rather busy and did no dangerous adventures but had a few wild and crazy ones. I loved to take the kids camping and teach them how to build a fire, put up a tent, fish and hunt. We went hiking, swinging on vines and cooked hot dogs over a fire and drank spring water whenever we found water bubbling out of the ground. To continue the legacy, one time at Promised Land State Park.

We were camped along the lake, and David and Tammy asked if they could take the rowboat across the lake to pick some wild blueberries for blueberry pancakes. I let them go but soon saw the rowboat coming back faster than I thought it could ever go. Tammy came running over yelling about a bear. Turns out, they must have invaded the bear's feeding grounds and the bear let them know they should leave. They did the right thing and backed away slowly out of sight, but then ran for dear life to the boat. We had no blueberry pancakes that morning.

Later we went back and picked some for the next morning. Diane and I pray for protection for our kids and grandkids like my mother and grandmother prayed for me. I hope their guardian angels will not have as much anxiety as mine did.

I day I realized my son Johnny would never enjoy all the outdoor thrills as I did. I knew he would never be a hunter since one time he was in a tree stand hunting deer and I saw from my tree stand that a couple deer had gone right by his stand and he did not shoot. When I went over, he was reading a book and never saw the deer.

He ended up loving computers and works as a computer programmer plus loves to read. He does part-time work for an entertainment agency doing hypnotism, mentalist, and magic. He also dresses up as a costume character and looks stunning as a pirate. He still enjoys going bike riding, kayaking, and canoeing though.

So, there is variety in my family so there must be variety in God's family. His sons and daughters will have different likes and dislikes. It is hard to accept sometimes because all of us fathers want our boys to be just like us, but I am happy they are not.

247

BACKPACKING THE WILDERNESS

Through the years I hiked, sometimes with others or sometimes by myself, parts of the Appalachian Trail, or various other trails in PA and went hunting. I went hunting to be a real backwoods man and provide meat for the family. Eventually I learned, after passing up some nice deer, that I just loved finding an excuse to be outside in the woods hiking and exploring new trails. I loved drinking from a mountain spring, hiking up and down mountains just to see the sights and wonder how they were formed. When hunting, I often preferred a flint lock muzzle loader just to relive the days of our ancestors. I doubt if obesity because of too much food was a problem with the pioneers using only a one-shot flint lock muzzle loader. Dampness, freezing temperatures and time involved to reload just makes it a real challenge to get meat.

I had all the kids out hunting with me. One time a beautiful 8-point buck ran by me as I took several shots, but it fell in front of David after he fired one shot. There was only one hole. There was a debate about whether I hit it and it fell in front of David or his bullet went through my hole. Diane also got her share of deer as well. The only difference was that after Diane shot one, she would go up to it and like in the movie "Avatar" she would go over, talk to it and apologize for taking its life but it would be put to good use in feeding our family.

As the kids became teenagers, Diane and I could get out ourselves more while the older one's baby sat. I wanted to backpack along a trail in the Allegheny Mountains and camp out for several days. It seemed like a real adventure since there would be the challenge of avoiding bears, snakes and exploring a ghost town along the trail and enjoying some magnificent views from overlooks. I took my fishing rod along, hoping to find a mountain stream with native trout in there to provide some fresh food and the excitement of catching them.

We hiked a day and found a perfect camping location along a mountain stream with a deep hole to fish and swim in. We set up camp, sprinkled some black pepper around our tent to help keep bears from investigating us and our food, which we hung up in a tree. I crawled up to the creek to not scare the native trout in there and ended up catching three or four beautiful colored native trout to provide a dinner for us, and then I took a swim in the cold water before building a fire for the evening.

It was beautiful but scary at the same time knowing we were miles away from any houses, cities, phones, cars, or any other help. But we were out in nature among God's creation, and we felt extremely close to God. We had a confidence in Him to provide protection and security as He always did before. This time I did my research, we had the right equipment; we left a map with the kids of where we were going, and we had a good idea of what it took to do wilderness camping. Our trip had no life-threatening events, but instead of continuing to hike for three days, we stayed at that spot since it was so perfect and did day hikes in different directions to explore. We went through the ghost town, which was just some remains of log cabins remaining from the early settler days and the lumbering, hunting, and trapping that took place there. Sometimes while out hunting, hiking or cross-country skiing, I have come across the remains of a house where some lived maybe a hundred or more years ago.

I love envision and imagine what it was like to live there. One place I found had a rock foundation, maybe twelve feet by twelve feet, which means a family lived awfully close together compared to our 3300 square foot house with 7 bedrooms and two baths. I saw a spring where they got their fresh water from, raspberry plants where they probably got fresh berries and an apple tree to provide more fruit. There was a rather large, cleared area where they probably had a garden to provide the vegetables. There were some remains of a fireplace which meant they cut and split wood plus tending a fire all day for heat and cooking. I could just picture a family living there like the show "Little House on the Prairie". Our trip was extremely rewarding and adventurous and after a few days we headed home.

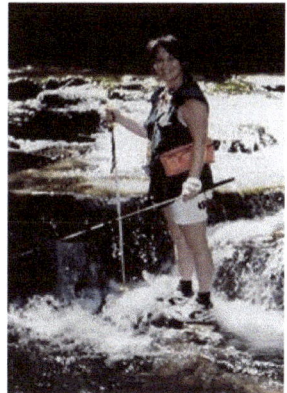

A MT. BIKE RIDE AND LOST IN THE WOODS

I had hoped to go back to the same spot someday to camp again or at least go fishing but was looking for a trail not so steep as we were on before, maybe even one I could ride a bike on or cross-country ski on. On a map I had, I saw what looked like a road that was shorter and thought I would investigate it if I had a chance. The opportunity came one weekend when I said I wanted to go camping with just my dog Rocky and do some mountain biking. I wanted to go pick up a surprise for Diane that would go with our western décor family room that I had seen at a country store when we were out camping in the Allegheny Mountains.

I picked up the gift late morning and had about five hours remaining before dark so I thought I could ride my mountain bike down the new trail with my folding fishing rod to our campsite, do some fishing and be back before dark. The trail was probably an old logging road and had not been used in many years. I rode the bike, and my dog ran aside of me from the top of the mountain down into a valley where I hoped to see the good fishing creek. Suddenly, I came to several enormous trees down on the road. I thought I was so close and hated to turn back, so I thought I would go around the trees through the woods. I could not let a few obstacles stand I my way. I went around the trees and but could not find the road. It appeared I was at the bottom where it ended, but there was no stream. I only had one bottle of water on my bike that I was hoping to fill it up when we found the stream since it was near empty.

Frustrated, I looked at the map I brought, and it showed the trail ending at the stream. There was no stream nor signs of one. Where is it or should I say, where am I? It appeared that my dog was too tired to go back up on the road we came down on, but it at least the road would get us there knowing it would be dark in several hours. That would be too easy for my exploring brain. As I looked at the map, I saw a direct hiking trail to the top of the mountain and ended near the parking lot. I looked all around and found what I was hoping was the hiking trail which would take us to the parking lot, but I would have to walk my bike. If this trail did not get me to the car by dark, I would have to spend the night in the woods.

As I hiked up the mountain, I was getting tired, hungry, and thirsty and for some reason brought no extra snacks or water. That was strange because I was always prepared for the worst. In another hour it was going to be dark and I had no idea where I was, and my family thought I was at a campground so I could be in trouble. I had a headlight on my bike and in my backpack I had the fishing rod, tackle, worms, matches and a garbage bag which I always carried with me that could be used as a raincoat or a poncho to keep me dry or warm in emergency. I could always be a real survivalist and eat the worms. Not that desperate yet. I figured if I did not my way back by dark, I would build a shelter and fire and spend the night in the woods.

I made it to the top of the mountain and had to carry my little dog part of the way since he was very tired and no signs of the bigger dirt road I was looking for. The sun had set, and I knew I would have to build a shelter soon before dark. I stopped and looked at the map and it showed the trail I was on meeting the dirt road where my car was, but I saw nothing. My heart was pounding in my chest and I was getting scared. This was one of those praying moments, so I did. I told God it was me again and I was in trouble and needed help to get out of there or protection during the night.

I saw an area where I could build a shelter out of trees, branches, and leaves so I was headed there when I saw some headlights through the trees ahead. Headlights meant a road and it appeared to be several hundred yards in front of me. Rocky and I kind of ran up the trail toward where I saw the headlights but of course they were gone now. What I found was the dirt road I was looking for since I saw my bike tire prints in the dirt. I do not know what they were doing there but to me they were heaven sent and I gave thanks for them showing me the way. I put Rocky in my backpack since he often road in there as a puppy and then rode the bike back to my car with the headlight on. By the time I got back to the car it was very dark. If it had not been for that truck, I would have camped out about 200 yards from the road and would have felt like a fool in the morning. I went to the campground and called my wife on a pay phone. We did not have a cell phone at the time. I never did get back there again. As usual, once and done.

A FREEZING WINTER CAMPING NIGHT

A friend introduced us to cross-country skiing, and we loved it. It was excellent exercise and allowed us to be outdoors in the winter, enjoying God's creation differently than we had ever done before. One place we skied was the Appalachian Trail. We found some shelters and campsites along the trail, and I thought what a challenge it would be to ski to a campsite and sleep out in the snow. So, we got our sleeping bags, a tent, hand warmers and whatever else we needed and did it. It was awesome to sit by a fire in the snow, cook a delicious meal and then look up at all the stars. It was so peaceful, quiet, and inspiring. We even hiked a little distance to an overlook that enabled us to see the lights of the whole Lehigh Valley, but especially Allentown was really all lit up.

We then retired to the tent, climbed in our sleeping bags with our insulated suits on and went to sleep. It was not long before we woke up very cold. We used the hand warmers all inside the sleeping bags, tried everything, but stayed cold. At one point I looked out and saw coals from the fire and we went out to add wood and get warmed up.

We spent the night shivering and in misery, wandering what in the world we were doing. This was going to be a praying moment, but after praying, nothing changed other than the clock kept ticking slowly. We got up early, saw icicles hanging inside the tent from our breath. We then built a fire, cooked our breakfast, and then headed down the mountain and home. We gave thanks we survived, but it was a miserable lesson to learn.

I did not like failing at winter camping, so I bought some books and did some research. I found out there were special sleeping bags, special clothes, small portable heaters, and insulation that was needed for the floor of the tent to keep out the cold from the snow. I went out and bought the needed equipment for winter camping and we tried it out in the yard which we should have done to begin with.

It worked great, and we slept without a problem, nice and warm. The winter sleeping bags and ground pads helped keep our heat in. We used a plastic sled to hold our gear and connected it with ropes and poles to a special belt I wore so I could pull it while on cross-country skis. We then tried camping on the Appalachian Trail, Weiser State Forest Land, near Jim Thorpe, where there were miles of trails to cross-country ski on and finally in Wyoming State Forest Land in the Allegheny Mountains of PA.

If we heard there was a snowstorm or blizzard coming, we headed for the forest with our skis and camping gear. One time the blizzard turned into an ice storm and we woke up in the morning with several inches of frozen snow and ice collapsing our tent. The tent collapsed from the 8" of snow and freezing rain, which made it crusty.

Everything was soaked, but we built a fire to cook breakfast and warm up on. We then headed back to our 4-wheel drive truck. When we arrived at our truck, it had about 2" of ice on it so we had no choice but to chip away to get in. Once in, I started the engine to get heat to melt the rest. We still had to keep chipping away. The way of the frontiersmen and wilderness people were not always a desirable life. But I wanted to experience it.

Most of the winter camping trips turned out to be a grand adventure with many exciting memories. There were quite a few nights when the temperatures dropped below zero. We carried small folding camping chairs to sit by the fire or sit and eat. We made it as comfortable as we could without carrying too much. One problem we had was that our drinking water froze every night, no matter where we put it. We had a small camping propane heater if we woke up cold, we could turn it on for a while to warm us up or to warm up the sleeping bags before climbing in.

When we were out winter camping, we would often hear Coyotes howling close by and seemed kind of eerie even though I do not think I ever heard of any attacks on humans by coyotes. It probably just reminded me of cowboy movies I had seen of wolf packs attacking settlers.

Once again, the people living on earth during Jesus's reign will not have to worry about wolf attacks. The Bible in Isaiah 65:25, NIV "The wolf and the lamb will feed together, and the lion will eat straw like the ox, but dust will be the serpent's food. They will neither harm nor destroy on all my holy mountain," says the LORD. How encouraging that is.

With any camping, one of the inspiring moments is being able to look up into the heavens at night and see all the stars. The sky is clearer during the winter months, allowing more stars to be seen.

One exciting time in the Allegheny Mts, we skied out to camp in about

12" of snow and close to "0" temperatures. I wanted to try using a hot water bottle to keep us warm at night like I had seen in Williamsburg, VA, where the settlers put fire coals in a pan in their beds to warm them up. Before bed, I poured hot water from our coffee pot into the bottles and put them in our sleeping bags. We eventually crawled into nice warm sleeping bags for a change. During the night, I heard Diane screaming and trying to get out of her sleeping bag. I must have not put the lid on tight and the water leaked out and soaked her and the sleeping bag. That was not good in freezing temperatures. Fortunately, she had a change of clothes but then demanded my sleeping bag and while giving me her wet one since I was the nut that left the lid loose. I do not think Diane thought of me as Johnny Angel that night. I think she accused me of being one dumb guy. That was a long night. It may have been another payback for my shenanigans.

I could never help but wonder what type of adventures await those that explore space. I wondered if all those planets, suns, moons, and other galaxies are just for us to look at or does God have a plan for them. Once we are spirit beings, will we be able to travel through the universe? Is there a chance that we may go to a planet and build it the way we want, or as God would direct us? Would we be able to make planets inhabitable so life could exist on them? If we oversaw a planet, how would we make it and what would we make differently than what is on earth? There are just so many things to think about as we look up into the heavens.

I once heard someone speculate, which means he was just explaining a possibility or theory about the future. In Isaiah 9:7 NIV, it says, "Of the increase of his government and peace there will be no end. He will reign on David's throne and over his kingdom, establishing and upholding it with justice and righteousness from that time on and forever. He speculated that possibly some beings may spread out across the universe and inhabit the planets out there after the bride of Christ, that is us, become spirit beings, find out what our jobs will be. Could it to somehow go out to recreate the universe? Some husbands like to have children from their wife and marriage. Can the bride of Christ have children? There has been some speculation about what spirit beings will be doing in Heaven, so why not imagine what work they will do through eternity? Like I said before, Adam and Eve were told to be fruitful, multiply and replenish the earth. Will Jesus and his bride be told to be fruitful, multiply and replenish the universe? I love to imagine things.

At one point we were buying cross-country skis at yard sales and keeping them for others to go along. Our kids have gone cross-country skiing with us, my chiropractor and his wife, several people from our church and even some older grandkids.

The photos below show us winter camping, cross-country skiing and during a blizzard, we made an igloo at our house and camped out in it. My grandson Ethan is building an ice hut.

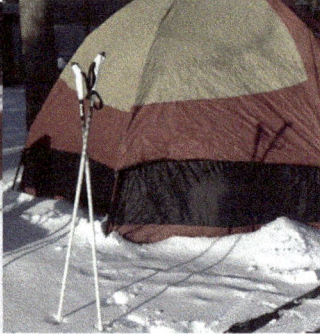

UNFORGETABLE RAFTING AND CANOE CAMPING

We went on a rafting trip on the New River in West Virginia. We rafted for a day and then camped along the river with a campfire and cooked steaks. That was my kind of experience with the sound of the river all night long. I thought someday I would like to camp by a river again. The next day we were rafting, and the guide allowed us to float in the river. He pointed out that there was a two-story high boulder a head right in the middle of the river with a tunnel under the rock with river water flowing under it. He said to be sure and stay to the left side of the rock to avoid the current that went under the rock. Somehow Diane and I got caught in the current that was taking us right for the rock. We tried to swim, but it did no good, we were going to hit the rock. As we got closer, we could see where the current appeared to be sinking under the rock. As the raft guide went out of sight around the rock, he yelled hang on to the rock until out of the current.

Here is one of those questions again.

What happened when we hit the rock?

A. We held our breath, went under the rock, and came out the other side.

B. Sam showed up with his wife Cindy, holding an umbrella over Sam, in a row boat and used her umbrella to pull us out.

C. We hit the rock and like Moses, the rock split and we coasted through the opening.

D. None of the above.

It was D. We hit the rock and felt the current trying to pull us under, but fortunately we had life jackets on and that helped keep us afloat. We grabbed the rock to keep from being pulled under and inched our way around it until free of the current and then floated free. The only trouble was that we went to the right instead of left, thus causing us to float through some huge rapids, but eventually came around this boulder and rejoined the rafters. I am sure the rafting guide was thinking how peaceful his trips were until we showed up.

Hanging on to the rock saved our lives. I have counted on rocks many a time in my adventures. Rocks provide a solid footing, stability, a foundation, and an overhanging rock or cave can provide a shelter. A rock sticking out of the top of a mountain can provide a viewpoint of where you have been and where you are going. The Bible compares God the Father and Jesus as the rock. That reminds me of Ps.18:2 NIV The LORD is my rock, my fortress and my deliverer; my God is my rock, in whom I take refuge. He is my shield and the horn of my salvation, my stronghold. Thank God for rocks.

The next adventure would be on the water. We always had a rowboat since we were married, but now, I bought a canoe. We canoed in lakes and in rivers and through rapids and really enjoyed it. My kids learned to love canoeing also; my two sons, David, and Carl, and my one daughter, Tammy, have canoes. Another daughter, Melody, often uses ours. I have three canoes, twelve kayaks, a rowboat, and a paddleboat for the family to use.

It seems every time I started a new adventure I had to camp out and canoeing was no different, especially after our camping, rafting trip on the New River in West Virginia. I wanted to go in a lake into a secluded spot and camp inside the canoe. Diane, being the loving wife she is, went with me. We would put sleeping bags on the bottom of the canoe and go to sleep. We paddled until the river was smaller and turning into rapids. We found a deep pool of quiet water and dropped the anchor where the river was about 30 feet wide and maybe fifteen feet deep.

We ate a packed lunch, watched a beautiful sunset, and waited for dark. It was a little early for us to go to sleep, so we fished and talked awhile and then figured we would go to sleep. It was not long before we heard all kinds of breaking branches, splashing and other noises. Secluded meant that there were woods all around us on the shore. We shined our flashlights around but saw nothing. We thought maybe it was deer drinking in the river or getting ready to swim across the cove when they may have seen or smelled us and startled them.

We laid back down and tried to sleep but shortly after heard leaves rustling and sticks breaking like strange creatures were walking on shore. We heard owls, coyotes, crickets and some kind of bird sounds, and it was rather scary. All the times we camped out; we never heard such commotion. There was no covering over us, and this was not a campground, it was wild, so we heard everything that goes on out there at night. Then we heard what sounded like something being attacked and eaten alive. I was thinking there would not be any peace or quiet that night. We were just lying there when we heard some strange sound above us in the air. It reminded me of old dinosaur movies and how a pterodactyl sounded. It sounded like wooosh-wooosh-wooosh over our heads.

What happened then?

A.   A giant pterodactyl came down and grabbed Diane, so I fought until it dropped her

B.   A whale like fish jumped out the water and grabbed the giant bird

C.   We got so scared, we tipped the canoe

D.   None of the above

It was D. Whatever it was; it sounded huge and seemed to hover over us, and then we heard it fly off. That was enough. We both agreed to get out of there and head home. There were never sounds like that in the Daniel Boone movies when he slept out on the trail. We were home by midnight, and we surprised the kids. No more camping inside canoes, but we wanted to try another canoe adventure. Diane must really love my good looks, big muscles, and superior intellect to keep going on these adventures with me even when they do not turn out to be as glorious as hoped for. You would think we would have had enough "adventures" and experiences of frontiersmen to stay home and watch Daniel Boone on TV. But no, keep reading. Remember Diane prayed to meet someone to take her on adventures. I will just say, be careful what you pray for.

ANOTHER CANOE ADVENTURE

The next canoe adventure was going down the Lehigh River in PA and camp out on an island. I knew just the island to camp on; I had seen it while paddling down the river. It had a nice sandy beach to sleep on, that we could swim from and land the canoe on. Trees surrounded it. We could be like Robinson Crusoe, pretending that Diane and I were stranded on this desolate island away from all life. Nothing to do but kiss and hug all night under the stars. (There goes my imagination again) So off we went again down the Lehigh to our little Paradise Island. We found a nice soft sandy area to put our sleeping bags on, built a fire to cook on and settled back to enjoy the evening. We searched for some nice smooth river rocks to be a pillow, like the cowboys' used or even Jacob had a rock for a pillow. Gen 28:10-22. That was an experience we did not want, so we used our clean clothes for a pillow.

Sticking with Jacob for a minute. Jacob used a rock for a pillow and had a dream during the night about God and angels. Jacob said because of the dream, he believed the place to be holy, to be the house of God. He took his pillow and made a memorial and poured oil on it. The place became Bethel. I am sure people thought it was a holy place. Jacob is not corrected for calling it God's house.

An amazing fact about Jacob's rock pillow is that a legend, tradition, or theory has it that Jeremiah carried that rock to Ireland. It then was carried to Scotland and finally to Westminster Abbey and placed under the coronation throne. But why all that trouble, if true? Some believe that Jeremiah took the stone there to keep it with the lost ten tribes of Israel. See why I love to explore the Bible and the mysteries in there. Not enough proof, as of now, to get fired from a job for.

Anyway, so back to the canoe trip. How could cowboy movies always show them with their head on a rock or a dead tree? That must have a good chiropractor business back then, or maybe that is why you always saw cowboys in a saloon with whiskey. It was a painkiller for their sore neck and head. We went to sleep under the stars and were startled by the sound of something swimming toward us in the river. We grabbed our flashlights and turned them on just in time to see several deer come out of the water and run right by us. We were wondering what this night had in store for us.

Once again, we fell asleep and during the night I rolled over and heard a terrible noise all around me. I guess during the night a flock of ducks must have moved in on the beach and did not know we were there. I think they were as startled as we were. We finally made it through the rest of the night with no more incidents. At daylight we both woke up all itchy and noticed we were covered in ants. The nice soft sand must have been ant hills, and they thought we were manna from Heaven.

We took a swim to wash the ants off, cooked breakfast and headed downstream through the rapids and back to where our car was parked. Along the way, there was a damn we had to take the canoe out and carry it around the damn before putting it back in. I always saw Daniel Boone and his Indian friend carry it on their heads on a trail. I never saw them carry their food, sleeping gear, paddles, life jackets, etc., up a steep rock riverbank, through uncleared woods and back down a rocky, steep riverbank into the water. I guess they could not get all that into an hour-long movie.

One of the safe adventures on the canoe was several sojourns we went on down the Lehigh River. I went on one with Diane, one with my son David and one with my son Carl and one with Sam Adam. I like to have fun, so I wore this huge spongy cowboy hat and had a huge water gun with me. I also tied a blow-up alligator behind the canoe.

To me, that made the trip interesting. They handed out awards for various things at the end, and I won a newly created award. Best canoe outfit. One paddler that hung around me really got a kick out of the gun and hat that when I went on the Sojourn again years later, there he was with the same gun and hat. Imagine that, someone trying to be a Little Devil, two nuts short of a fruitcake and use my wild, resourceful antics for himself. Maybe I was his idol. I was becoming infamous, that is more than famous, I think. Poor guy.

EXPERIENCING WHAT SATAN CAN DO TO A CHURCH

Satan from the beginning has been trying to hinder and stop God from accomplishing His plan. In time, Satan must have given authority over the earth since Satan offered the kingdoms of earth to Jesus. He is the prince of the power of air. Through the years I have heard many a pastor say that they felt like they are actual targets of Satan. Satan knows that if he can weaken the leader, the congregation may get confused and question God, leading to a deterioration of their relationship with Him. He may also use the desires of the world, so people get so caught up in seeking those pleasures and they neglect their relationship with God. I have seen so many churches that once had a church full of people and now have either closed their doors or have so few people attending that they have trouble accomplishing their goals of serving others and preaching the gospel to the world. They are just barely hanging on serving themselves and have little love for others. What happened? Did Satan destroy all these churches or was it something else? People seeking power and position can do it. People wanting to hang on to the past even though the future is here can do it. People not wanting to change when change is needed can do it.

Here is the story of one church I saw that happen to. One of the most painful experiences of my life. During our attending the same church for 25 years, we saw people with their own ideas leave and start their own church, people get their feelings hurt and leave, people question God because of death, sickness or lack of healing would also leave the church. Everyone, including myself, has questioned whether there is a God, where was He when I needed Him and what in the world is going on in my life and the world around me.

After about 22 years in this church, our head pastor died. We called him a pastor general since he was the main one in charge. In his search for a church, he claimed to find a small church with the name Church of God and had all the teachings he was looking for. They also traced their roots back to the apostles. He became a pastor, and the church grew to be worldwide with well over 200,000 members. Before his death, he appointed another pastor to take over after his death. For about 3 years, everything stayed the same, but then gradually the new pastor taught that our former beliefs were wrong. He taught the doctrine of mainstream Christianity were the true doctrines. I knew we were not one hundred per cent correct but I also knew neither was anyone else so why change one hundred per cent.

To make a long story short, after about 3 more years, about half of the church broke off to keep the old teachings and about half stayed to hear more about the new teachings. That has happened to so many churches through the years. It is sad to hear about it, but worse to experience it. This breaking off into two groups split friends, families, marriages, and children. Confused pastors, not knowing what to teach, had to make a decision that would affect their congregation, employment, job security and even their future retirement plans. There was a lot of hostility, questioning of others and even condemning others who disagreed with them.

Diane and I wondered how could a group of people that claimed to believe what the church taught, had searched the Bible like we did, had given up a lot to live out the way they believed, just turn their backs and believe something different which was the same as what mainstream Christianity believed.

A close friend, I hunted, fished and went camping with told me that if I switched churches and did not believe what he believed in, I would face the judgement, which means I would be burned in the fiery judgement. I think he meant that since I already knew the true gospel and was now turning my back on it; I was doomed. Where did that come from? Who told him that? What was happening to people? I do not understand what made some stay with their original beliefs and others so easily change their beliefs.Diane and I looked at the Bible to see what we believed and finally because of the hostility in both churches we decided to not attend either of the churches. It was probably the worst time in my life and was difficult on Diane and our 6 kids as they all saw friends turn their backs on them as well. My one daughter, Tammy, was at our church college right in the middle of all the changes, so it was a terrible experience for her while there.

My guardian angel probably wondered how he could protect us from the hurt that was taking place and after much prayer, counseling and studying we thought it was best to leave.

One church was changing back to teachings taught twenty years before, some back to thirty years before. Our church always changed as new proven knowledge became available about a scripture. No everyone liked that. Some wanted things to stay the same as it was when they became a member. I have heard that many times in various churches I have attended. Some want to keep things the same regardless of right or wrong, like I said about traditions. The church with new beliefs was teaching new doctrines so fast that there was no time to research them. They were tearing down traditions without an explanation. Through the years, I thought the church was a little too strong on obedience and legalism, giving too much authority to the ministry. I wanted to see some changes but not to tear down the entire belief system to go to something like the church I grew up in and had rejected it.

With no central figure to keep things straight, every man left to his beliefs, there continued to be more and more splits as some people thought there were too many changes and some people thought there were not enough. After 25 plus years since the split, the churches still exist but are much smaller and have continued to split even more. Through the years, I have seen other churches have experienced similar circumstances. As some churches try to adapt to what is happening in society, there are disagreements and sometimes a split. One thing is for sure, the Devil is alive and working hard to destroy God's plan with His church. Remember, it is to be the bride of Christ. The Bible seems to show that Satan has produced a counterfeit church to look just like the true church. I think he also has a plan for mankind, which is not good. God's plan will be good for us in the long run. Once Satan is locked up, it will all be over until they release him after the millennium.

After all our research, we were hoping we had found the church with beliefs like the historic church, but now which one was it? There are always choices in life. When Eve wanted to taste the fruit of the tree of the knowledge of good and evil, she sure got a mouthful. It is a sweet tasting fruit to begin with but sure gets bitter soon. Even in my case, with my curiosity, I wanted knowledge; I wanted to experience and explore life with its dangers and sometimes evil results just to know what was out there. I chose the tree of the knowledge of good and evil and have experienced the consequences of that, just like all people have.

When I accepted God's salvation, with limited knowledge and truth,

I did not understand that there was so much to learn about God. After many years of study, I understand that plan better but am still learning. There are many theories out there of what God's plan is and what the Bible says about it. I believe God put in us a desire to seek Him and believe in Him, but Satan has put obstacles in front of that desire to hide, confuse and frustrate us in that search. I believe God reaches out to us, like it was for me by seeing creation. We must be ready to respond when He does. That is where Satan tries to keep us distracted or so busy that we do not see God calling us. I believe that I still do not have all the understanding I wish I had. So how could God expect all of mankind to make an informed decision on salvation, a search for God, and what that means if the understanding of what it means is so hard to find?

That is where faith comes in and if we love God, we believe He will do the best for us, He will be sure we have what we need to do what He is training us for. In the Marines, I found some leaders wanted all his men to be like he was, love the Corps, look sharp, fight to win and be like we used to say, a mean, green, fighting machine. That produces a unit that is identically the same. A father may want his boys to turn out just like him, a mother may want her daughters to be just like her. I believe God wants variety in his family.

After the church break up, I studied once again to prove what I believed. I found it hard to consider that I had been wrong about what I had proved before. I bought a new Bible that was not all marked with my notes of what that scripture meant. I wanted to find out if the Bible really said what I had concluded with no helps from previous notes or other markings in my Bible. It was amazing what I had missed in my first 25 years of reading. I believe God was about to open my mind to more truth and what is important to God.

We did not attend church anywhere for a few years but went back to visit the two churches occasionally to see what was happening and see our "friends". One church had become just like a protestant church, so why would I drive 30 miles to go to a small church when there were closer ones. It was nice to see people we knew, but it seemed we no longer had that same bond. I wondered how they could change beliefs so fast.

The other church had taken a hard stand in getting its teachings back to where it was maybe 30 years ago. Anger and hurt were present. People became hard and steadfast in clinging to what they believed. If we brought

265

anything up about changes, it was not received well. It was nice to see friends, but they seemed to be more cautious, not as trustful, and less open to discussion because it had hurt them and called names for sticking to what they believed. So eventually we made a permanent decision to not attend.

For the next two to three years, we did not attend any church nor have fellowship with other believers as we continued our study into examining our beliefs. Through the years, I believe God showed me where I was wrong, which I will talk about later. Twenty-five years after the breakup, about half the church just gave up, got confused and quit attending all together.

Chapter 21: OVER THE HILL ADVENTURES

As we got older, the canoe seemed to get heavier and kayaks were becoming more popular. The next adventure would be with kayaks. Our family rented kayaks at Ocean City MD and went on a guided tour of the marshlands and creeks and then off to the ocean to ride waves. We received instruction on how to ride waves, and this was my new passion. We all loved it and went out and bought kayaks. We had a lot of fun on the lakes, in the ocean riding waves and going down the Lehigh River through the rapids. I cannot think of any out of the normal incidents other than the wild and crazy way we lived. We always look forward to sharing our love of boating with others. We still have many pairs of cross-country skis and enjoy sharing our love of skiing with others. We both cycle and have many bicycles also and enjoy sharing our love of cycling with others. My garage is filled with bikes, my backyard filled with watercraft, and my basement is storing many skis, boots, and poles.

The photo below shows Diane and I still enjoy going to a beautiful, inspiring spot where we can feel close to God. At one time or another, we have taken all our kids to our favorite spots.

PARALYZED IN THE ICE-COLD OCEAN

However, there was this one time when I was about sixty years old and a Little Devil raised his head again for a rather nutty act. We were down in NC for Christmas and I wanted to ride some waves in the ocean. The air had warmed up to about seventy, but the ocean was freezing. I hardly ever fell off a kayak, so I just wore my insulated water boots, wet suit shorts and a waterproof parka. Besides, if I fell off, the waves always washed me into shore, and I would just get out. I went out and was having a great time paddling out through the surf and riding over a wave just as it crested and broke; I went over the lip, got some air, then came crashing down on the back side of the wave.

That was a real radical trip. Being raked over was awesome. Sometimes I would ride a wave back in and paddle out again. That is surfer talk, I heard. I wanted to rest a bit, so I paddled out through the surf and just sat out in the open ocean relaxing. I was the only one out there and Diane was on shore in a lounge chair soaking up the sun. I looked out in the ocean and saw an enormous wave coming. I figured it would be better to paddle out to it and go over it rather than trying to ride it. I paddled out and made it over it only to see a bigger one getting ready to break so I quickly turned around hoping to ride it in. It was not a good riding wave; it curled up behind me and dumped right on my kayak, knocking me off the kayak. It was a wipeout.

The cold water went into my parka and covered my head. It was so cold I could not swim. I came up holding my paddle and then grabbed my kayak, which was right there. My body was like paralyzed and I could not get back on my kayak and I could not swim. I was so cold that I was having trouble breathing. Diane saw me but did not know I was in trouble since I usually just swim back to shore if tipped.

I knew I was in big trouble and just remember saying God please help me, I cannot move. Suddenly, I heard a voice saying, "Can I help you?" I answered instinctively, "Oh, yes Lord." I turned and saw a surfer in a wet suit was aside of me and asked if I needed help. I said yes, I cannot move and asked if he could push me into where I could touch bottom. He did, and I could walk out.

The whole time I was out there, I saw no one around. Where did he come from, I wandered? Was that my guardian angel in a wet suit? Did my guardian angel twitch his nose and instantly he had a wet suit and a surfboard? Was he a good surfer? Was there a heavenly surf somewhere he went on his day off? Will I ever learn? There goes my imagination again. If it was my guardian angel, he had a very muscular body and was rather handsome. Wherever or whoever, I thanked God. I bet the dolphins shook their heads and said "Yo, Dude, that was one rad barrel dumping on you out there in that freezing water". Of course, as my custom was, I never went kayaking in the winter again. My name should have been Wan Dum Guy. That is not true, I did break the thin ice one time and kayaked a little just to do it. Definitely. Wan Dum Guy.

RETIRED AND CYCLING THE ROCKIES

I had done much riding of a bicycle as a kid. Almost anywhere I wanted to go, I rode a bike. I rode a little during our married with the children but not too far.

By age fifty I was about fifty pounds overweight and feeling sluggish. I had done some mountain biking on several easy trails and saw I was losing weight. I also had started to country line dance, which helped burn the weight off. Every year we performed at the Potter County Fair about 250 miles from our house. I made a commitment that if I could lose fifty pounds; I would ride my bike home from Potter County that year. I started riding my mountain bike more and increasing the distance. I would ride with my wife up to Wilkes-Barre PA and ride home through the mountains about 60 miles. I also controlled what I ate.

I lost fifty pounds during the year 2000, so after the fair, they left me there with my bike and about fifty pounds of necessities I carried on my bike. I planned to stay in motels or camp out if needed. I rode the bike from Millport, Potter County to Easton, PA to make it about 350 miles. Although riding a bike 350 miles is enough of an adventure by itself, there were no dangerous situations or out of the ordinary except for one.

I was riding through Potter County on Rt. 6, which they call God's country. It is beautiful, but I see God's beauty everywhere I go. Late in the afternoon, I came to the Grand Canyon of PA, the Pine Creek Gorge. I did not plan to ride it, but I do not live by plans very well. If I get curious, I will investigate immediately. I had ridden through the Lehigh Gorge several times, so I figured I would ride through the Pine Creek Gorge, which was about 18 miles one way.

Since I had my mountain bike, I could ride the hard gravel trail with ease. I had an enjoyable ride down to the end, stopping along the way to admire the view and to take photos. It had taken longer than I thought to get to the end, and it was now early evening. When I turned around to go back, I saw black clouds coming and heard thunder. I rode back through the Gorge when suddenly it poured with thunder and lightning. There was no safe place to hide from the lightning, so since I was low in the canyon, I would hope for the best. I put my rain gear on and kept riding.

It was getting dark and with the fog and heavy rain, I could hardly see. To go the 18 miles back, I knew it would take about 90 minutes and I wanted to get back to Rt. 6 to find a motel before it got too late, so I pedaled as fast as I could. The rain came in my helmet and neck and soon I was soaked and getting cold. I turned my headlight on to see the trail better but was very scary with the fog, lightning and thunder which seemed to be all around me. The trail was getting puddles and water was flowing across the trail, slowing me down. Once again, my curiosity seemed to get me in trouble. I had hoped to be safe in a motel by now. This was once again a praying moment. This was just a prayer for safety and being able to find a motel. That was a ride to remember.

I made it back to Rt. 6 safely as the storm stopped about nine o'clock at night. I realized I could not make it to the next town to find a motel, so I rode and looked for the next motel along the way. Soon I found a motel but was a mom and pop type with a no vacancy sign and closed sign on the office. I went up to the door of what appeared to be the owner's house and stood there soaked as he answered the door. He said he was sorry but had nothing available. He was probably a little fearful looking at a water drenched man holding a bike helmet standing at his door. He probably thought, what a fruitcake? As I walked off, he called me and said he had a room available that was being worked on, but it had no air conditioning. I did not care about A/c; I wanted heat for me and my clothes. I took the room and warmed up immediately. He even cooked me a meal, no charge, and brought it to my room since there was no food available anywhere around. Up in the mountains, everything closes early with not much night life happening.

When I was on the trail praying, God did not stop the storm but allowed me to go through it to the end. Whether He wanted me to develop more faith in Him or see that I can do things I do not think I can or just to let me experience the consequence of my actions, I don't know. Obviously, I was protected from any life-threatening events but also found a close motel room with a meal. I have been to Vietnam and Japan and have seen many religions. Some have a place and a time to pray, even the Jewish people in the Old Testament had a place, a time, and a way to pray. I give thanks for a God that allows me through Jesus Christ to pray to Him any time and any place. I sat by a heater wrapped in a blanket giving thanks to God.

I can pray on the top of a mountain with a beautiful view, or pray in a valley along a peaceful stream, pray when I'm out in the woods watching wildlife or pray when deep in a cave while lost and in complete darkness, on a speeding train, or in a kayak in the ocean, or pray while riding a bike through a storm, when lost in the woods or even when I've had enough of the way I've been living and want a change.

A lifetime of experiences has taught me to love and trust in a great Creator God and a loving God. I hope all my grandkids will put their faith in that God. As I read Psalms 23, I see the Lord leading David to places where He and David could have fellowship together. That is David praying and talking to God while God gives David peace and strength through His Holy Spirit.

Other than that, it was a delightful ride back home. I saw deer, porcupines, fox and many other animals and birds. The advantage of riding a bike is that you are aware of your surroundings. You smell the distinct odors in the air, see the unique sights close up, you know the condition of the road; you experience the steepness of the hills, feel the joy of downhill coasting and most important, you know the wind speed.

When the local newspaper found out about my trek, they wrote an article called "A Change of Heart-Picture of Health". Two local TV stations came out and filmed me riding and asked me some questions for the news.

A CHANGE of Heart ⩘ Picture of Health

JOHN CRESSMAN, 53

CESAR L. LAURE / The Morning Call

John Cressman
Featured In: The Morning Call
October 5, 2000

A local girl saw the article and called me to tell me about a 3 day/300-mile bike ride across PA sponsored by Focus on the Family. I signed up and rode that one on my mountain bike, uneventful as far as me getting into trouble. To follow along in my legacy of imagination and trying to get a laugh, I won an award during the bike ride. I had a black bear backpack on that I had bought while in Potter County. I made a sign that read, "Grin and bear it" for the other cyclists to read as they went by me up the hills or as I passed them on the way down. Everyone thought it was cute, so my very manly award was for the "Cutest Accessory". It turns out that all most everyone went cruising by me, so I had to "grin and bear it".

Then I heard they were also having a 3-day, 350-mile bike ride from Vail, CO to Colorado Springs, CO. I signed up for that one also and began training for the ride the next summer. This time I saw I would need a road

272

bike to make my ride more efficient and easier. Most of the day we would ride up and down valleys and gaps, going between 9-12,000 feet. It would exhaust me, especially in the higher elevations with less oxygen.

When the time finally arrived, Diane and I drove out to Vail and Diane went along with me to help along the route by giving out water and snacks. She would be there waiting along the road when I rode in each night. It is exceptional to have a mate that encourages and believes in what you are doing. I would hear her singing as I came by "Oh here comes Johnny on his bicycle, oh here comes Johnny on his bicycle, I wonder where he's going, I wonder where he's been as he goes flying down the street". (That is an old song I remember from the 50s.)

I pray that all my grandkids will take the time to find a mate that will do the same for them. It was scenery that I could only imagine. There were some spectacular mountains with the highest peaks of 14,000 feet having snow cover with beautiful valleys of green everywhere. There were many streams and creeks all flowing with clear mountain spring water. The second day we went over a suspension bridge that hung over the Royal Gorge, a deep gorge with a river at the bottom. It was so awe-inspiring that I could not seem to move away from the view. The bridge is 956 feet high over the turbulent Arkansas River below, almost one quarter mile long, and is one of the highest suspension bridges in the world.

Earlier that day, I was riding through a canyon and saw all this sparkling from the rocks in the canyon wall. Could it be gold? My curiosity got the best of me again and I had to see what was up there. I could be rich if it was gold.

What do you think happened next?

A. I called Diane and told her to buy the land.

B. I hired a crew to dig some and take it to an assay office.

C. I rode on down the road and forgot it (Little Devils do not give up a chance to be rich)

D. I climbed up the canyon wall to check it out

It was D. I parked my bike and climbed up the canyon wall to the precious metal calling out to me. I heard it say, John, come get me, you will be rich. When I got there, it turned out to be iron pyrite, fool's gold, and suddenly, the hillside collapsed, and I went tumbling down. Having hard sole biking shoes on, I felt a real sharp pain in the bottom of my foot. I guess they added my name to the fool's list, that look for quick riches hoping to find gold. I am what I am. My foot was really hurting when I walked but did not hurt when I rode my bike, so off I went.

I was the last one to leave Royal Gorge, and since the vehicles that followed us were not allowed across the bridge, they went ahead to the motel. Between staying so long at the bridge, my search for gold and a hurting foot, I was way behind everyone else. It was after dark when I got to the motel and Diane had been checking around to see where I was. They were about ready to organize a search party when I came in. Dinner was over, but they found some food for me. My foot was really hurting when I walked so, I just soaked it in ice water.

The next day was our last journey through Colorado Springs and The Garden of the Gods. What an amazing, unforgettable place it was with the various colored rocks and incredible shapes. No wander they call it The Garden of the Gods. They should have called it The Garden of God, not gods. I once again gave thanks to God for the beauty and just wandered how all this was formed. I cannot wait until I find out.

I rode into the finish at the Focus on the Family Headquarters and greeted by hundreds of people. While standing in line for the speeches, I almost passed out from the pain in my foot. Some other cyclists helped me to the emergency medical tent, where they checked it out and sent me to the hospital for x-rays. Turned out I tore some ligament on the bottom of my foot and collapsed my arch. I went home to PA with a cast on my foot, Diane driving, many splendid memories, and a pocket full of fool's gold. It crushed my hopes of being a rich Little Devil. At least I had a new adventure and experience. For a moment I knew what it was like to feel what people experienced during the "Gold Rush". To imagine what I could do with a gold find.

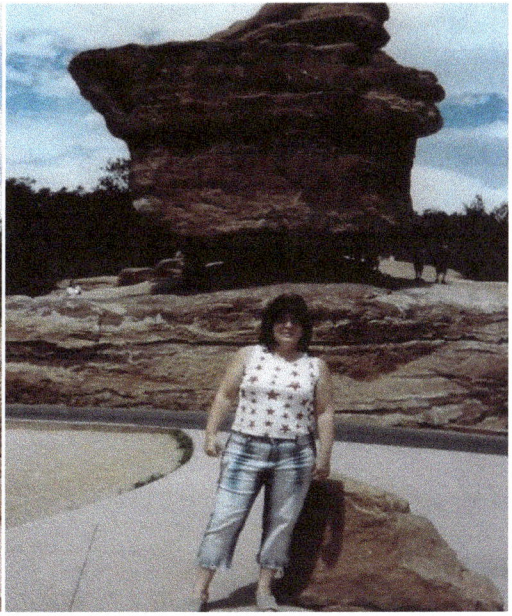

MY HOT BODY BRINGS THE FIRE DEPARTMENT

I know you are thinking that I am so hot that when Diane looks at me; she burns up with desire. That is not what happened here. True but not the case here. After our church of twenty-five years broke up, we did not go to any church for several years. We continued to study the Bible to see if we were right or wrong in our beliefs. One man who followed our shows invited us to his church. He like our shows because we talked about God, His greatness and we stressed the importance of family. We attended there for about 8 years. It was an independent church and had many teachings we agreed with. They had a praise band and praise music and that was hard to get used to since all our lives we had piano and organ hymns.

Eventually, I played trumpet and sang in the praise band, not both at once of course. People were friendly and there was little talk of doctrines just loving God and His grace through Jesus. We went through a membership class and there were some requirements to become a member, but not as many as the last church we were in. It was kind of left up to the individual church members to be right with God and allow the Holy Spirit to lead them. There were differences of opinion, but I saw people could work together. We continued to get more involved in the church.

At some point they had asked us to perform, sing country music and teach country line dancing at a chili cookoff social they were having. They had an enormous room that they had services in on Sunday and during the week for a general-purpose room. Things had changed since I was a kid. Would things have been any different in my life if we, as teens, could have had a dance in the basement?

We did our usual show, which included doing Honky Tonk Superman. I must have really looked hot or the women just loved my good looks, muscular body, and superior intellect that the temperature rose in the hall and set off the fire alarm, bringing the fire trucks. I wish it were because of me, but my son turned the smoke machine on to add some effect during the song and it set off the smoke detector alarm which automatically brought the firemen. That was embarrassing, but many years later, people remembered me as the Honky Tonk Firemen. It is so confusing to know who I really am. Will my legacy be a tree climber, a snake-man, a honky-tonk fireman, a person who falls off the stage or a Stud?

Chapter 22: AN ADVENTURE WITH SURGERY: ANESTHESIA-MASKS-SURGERY "NO WAY JOSE"

About 1995, my daughter Melody introduced me to country line dancing. I loved good clean country music and now fell in love with country line dancing. It was great exercise; I found some friendly people and the way everyone moved together during a dance was inspiring. People from differing backgrounds, beliefs, colors, opinions, and ideas came together to operate as a group with no complaints. Why could not the church do the same? Probably because Satan is not trying to destroy country line dancing but is trying to destroy the church. However, I have seen dance groups splitting into smaller groups because they thought another instructor could teach better. Originally, we danced to country music, but later some line dance choreographers started making up dances to pop, then rock and them hip hop music. Some dancers went there to learn dances, get exercise, and have fun, which did not include alcohol. Other dancers went to other places where drinking a lot was normal. We started teaching country line dancing at our shows and doing it on stage to the songs.

About 2009, I was dancing and suddenly tripped over my feet and fell. I got up and continued, but it kept happening with more frequent occurrences. My chiropractor ordered some MRI's and then said I should see a Neurosurgeon since he saw the problem causing my clumsiness. In 2010, after years of gradually losing strength in my legs and arms, they diagnosed me with 2 areas in my neck where my spinal cord was being pinched. One was by a bulging disc and one by a boney growth out of my vertebrae. When I saw the MRI, it looked like sausage links with the two areas pinched so bad that no spinal fluid was getting to those areas to keep the spinal cord replenished. The result would be the decay of my spinal cord, which would be irreversible.

In the meantime, if I had an accident, it could cause the severing of the spinal cord which could cause death or being paralyzed from the neck down being a quadriplegic. I had avoided any use of anesthesia all my life since that experience at the dentist's office of holding me down, squeezing my nose shut and forcing me to breathe ether gas. I opted for local numbing for stitches, oral surgery and anything normally put to sleep for. I also did not like the idea of not being in control of my circumstances while put to sleep. I think my fellow Marines putting me in that box at the training school, for what I thought would be overnight, gave me even more claustrophobia type feelings if not in control of circumstances.

After much counseling and research, I reluctantly set a date for surgery about two months later after the surgeon returned from surgery. I was concerned because of the risks of surgery and a chance I would be no better. After all the things I had done in life, you would wander why I would now think about risks. I suppose because it was risks caused by another person, not my own. I started having nightmares every night of knives, masks, and people holding me down, in much pain and from the ugliest doctors and nurses I have ever seen. The photos below are my granddaughters helping to illustrate my nightmares.

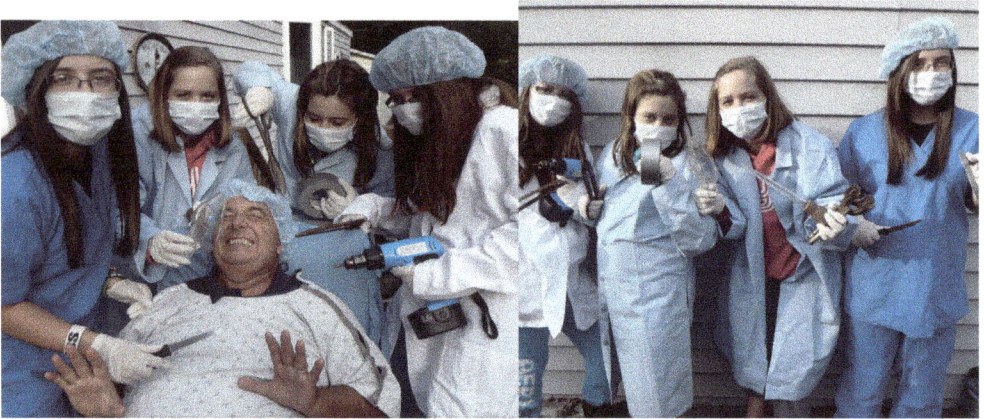

I was also torn between trusting in God completely for healing or allowing a surgeon to make the repairs and ask God to heal the recovery of the spinal cord. I had seen many healings and believed in healing, but what do I do now. I was terrified, and that is all I thought about. I was exhausted when the day finally came. The day before surgery, I went for a bike ride to relax and got sick to my stomach. I had a terrible headache, my heart started racing, and I had trouble breathing, basically a stress attack. I made it back to where I had parked and just started crying and yelling out to God that I was sorry for my lack of faith, but I could not do the surgery and I was going to cancel it. Suddenly, I felt better, like a burden was lifted off me and I was now at peace.

I went home and told my wife, and we called the hospital and cancelled the surgery, realizing I was putting myself in danger of being paralyzed. I was now at total peace and I was hungry because I had trouble eating since I had so much anxiety.

The next day I called my pastor from our Church to talk to him about my decision. He helped me analyze my thoughts and put together a plan of action. I did more research about the surgery and to see if there were any alternatives. I would also get second opinions and then go from there. I wondered why I felt guilty of having a lack of faith in God to heal me. Why did I believe that? Was it something I read in the Bible or did I hear it from a religious leader? This would be the beginning of asking why I believe the way I did. Did I read and prove it to be true, or did I hear it from someone I trusted and accepted it as truth?

To answer some of my questions, I headed to the mountains where I felt close to God. I spent three days at a rented cabin in World's End State Park. I believe that I was such a basket case that God called me up to the mountain so he could talk with me. I just thought it was my idea. I prayed and read my Bible; I hiked the trails and sat by streams, waterfalls, and inspiring overlooks high in the mountains. I had seen miraculous healings within my family many times, and Diane even wrote a book about them. Was I abandoning my beliefs? Was I turning my back on God? Did I have faith to wait for others to be healed but not my own? Does God use doctors instead of outright healings now? Should I just turn myself over to the doctors and trust their skills to repair me and our bodies can heal themselves with God's help?

One afternoon I had driven to a secluded area and went hiking along a creek with some beautiful waterfalls and views. I came out of the woods just before dark and found I had lost the keys to my car. I always kept a spare key hidden in case I ever locked the keys in the car. I found it, but it only opened the door but did not operate the ignition. I was in trouble since I had no cell service, no one would miss me at the cabin and my family knew I could not always call them because it was hard to get cell service. It was too far to walk to a major road, and I was tired from hiking all day. This time of day, there was little or no traffic on this road. At night it was going down to freezing temperatures and fortunately I always carried an emergency blanket, matches, a flashlight, some beef stick with cheese and a few packs of crackers, I could have survived the night but I was not looking forward to it. Knowing that God is always available to pray to, I talked to God about the problem and how I needed to find the keys and get back to the cabin.

I took the flashlight and hiked to the first waterfall where I had taken the camera out of the same pocket that my keys were in, hoping they fell out there. I hiked to the first falls and looked around, trying to remember where I took the first photo. As I looked around, the flashlight beam showed something shiny and sure enough, I saw the keys right on the trail. I gave thanks and headed back to the cabin. That was an encouraging event to let me know God was concerned about me, even though I had my doubts about His healing since I had not been healed and was concerned about whether I had faith. I seemed to never have a problem having faith that God would heal others, but it was harder when it is was me, so this was a new adventure.

One thing I noticed while hiking was all the damage in the forests and along the streams from wind and flooding. God did not come down and repair those creeks and clear the downed trees. If anyone made repairs, it was people who wanted the area to look better and be usable again. Was this a sign that I should allow a surgeon to correct the damage done by my aging body?

When I went home, I decided to try alternatives like traction, exercise, weight loss and pain management for maybe a year and then get a second opinion and a new MRI. I would continue to ask God for healing. I did that and many of the symptoms disappeared and I was excited thinking I was healed. During this time, I had asked everyone I knew to pray for healing, including the 700 Club. I saw in the Bible in James that if sick; we are to call for the elders of the church and be anointed. I did that.

I went to see a new surgeon and got a new MRI. It took about 6 months to get an appointment and work up the courage to get into a claustrophobic MRI even with the help of pills. It was now about a year and a half since my first scheduled surgery. It showed the pinched areas were still there but had gotten no worse. He recommended immediate surgery, but I explained my fears and concerns. He said he could give me relaxing medications to be sure that I would show up this time. He also said I could continue my alternative methods and hope for the best or have the surgery and hope for the best.

280

I set a date for surgery about thirty days away. Almost immediately the nightmares, the extreme anxiety and worry came back. My family was supportive and would back me up, whatever I decided. I spent many a night talking with Diane about my fears and concerns and she was so supportive, so encouraging, she was and still is so amazing.

Since I was in the music ministry at church and our assistant pastor was our leader. Almost every week the ministry prayed for me and I sought counsel many a time.

Two weeks before the surgery, I went off to the mountains again. This time I would cross-country ski out to a cabin in the woods at Crystal Lake Ski Area near Williamsport, PA. I wanted to be close to nature, so I chose a cabin with the only way to get there was by skis and you had to carry or tow your gear on a sled. There was no running water, no electricity, no heat, or any other modern conveniences. There was a set of bunk beds, a wood heater, and a nearby spring for water. There had been recent snow so it should be nice cross-country ski trip to once again be close to God. For me, it is easy to get close to God while amongst His creation. I did some skiing, some Bible study, and a lot of praying.

The second day I was out skiing when I came to a high area overlooking some other mountains and valleys. I stopped to rest and talk to God. I was kind of mad because I did not know what to do; I just wanted to get back to normal. I was angry at my body for doing this to me, angry at God for not healing me, angry that I still had this fear and anxiety. I was kicking snow, throwing rocks and sticks. I was talking out loud, yelling and crying. I did a lot of crying in the last year as anxiety would get the best of me. In Psalms 56:8, it says God is aware of our miseries and saves our tears in a bottle to go in His book. During the last year, I am sure He had to get a bigger bottle with my name on it.

After I finally got my frustrations out of me, I sat down on a stump exhausted. I was just sitting there awhile when I heard a voice say, "I will heal you". I jumped up thinking some another skier had heard me talking and was now playing a joke on me. Then I heard it again "I will heal you". It sure sounded like an audible voice, but I did not see anyone around. I wondered if it could be God speaking to me. I had heard of people claim to hear audible voices from God, but I was not sure if it was possible.

As I stood there thinking, I figured it was God's voice, whether audible or just a strong thought from God; I did not know for sure, but I felt more positive to trust God for my healing and cancel the surgery again. In Ex. 3:1-17. It says an angel was there in the burning bush, but then makes it sound like the LORD spoke to Moses. Did an angel deliver a message to Moses, or did God speak the words? For me, I just heard a voice which I thought was audible.

A MIRACLE AT A METHODIST CHURCH

I went home the next day feeling all together, uplifted, positive, inspired, and energized knowing God was going to heal me. That was a Saturday and the next day, Sunday, I went to my son's church, a Methodist Church in Wescosville PA, to hear the grandkids sing in the children's choir. It was a church like the church I grew up in, and I had not been in a protestant church in about 40 years. Between not wanting to have anything to do with my mother's church and being asked to leave the church Diane, and I got married in, I wanted nothing to do with protestant churches.

During the service, the Pastor took time to pray for the sick, the shut-ins and those in the military. I imagine they have a rather large membership, so there were quite a few people with various needs. It was not just a quick coverall, heal the sick and move on type of prayer, but a very detail prayer of their needs, including sometimes their names and their exact needs. As I listened, I felt a lot of compassion for those people. I realized not all of them had the luxury I had of thinking about and debating whether to have surgery, but some had no choice. It was either have surgery or die unless God would heal them. Other people had multiple surgeries and needed more surgeries to make them well again. Some were facing death or slowly dying and lived a life of pain and suffering. Some had lost a child or a mate. I am sure they had a lot of anxiety, like me, about their situation.

Suddenly, my problems seemed so small, I felt so humbled, so lacking in faith, such a cry baby so ashamed that I had allowed myself to dwell on the negative aspects of surgery instead of the positive. Where was my hope and faith? How did that spirit of fear get into my head? How did the enemy catch me unaware? For the last year I had been thinking of myself, there was no room or time to think about others, let alone pray for others. I thought about the roller coaster of emotions I had caused my family with the constant on and off again lack of decision for surgery. I knew I had caused my wife to hurt as bad as me since she has a gift or curse of being able to feel the pain of others. I realized that it held me captive to this fear and anxiety my entire life, and it was controlling my life.

Wow, my brain was in overdrive, racing a mile a minute. During the rest of the service, I felt such a peace as it seemed all negative thoughts of the surgery were leaving me, and I could see that surgery was the best option; I needed it. I could think about it without freaking out. I was healed as I heard the voice say in the woods but not of my spinal condition but of my anxiety. Ooorah.

I wondered if it was possible that God had arranged circumstances and events to bring me to this point. It helped me understand what I was searching for. I was searching the Bible for what it said but sometimes a statement can made about what it does not say. It was like when God showed Peter, he should not judge what people are clean or unclean.

WHAT'S UP DOC?

Monday the surgeon called again to see how I was doing, and I told him what had happened with all the anxiety leaving me and I decided to go through with the surgery. He said he was glad to hear that, but he sounded like he was a little skeptical because he said he would still prescribe anxiety medication to be sure I showed up. I heard later that the Dr.'s office staff had been talking about me. Once again, it was not about my good looks, my muscles, or my superior intellect, but they had bet that I would not show up for the surgery. The doctor's assistant lost $25 when I showed up.

Later that day, a representative from the 700 Club called to do a follow up on my prayer requests since I had asked the 700 Club for prayers many a time. She prayed again for me and was happy to hear that my anxiety was gone. A day or two later, I received a personal card of encouragement from the 700 Club.

Our assistant pastor, who had involved in my anxiety problem and had often prayed for me and with me. Since I was involved in music ministry and she was the leader, she often asked for an update on how I was doing. She and her husband had prayed privately for me and publicly usually at music ministry practice. I even asked to be anointed with oil, as the Bible says to do, by an elder, if we are sick in James 5:14. After I heard from the 700 Club, I received an email from Music Ministry Pastor and for no apparent reason she just mentioned that I was a blessing and appreciated having me at music ministry. I am not a talented singer and because of my anxiety all the time; I was not an overly friendly or a cheerful person. Why would she say that? I asked her and she said, "God put it on my heart". That did not make sense. Why would God do that? I would have to think about that since everything always must make sense to me.

A few days later, I received a call from the Pastor of the Methodist Church I had visited on Sunday. He calls all the visitors that are first-time visitors. I mentioned what happened in church and the problem I was having with anxiety and he mentioned that God does not give us a spirit of fear but of a sound mind and that some anxiety was normal but extreme anxiety was not of God's spirit. He prayed for me before hanging up, and I felt better.

As I thought on all the things that had happened, especially in the last week, I realized that when I heard the voice say "I will heal you", it did not mean healing of the spinal problems without surgery. It also could have meant that God was going to heal me of the extreme anxiety disorder so I could have the spinal compression removed, and then God would also heal me back to a state of pre-spinal compression condition. This seemed to make so much more sense and gave me such peace; I was finally happy and had a real peace.

I thought about the phone calls from my surgeon, talking with the various pastors and the card and phone call from the 700 Club and what it all meant. I realized how much it meant to me and how encouraging it was to have someone show concern and be positive.

My anxiety was gone, and never returned. I never did take any medications, but they gave me some just before going into the ER. That was because they told me that I would be awake when they wheeled me into the ER to undergo some tests. Then I would have to wear a mask to breathe in plenty of oxygen before the surgery. I was ready to run out of the hospital in my cute gown and my awfully long nylon stockings that helped with circulation in the legs. My daughter and wife encouraged me not to do that, so I did not. I made it through the surgery and the recovery went very well.

After the surgery and I gained much of my strength back and could ride my bike on trips of 30-40 miles, go kayaking and hiking again. I have a lot of arthritis up and down my spine, so I am still limited in what I can do with some numbness in my fingers and legs. I never got the coordination back to do country line dancing very well, but the danger of being paralyzed from a broken spinal cord is gone. My surgeon said to see him in a few years about fixing my lower back.

I would wander of all the things I tried and of all the people I asked prayers from, why was I healed at a Methodist Church. Why did it take 3 years to be healed of the anxiety? Was this a message from God to show me I should not judge if God is working or not working in any church? I believed for 25 plus years that God was not working in certain churches; I thought I was wrong when I wanted nothing to do with protestant Churches. I knew I had hurt my mother when I refused to go to her church. It also hurt her to know I would never again play my trumpet with her accompaniment. I would have to repent of that and which I could go back and change things, but we cannot.

The photo below is when my granddaughters came to visit me after the surgery, and I decided to make it look like I was in bad shape. Their look of compassion when they saw me was overwhelming. I had to tell them I was feeling great and we all had a good laugh. My humor may get me in trouble one day.

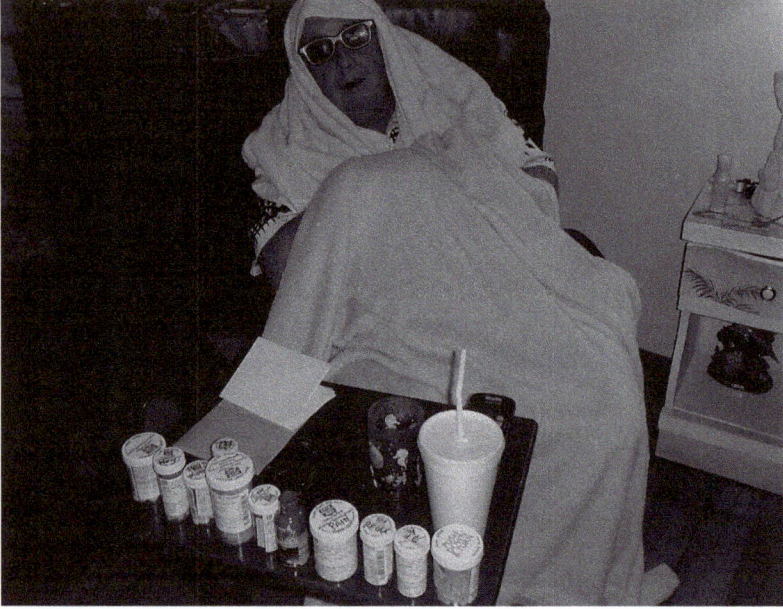

SENIOR CITIZEN CYCLING

About age 63, cycling was one exercise I could do without bothering my lower back disc problems. I trained and went on the "Hot 100" bike near Burgaw, NC, which was a 100-mile bike ride. I made my usual stops to read the historical signs, take photos, and explore any side roads that aroused my curiosity such as Moore's Creek Battlefield National Park. I got back to the starting point late expecting a hot meal, but everyone was gone. I found many of the cyclists go to these events to see how fast they can ride the distance. I go to see the sights and get exercise. Just think of all the sights those fast cyclists missed. That reminds me of when I went on the Colorado Ride. We were told there are three typed of cyclists. One stops to smell the roses; one slows down to look at the roses and one says, "what roses".

At age 64, I wanted to ride the Allegheny Passage Trail in PA to the C&O Trail in Cumberland, MD, and continue toward Washington DC. I started at Confluence, PA and quit at Williamsport MD since that was all the time I had. Once again, I rode by myself and enjoyed all the sites from the towering heights of the Allegheny Mountains and the breath-taking views, going through 3 old railway tunnels along the way, crossing the continental divide and resting at motels along the way. At Cumberland, MD, I took a steam locomotive ride back up close to the continental divide and then coasted with my bike back down. That was exciting to remember the old days of riding on the outside of trains. On the way up the mountain, the train came to a slow stop. The conductor announced that we had run out of steam and it would take a while to build a hot enough fire to make more steam. That reminded me of times my dad would say that he had run out of steam and needed to rest. I never knew what that meant, but I guess in the days of the steam locomotive, that was just a common saying for not having the energy to continue.

After the Allegheny Trail(GAP Trail) ended in Cumberland, MD, it was on to the C&O trail where there are camping sites along the way for bikers or hikers to stay in. It was a different type of exceptional views riding through valleys and gaps in the mountains alongside the Potomac River.

I hope to go back some day to ride the entire trail from Pittsburg to

Washington DC. It would be delightful to go with Diane, one of our kids or possibly a grandchild or two.

The photos below are at the Paw Paw Tunnel on C&O Trail and highest point on the GAP trail.

WELCOME HOME

One spring we were in NC and my daughter came to visit. She wanted to take her kids to a church with a Sunday School since the church we were attending did not.

She was going to attend the church where we were married but we were not sure if we would go along. We had not been back for 45 years and were hesitant about going back. We did not leave there on the best terms and were afraid people would attack us. We had not been in a Protestant Church for about 40 years until the miracle at the Methodist Church. We went with them but had anxiety about it. As we got out of the car, scared to death, we heard someone yell "WOOOHOO, good morning, good morning". Immediately, I felt at ease and walked up to the greeter who was the pastor and the person who yelled. As we walked in, no one stoned us or told us to leave, which was a relief. We did not recognize anyone there; it had many more members and was now a lot larger church building with several additions.

We began attending there since the pastor was preaching exactly what I was coming to believe. He was preaching differently from what I heard forty-five years before. He said the church was the "Called Out Ones". not a building. He questioned traditions and asked "WHY" do we do this? They had a traditional service for people who liked that, mostly older, and a contemporary service for people who liked that, mostly younger. When mixed, they got along fine. There was no judging, condemning of others who worshipped differently. I was comfortable there and enjoyed attending. They had fun filled socials and even had a dance in the church building where we got married in which was now a fellowship hall. The funny part is that I was the DJ for several dances.

If you remember back when we got engaged, I made an engagement ring in the machine shop and put a cross on it. While being a DJ at a dance around our 45th anniversary, I hid a real diamond engagement ring in a rose and gave it to Diane on my knee in front of everyone. I loved her look and surprise. I just love the way God works things out. Life is full of wonderful surprises. We also have the growing periods when we are in trials and tests. After explaining what happened in the past there and us not coming back for 45 years, he always said "welcome home" every time we came down from PA. It was like a full circle was complete. Like we had left on a journey to explore and now returned. It was like Lewis and Clark returning from a mission to see what was out there, to find a path to the west. In our case, it was to find what we were looking for. When Lewis and Clark returned, they gave the President a report of what they found. After a few more adventures, I will give you a report of what we found. It would still take a while to tie things together.

NIGHTMARES FROM VIETNAM RETURN

Shortly after we retired and leased a cottage along the Intra Coastal Canal in Surf City, NC. It was only about one-half mile from the house we rented after we were married. A friend was helping me apply for VA Disability thinking Agent Orange had something to do with my nerve problems in my back, legs, and arms.

We were in NC and one day I was out kayaking and often see Marine Corps helicopters flying overhead since Camp Lejeune is close by. In the distance I heard a sound that caught my attention. It was the unique sound of a Vietnam era Huey Helicopter. Suddenly, I started to shake, got anxious, memories racing through my mind. I was moving around so much I thought I would lose my balance and fall in the water.

I paddled to shore and was a nervous wreck. I ran in the house to get away from the sound, but it just got louder until it passed over and went away. After that I started getting extreme nightmares at night which would wake me up and I could not go back to sleep. I saw the wounded and dead either from a battle or as I helped unload helicopters. I finally had to go the VA Hospital. While I was checking in, I noticed the VA Hospital was all men, for the most part and everyone seemed to have an injury of some type. There were photos of war and war machines all over and suddenly I freaked out and could not even check in. All types of memories were coming back, and it got so bad they sent me to see a Psyhcologist right away. I never would have believed there was so much hid inside of me. The VA was a big help and in time the nightmares went away. The biggest help was the Warrior Ride and the kids that showed up to greet us.

They said sometimes we bury our fears and traumatic experiences but there can be a trigger to start it up again. When repented and Jesus changed my life, the bad experiences disappeared and never had any memories. I never joined any Vietnam Vet organizations nor went to any bars to talk about the war.

Some memories of Vietnam protestors also returned from the crowd control experiences I had. It also bothered me to watch the police as they used crowd control techniques like in Ferguson, MS during the riots. They did the same thing we did, and that was to stand shoulder to shoulder, rifles at the ready, gas masks, helmets, and bullet-proof vests. We also used bayonets on our M-14 rifles. If we needed to move a crowd, we stomped forward to make a noise in unison and moved the protestors out of an area. The hard part was standing and taking the abuse from the protestors. It stuck in my brain all those years. That is why I went AWOL.

The psychologist said I had never dealt with the hurt, anger, and terrible things I had seen and was still in my brain. They were hidden away all those years, and now the helicopter brought them back. She gave some techniques on how to deal with them. The hardest one was to forgive those that had hurt me. I was a Christian and could forgive them. Before, I could do that, so I went around all the places where I remembered being hurt at and asked God to forgive them. Many places had changed or no longer there, and the people were long gone. As I asked God to forgive them, it gave me peace and never had another problem with it again. I prayed for God's kingdom to come to end all wars and do away with the pain and suffering involved with it. Once again, I had peace with it and had no more nightmares about war. I also went to all the places that hurt me or did me wrong because of my beliefs and forgave them and asked God to forgive them. As I went through more exams by the VA, they agreed that I had PTSD and the effects of Agent Orange causing my nerve problems.

Just like David, God as the shepherd was leading me through the green pastures and though I was passing through a valley of fear, I had peace because he was with me. Many things were being revealed to me and saw that I was wrong in many of my beliefs.

Chapter 23: DISABLED BUT STILL SEEKING ADVENTURES AND STILL A TROUBLEMAKER

Several years after the surgery, I went back to the surgeon to get help for my lower back. Upon getting MRI's of my brain and entire spinal column, he said there is too much degeneration, bulging discs and herniations to do anything that would help so I will have to live with many lower back problems. I saw two more surgeons who said the same thing. One added he would put a rod the total length of my back to support it.

In 2018, they diagnosed me with exposure to Agent Orange in Vietnam, which was causing many of my problems of nerve damage. I was now classified as a disabled veteran since I had been diagnosed with PTSD and now Agent Orange exposure.

I have found the best relief for the numbness, pain and weakness is to ride a bike, kayak, swim or do aqua aerobics. It helps keep me mobile and lower the pain level. I like to go on bike rides with others whether it is with the family, friends, or other veterans. I had to find a bike and kayak that did not put pressure on my discs, or my legs would go numb. I found some veteran groups that helped. They call it adaptive cycling. One such group was The Warrior Ride which organized bicycle rides for veterans of all wars. Many Wounded Warrior groups do not help Vietnam vets.

THE WELCOME HOME EVERY VIETNAM VET NEEDED

One such ride, I enjoyed, was with a group of wounded warriors and disabled veterans called The Warrior Ride, out of Oak Island, NC. It was made up of vets from any war. We did several rides a year as a group visiting schools and veteran organizations. That was very enjoyable to see the appreciation shown for us. One such ride was to visit an elementary school in NC. As we approached the school a block away, I heard the kids yelling USA-USA-USA. My eyes teared up, I got all congested and became so emotional that I could not ride my bike. It was like 45 years of hidden pain was being released and I could not control it. Another vet helped me walk my bike up to the school.

Everyone else road along the driveway filled with children holding flags, waving banners, yelling USA, and hi-fiving the vets as they road past. Eventually, I got composed and rode my bike down the driveway but stayed away from the kids. I went around and decided to walk my bike through the gauntlet of smiling, friendly yelling kids. I stopped and my photo taken with some, some gave me cards to thank me for my service, some gave me a hug and the teachers shook my hand. I was glad I had sunglasses on because my eyes were soaked. I was a real basket case. Their very sincere welcoming and showing of appreciation gave me the "Welcome Home from Vietnam", I never received.

I cannot help but wonder what my life would have been like if I received a proper welcome home. I do not think protestors are aware of the lives their actions will affect for a lifetime. We also rode our bikes in parades and received more welcoming, thanks and signs of appreciation from the people gathered to see us and veteran organizations that fed us and supported us. Seeing other veterans with their own disabilities helped me to appreciate the fact that my problems could have been worse. Every time I went on a ride or to a school, it was a healing to me.

It was an honor for me to be asked to start off the daily rides with prayer with the entire group. There was a lot to be thankful for and many dangers out there to ask for protection from. I also was honored to give thanks for the provided to us and ask a blessing on it.

ON THE BUCKET LIST: ONE LAST ADVENTUREST BIKE RIDE 6 DAY-365 MILES

For about ten years, I dreamed of riding my bike from Pittsburg, PA to Washington, DC but could not figure out how to do it since it involved where to sleep and eat, shuttle from DC back to Pittsburg, how to carry luggage, plus I was no longer strong enough to pedal long distances daily. Also, I could find no one to go with me in case I needed help. In the old days, I would have packed up my bike and camped along the way eating survival food and ride back to PA. But now I need a bed, a mattress, a shower, hot food, shuttle service and a plan in case of emergency.

Then I found an organized tour group, Wilderness Voyageurs, that would arrange motels not campgrounds, arrange or provide all the meals, provided a guide to ride along with the group of 12 and another guide that drove a van with a trailer with extra parts, bikes and our supplies for the week and finally shuttle service for our luggage to the motels, restaurants and back to PA when done, The best security for me was a van to ride in if I become unable to bike or just needed a break. Since I was then 72 and disabled, they recommend a battery assist bike to help keep up with the others. I would still have to pedal the bike to go, but the assist would make it feel easier. I could use it or not and could add more assistance if I needed it. I think they had to recommend it because of my age and being disabled. They wanted everyone to succeed and not fall behind. The trip of 365 miles would take 6 days. I booked my place for June 23 of 2019.

It turned out to be a hugely different ride than any other adventure I had ever been on. Doing it this way sure removed a lot of anxiety for me with still having the sense of accomplishment and security. I got to ride the 150 miles of the Great Allegheny Passage Trail from Pittsburg to Cumberland MD. It soars over valleys, snakes around mountains, and skirts alongside three rivers, the Casselman, Youghiogheny, and Monongahela.

We started in Pittsburg, PA and rode along the Youghiogheny River and then through Chestnut Gap, which was a 1400-foot gorge in the Appalachians of PA. After crossing a 100 ft. high bridge, we ended our first day of 57 miles. We spent our first night in a lodge on top of a mountain with a beautiful view of the very colorful sunset.

Day 2 would be a 72-mile journey along the river where George Washington once explored. Now that was my kind of exploring. About 10 miles into the trail, I remembered I left my wallet, phone, and car keys at the lodge. There were no locks on the doors, so I had hidden them and forgot until I looked for my phone to take a photo. I turned around to go back when I met the guide, and she called the lodge and had someone meet us on the trail. That was very considerate of them. In my old age, I forget things unless I see it. I rode hard and caught up to the others just in time to ride across the Salisbury Viaduct, where it crosses the Casselman River. They constructed it in 1912 as a railroad bridge. We then rode uphill to an elevation of 2392 feet, which is the PA Eastern Continental Divide. Water on the east side flows into the Atlantic Ocean and water on the west side flows into the Gulf of Mexico.

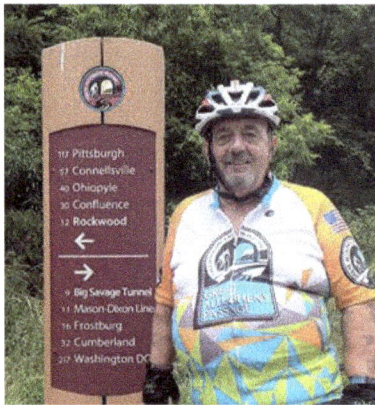

We then rode through a very foggy 849 feet long Pinkerton Tunnel and then the 3294 feet long Big Savage Tunnel, which was built in 1911. Going down the mountain, we crossed over the Mason Dixon Line as we entered Maryland. Finishing the day, we enjoyed a well-deserved night's rest in Cumberland, MD thus ending the GAP Trail.

On day 3, we would ride 59 miles on the C&O Canal Towpath Trail on our way to Washington, DC, about 200 miles away. The trail was muddy with puddles, rocks, holes, ditches, snakes and turtles so it was a messy, slow ride. I heard the State wants to keep the trail with little maintenance so we could experience the same conditions the early settlers faced while traveling it. We did. The highlights that day were the 3118 feet of the Paw Paw Tunnel built in 1836, by hand, for the canal to go through the mountain instead of around it. I noticed there were camping sites along this trail with porta-potties and well water. To camp, you would carry all your belongings with you. I would have enjoyed that when I was younger.

We spent the night in Berkeley Springs across the Potomac River in West Virginia. Years ago, people came to soak in the healing powers of the spring water, including George Washington. One thing I noticed from the past was that there was one pool for the men and one for the women. I soaked my feet in the healing waters, hoping for relief, before getting a night's sleep.

On Day 4, we would ride 54 miles and would ride on a well-maintained trail. About 15 miles into the trail, I realized I forgot to turn in the room key. It was not a card key but a big, beautiful, shiny bronze key. I was in trouble again. The guide took the key and said they would return it by mail or next trip. I do not think I was creating a good impression. Especially later that day, I saw a paved trail running parallel to ours. I heard a little voice in my head say, John, you good looking thing with big muscles and an intellect much higher than your guides, just get on the paved trail and enjoy it so I figured I would ride it since I was tired of mud, stones and holes. I could ride fast and was just cruising along, occasionally looking through the trees to be sure I was parallel to the canal trail.

We had mounted on our handlebars a GPS that had been programmed to the trail and beeped if we got off the trail. It was just beeping away, but I knew better and kept going. After several miles, the trail turned and went downhill, and I no longer could see the canal because of thick brush and trees, so I stopped and turned around to head back.

Eventually I could see the canal but there was thick brush in between the trails so I ended up going back to where I got on the trail at. I was dead tired; my bike battery was almost dead and the guide who follows behind us had probably passed already and she had the extra battery. My battery went dead about 10 miles from the lunch stop, so I had to pedal this heavy bike to the rest stop to get a new battery. When I got there, they had already eaten, some had hit the trail, and the guide was about ready to go looking for me. What a lesson to learn because of trying once again to do it my way; tired, sweaty, dirty, thirsty and hungry.

The group was not impressed with my explanation and my idea of a simple path and thinking my way was better. I was getting the idea that I would not be remembered for my good looks which were maturely wrinkled, my big muscles which were slightly under-inflated or by my superior intellect which to them seemed to be like an elevator which did not go the top floor.

With a new battery, a delicious meal and lots of water, the highlights for the rest of the day would be a visit and tour of Fort Frederick, a restored fort from the French Indian War, The American Revolution and the Civil War. Also, a visit to the Antietam National Battlefield where 23,000 soldiers were killed, wounded, or missing after twelve hours of savage combat on September 17, 1862. Another tiring day, but the Bavarian Inn made up for it with its pool, pool side meals and jacuzzi tub in the room.

Day 5 would be a 40-mile ride which would include a stop and tour of Harpers Ferry, a trip across the Potomac on White's Ferry, the last operating ferry on the Potomac. Also, for a while we were on the same trail as hikers where the C&O meets the Appalachian Trail. We ate a delicious lunch by the picturesque Point of Rocks and then enjoyed the pool and jacuzzi of the Homewood Suites by Hilton in Leesburg, VA. The photo is crossing the Potomac on the ferry.

Day 6, our last day would take us into Washington, DC, 37 miles away. One of the best highlights of the entire trip was The Great Falls of the Potomac, Washington DC's most spectacular landmark! We would ride through Georgetown and end up at Thompson Boathouse, the end of the C&O Trail. The same old me was intrigued by the sites and missed a turn because I was not paying attention and I ignored the beeper on the GPS once again. I was on the trail. What could be wrong?

I got suspicious when I saw the other bikes on the other side of the canal but knew I was definitely in the wrong area when I rode my bike with my dirty, sweaty clothes right into a fancy restaurant patio area along a restored section of the canal. I was told I could not ride through there and had to cross to the other side miles back where there was a bridge with a ramp for bikes. The other bridges had steps which I would not have been able to carry my bike over. So once again I was the last one to finish and

298

my bike battery and GPS battery died about a mile from the end, so I was on my own. My anxiety level was building as I rode through Georgetown with no visible sight of a canal trail I had been riding on before, just a dirt trail along a ditch which I guess was the remains of the canal in a city. Everything was under construction. I am sure my guardian angel, now old and in a wheelchair and in poor health from all the anxiety I had caused him through the years, took a deep breath from his oxygen tank.

At the end of the C&O Trail there was a road, an interstate highway and a sidewalk going right and left but no sight of the group. There were cyclists riding on the sidewalk and road, but no sign of my group. Am I be lost in DC? I tried to call the guides, but no answer. This was a praying moment once again. It seems no matter how many mistakes I have made in life, or how many times I get into trouble doing things my way, God is still there and ready to help one way or another and sometimes slower than other times. Abraham prayed and waited 40 years about his wife getting pregnant. Once pregnant, Abraham's wife, Rebekah, prayed about a rumbling stomach and God answered immediately. This was a Rebekah moment, not an Abraham moment. I needed help now. This was the end of the trail, so where was everyone? Suddenly, the one guide and two cyclists rode up to me saying they had a series of flat tires and were just finishing as well. The guide led me to the meeting spot where we ate, swapped stories and packed up for the journey back to PA.

There was little hope of the other cyclists remembering me for anything but the muddy guy, the bald guy, the weak muscle guy who can't keep up with the others, and the guy who gets lost thinking he knows more than the guides. They probably thought I was as bright as December in Alaska.

We had an outstanding ride; I met some world class cyclists, and I accomplished a desire I had for years without causing too much trouble. We had a 6-hour ride back to our cars, said our goodbyes and off we went to our homes.

THE CROSS UNBURDENS ME

Lake Junaluska, in the mountains of NC, has this huge Christian cross on a hill overlooking the lake. We were there for a marriage retreat and one night, the facilitators took us out to the cross one night so we could confess to each other anything on our minds. I was having great difficulty saying or doing anything because I felt uncomfortable. Why was that? What had I learned or been taught that made me feel uncomfortable?

If you look up the history of the Christian cross symbol, you can find various origins and uses. One was when Constantine had a dream to use a cross symbol to conquer his enemies. In our younger years, I made Diane's engagement ring with a cross on it instead of a diamond, my little chapel had a cross in the midst and our wilderness camping site had a cross there. Maybe I felt like a cross was a symbol to remind me of God's love for us, like in Jn 3:16. Maybe it was that I thought Jesus was there with us and was a symbol of what he did for us.

As I learned more about the cross, I saw there was a debate going on as to whether Jesus was crucified on an upright stake or a stake with a cross bar. I had come to believe that having a cross on my neck or in our house added nothing to our relationship with God but sometimes made me look to the cross as an object I connected with God. I prayed and acted like there was some supernatural power in it, so I discontinued the use of it because I was concerned how the pagans used it.

At the cross, I wanted to apologize to Diane for any hurts I had done through the years but could not say a word and felt bad about that. During the night, I kept waking up hearing in my head "Go to the cross, go to the cross". Over and over all night long. We had to leave at 5am and I was exhausted from the lack of sleep and these thought in my head but I stopped at the cross and knelt on a knee and told Diane I was sorry for the hurts I had caused her through the years. Being married to a spoiled brat, a Little Devil, a Holy Terror, and a guy 2 nuts short of a fruitcake, there was a lot of hurt I had caused. Diane response was overwhelming and was one of the most memorable moments of our marriage. I had said the words before but why such an effect now at a cross. Why not a vista overlooking a mountain range, at a sunrise on a beach, or while on a bike ride? I eventually concluded that God was trying to tell me to be careful how I make judgments once again about where and when He is working. The scripture came to mind when Jesus' disciples complained that others, not part of their group, were preaching and casting out demons in his name and Jesus said "if they are not against us, they are for us" in Mark 9:38. Also Paul said that regardless of people's motives for preaching, as long as Christ is preached, Paul would rejoice. Another lesson learned and God is slowly correcting me in a loving way not beating me over the head.

TWO MORE WHITEWATER KAYAK TRIPS

I missed whitewater kayaking but had not been able since my neck problems. It left me with poor balance and strength problems. I could kayak on a lake or calm river water but that is about it. I have a special kayak adapted to my disabilities. Other than loosing balance and falling in the water while getting in a kayak, I was not getting into any trouble. In the summer of 2020, I bought a pontoon kayak which was very stable and comfortable to my back.

One weekend my kids and grandkids were going tubing down the Lehigh River, so I decided to go along. It has class 2 and 3 rapids, but the water was low and slow flowing. We all went and had a ball together. I had no problems and was able to sit in my kayak for two ours without pain or numbness. I was exceedingly happy to be on the river again and enjoying everyone's company.

Labor Day weekend, they decided to go again so I was ready. We were all having a blast, and everything was going great. Before we got to the best rapids, some of the family were headed for rocks so I pulled them back in the main river current. I did not get into the best current for a wide pontoon kayak and was headed for a narrow passage between two big rocks. As I went between the two rocks, my one pontoon was caught in the fast current while the other hit the rock and spun me around throwing me off into the rapids. This was my worst nightmare, falling off the kayak, knowing I would not be able to get back on the kayak until I got it to shore.

Fortunately, I came up out of the water holding my paddle and was close to me kayak. I swam to the kayak and held on for dear life as I went through the rapids. I knew I should not try standing up because my feet could get caught in the rocks and the force of the water would push me front facedown and I would drown. I let my feet follow behind the kayak as I my knees bounced off rocks, getting splashed with waves coming over my head all the way through the best rapids. Once again, I prayed, I would have the strength to hold on until I was through the rapids. I think my guardian angel, in his old age, may have sat on my kayak holding my wrists so I would not let go.

Finally, I was out of the rapids and made my way to the shore where I could stand up and get back into my kayak which I did. Seeing I was not on my kayak, the family was trying to get to me to help but the current was too strong. Everyone was glad to see me back on the kayak, safe and sound. I gave thanks once again and was careful the rest of the way.

Next year I will use straps over my legs to hold me in case of a sudden stop. I used to use them while kayaking in the ocean and riding waves. Since I use a sit on top kayak, it is easy to slide right off. The straps just help give you some support, but I can get out quickly if needed.

I FIND THE ANSWERS I WAS LOOKING FOR AT WORLDS END STATE PARK

After Thanksgiving of 2019, I went to a cabin at Worlds End State Park. I used to say that I was going to the mountains to get close to God. That meant I would pray and spending time in studying my Bible. Just getting away from society is a help. For me to be among God's creation, meant I would be greatly inspired and would find it easy for me to put my thoughts together with the help of God's Holy Spirit.

I used to think it was my idea to go off my myself but a pastor said one time that it was not me seeking God but God seeking me to come up to Him and tell Him my concerns, desires and questions. I never thought about it that way before, but it goes along with my belief that the entire purpose of mankind and every physical creation is to lead mankind to Himself for fellowship. Like me as a father, I love to have fellowship with my kids and grandkids.

As I read the book of Acts, I saw that were subtle changes were usually by revelation or observation of what God is doing. Unfortunately, there were no tablets or scrolls to describe the Christian church. Peter and others saw the Gentiles receiving the Holy Spirit. When Gentiles came into the church, I did not see any problems or major questions if they had to adapt to the Jewish traditions. But neither did I see the Gentiles were told to keep up traditions of their pagan religions. There were Christians coming from the Jerusalem Church to teach Gentiles to keep the Jewish traditions, so the Jerusalem Church must have been keeping them just like I had done.

I saw where the Apostles mentioned doing things on the Sabbath and Holy days but was it being observed by them? Was it mentioned to show a time of year when an event was happening? Was it mentioned because that is where the people were, they wanted to preach to? I did not see proof that I should or should not observe the days as far as obedience goes. At my next get alone with God, I will tie everything together that makes sense to me.

Chapter 24: AN ADVENTURE IN WHAT THE EARLY CHRISTIAN CHURCH BELIEVED

It would be cool to jump in a time machine and go back to after Pentecost and see what the early Christian Church was doing. Maybe a stop to see what Paul is teaching gentiles and maybe stop at 325 AD at the Council of Nicaea.

I believe my research shows that the apostles and early Christians were converted Jews for the most part, so they continued to keep the Jewish law, the Sabbath, the Holy Days and all the traditions. There has always been Gentile converts to Judaism and they started keeping the same laws as the Jews. They preached the gospel of the Kingdom of God and that the Jesus that they crucified was the Messiah and the Son of God. Jesus also sent the comforter, the Holy Spirit, on Pentecost to lead them as if Jesus were on earth. During this time Jesus revealed to Peter that Gentiles could now receive the Holy Spirit. This was not written nor spoke to Peter, but it was revealed in a dream and circumstances. There were no written laws of the new testament church like there was for Israel. They were learning by revelation, so we have to trust what the Bible says about those revelations. I believe that my healing at the Methodist church was revealing something. I believe it was that I should not judge where God is or is not working.

Then Paul came along, called by Jesus, taught by apparently the resurrected Jesus, and then claimed to have a gospel that people would be saved by. Jesus' gospel was about a coming kingdom. Paul preached to the Gentiles, and many Gentiles believed and were brought into the church. It must have been difficult for the Jerusalem Church, made up of the Apostles and mostly Jewish converts, to accept Gentiles coming into the church. Jesus said to not go to Gentiles in Mt 12:5 where Jesus sent the 12 out but to gentiles. History says the Gentiles brought in traditions from how they worshipped their gods. Is that ok or not? In Rev. 2 where Jesus wrote a letter to the seven churches, he warned of false apostles teaching false doctrines, worldliness coming into the church, a belief that grace was a license to sin and lusting after the pleasures of this world.

The church was under attack from the beginning from Satan and men wanting power. I wondered after the apostles were all dead, what happened to the church, where did it go and what did it look like? Too bad I got a time machine working.

By 300 years after Jesus' resurrection, there were many versions of Christianity and Constantine, the Roman Emperor, wanted to make the Roman Empire Christian. He appointed the Council of Nicaea to come up with one set of beliefs to end the variety of beliefs. I wonder if the beliefs being considered were from the Jewish converts, much like the Messianic Jews of today, who may have been keeping the Law, the Sabbath, and the Holy Days. Was there also a group of converted Gentiles believing in the grace that Paul taught, but were there also other groups mixing in various traditions from other religions? I wondered if the true beliefs survived the Council and Roman Christianity. It had to.

Before the council, some churches kept the Saturday Sabbath, and some kept Sunday in honor of Jesus' worship day or resurrection. The council ruled that Sunday would be the official day of rest and worship of Christianity. Sabbath keepers did not agree that man could change the Sabbath to Sunday, so they stuck with their beliefs and received persecution. There were other groups that did not go along with the Christian Church of Constantine, the Roman Church, and they were persecuted as well. I wonder if the church during Constantine's time became the church we see today.

The invention of the printing press allowed more people to read the Bible, which led to questions and church splitting. Then there was the Protestant Reformation, which caused even more church splitting and more differences of beliefs. There have been many church splits through the years and many more during the Civil War. Some say the protestant reformation did not go far enough in removing beliefs not in the Bible. I wondered if what Paul taught survived and where was it today.

I LOOKED FOR GOD IN MY CHILDHOOD CHURCH BUT NEVER FOUND HIM-WHERE IS HE?

I mentioned how when I was young; I searched God's house to find God. I was told the church was God's house, and He lived there. I never found Him in a physical form nor any signs that any spirit form which I considered at the time to be like a Casper the ghost. I think people thought that because Israel believed God dwelt in the Temple and that Jesus called the temple his father's house, that people assumed God dwelt in the local churches. I am not sure where the idea came from that God dwelt in the church building. Maybe it was to keep control of us wild and crazy kids.

I was recently watching the restoration of Notre Dame and how it made people stand in awe and amazement as to be where God dwelt and cause people to surrender to this God. I guess that is all part of using emotion to turn people to God. There sure are many beautiful churches in Europe and the USA, and you cannot blame people for wanting to build a beautiful place for God to dwell in. That is probably where all the rules came from of how to act in God's house. But I must ask in my search for God, does He want to dwell in a church building, or does He want to dwell in us? Was the church a building or is it the group of people. I needed to search more for the answer.

When outside at night with my dad, he told me God lived in heaven past the stars. I took my official Tony The Tiger binoculars and searched the sky for God but never saw Him, but I did see some lights going through the sky, which I was told were angels coming down to check up on us. Later, I found out they were meteorites.

I lived through the God is dead movement during the 1960s. Maybe at that time, is when people replaced God with science. Science was mixed with Christianity as well. By 2020, science would be like a god to some.

Being born and raised in a Christian family and until my mother got an organist job, the entire family attended church together including my family, my grandparents and my mother's sister's family. Because of that, there has never been a day that I did not believe in God and that He created everything. The only thing that has changed through the years has been my

306

knowledge of who God is, what His plan is and where I attend church.

Until about age 21, I mostly thought about God as a force way out there in space who made everything and was there to help us. I especially realized there was a God when my prayers were answered. I also realized that God must love me since He cared enough to answer my prayers. One of the first scriptures I memorized was John 3:16, which says He loved the people in this world so much that He sacrificed His only son so that if we believe in that sacrifice, we will not perish but have eternal life. I would say God did not want Adam and Eve to sin in the garden, but when they did, He provided a way that they could still get eternal life.

Evidently, He must have given us a temporary existence because He says we can perish. Some believe that means we burn in hell forever, and others believe we are burned up and cease to exist. Whatever perish is, I would choose eternal life. Just a disagreement on whether people have eternal life at birth or can cease to exist has caused churches to split because of different beliefs.

When Lewis and Clark were commissioned by the President to explore and search for a passage to the west, they had to report back to the President what they had found. Here is what I found as I explored and searched for God and His church:

Chapter 25: AFTER SEARCHING FOR GOD, HERE IS WHAT I FOUND

One of the most interesting adventures of my life was to find out what God is like, what he thinks and what is plan is. I do not claim to know everything but it is exciting to learn. I will keep my mind open to learn more and not get locked into one belief. So, what is God like?

GOD IS THE CREATOR

Eventually, I would realize that everything I saw required a Creator. As I pondered upon the mesmerizing stars and moon, I wondered what it would be like to go there, like Captain Kirk, and explore the unchartered universe where no man has gone before. Once again, I marveled that many people, including me, could just look in the sky and feel so good and inspired by what He created. I wondered how I could search and find a God I could not see.

When Sam and I were speeding along the railroad tracks and we had our prayers answered, I realized answered prayers require a power to hear and carry out what I requested. I saw this power, which I called God, like a father that comes running when his child is in trouble. That perspective of God I had, has never changed. As a young child, it seems I had many prayers answered, which was strange because I got myself into trouble and then needed rescue. So, this God I was searching for would continue to answer prayers and show love repeatedly, even when I was not doing things correctly.

GOD IS LAW GIVER AND SUSTAINER

Another thing I noticed as I searched for God was the forces that shaped this earth. What broke the strata apart and pushed it up from deep in the earth? What carved the valleys, lakes, oceans, and gaps in the mountains? What gave me feelings of enjoyment when I swung on a vine making use of the laws of motion (Called Newton's laws), like gravity, acceleration, momentum, inertia, centrifugal force, and centripetal forces. All these laws had to be created and sustained. When the vine broke, gravity caused my body to fall toward the rocks. When I hit the rocks, momentum tried to keep my body parts moving or transfer my energy to move the rocks, but the rock stopped me and threw my body out of whack, thus causing pain and inability to move. The same laws are used to make rides at amusement parks exciting. One thing I know is that when we know God's laws and get in harmony with them, we are happy. Violating or being ignorant of the laws of God brings pain and suffering. Like if I had fallen off that cliff and gravity pushed me down to the rocks below. That would have caused pain and suffering.

Why did I feel so good and at peace when I sat by a waterfall on top of a mountain and smelled the forest after a rain? Why did I, at age 11 or 12, while sitting around a campfire at church camp, feel something inside of me that made me feel like I wanted to be part of what God was doing? I found a part of God by feeling the effect of His laws as He rules and sustains everything. Airplanes fly because men use God's laws, ships float because of God's laws, and rockets go to the moon using God's laws. Something I love to meditate on is how God's laws effect everything I do and everything I use. I also wandered if there were laws that governed things like marriage, child rearing, health, etc.? I often wondered if I got a headache from banging my head on a wall and I asked for prayers to heal my headache, would anyone say stop banging your head or would they just keep praying for healing? There is cause and effect. The problem I saw with knowing about God's laws is people judging others. If you are sick, people asked what health laws you broke, if you have unruly kids, they ask what child-rearing laws you broke. For me personally, if something is not working, I ask if there are laws governing that result and what did I do wrong? When I needed surgery, I asked what did I do? I finally realized that I will never know if it was something I did wrong, heredity, an accident, environmental, Agent Orange or anything else.

GOD IS A HEALER

This book is about the many times I was in trouble and God answered my prayers, there were also many times I was in trouble and no immediate answer came, I think it was probably for my good that I learn patience and think and pray before I act. Many men waited for God's promises or an answer to prayer or to see a purpose for their lives. Abraham waited 25 years to get an answer to God's promise of a son. Isaac prayed for 20 years for Rebecca to get pregnant, Joseph waited 15 years, Moses waited 40 years to free Israel, and Jesus waited 30 years to preach. It seems patience, faith, trust is something God wants us to have. Until about age 21, I thought of God as my spiritual 911. When in trouble, I just called 911-Prayer? I believed this God had created everything to sustain life, but also for our pleasure, or at least I was enjoying God's creation. Abraham, Isaac, and many others had their wives healed so they could have children. Diane's father told me before we got married that she had some internal problems that the doctor said may keep her from having children. We prayed about it and five months after our marriage, she was pregnant. We did however forget to ask for a limit to His healing, since we ended up with six children. We have seen and experienced many healings in our lifetime.

God healed my anxiety so I could have surgery after two years. As you will see, God healed me of the many false conceptions I had about Him, churches and is still at work.

GOD IS FORGIVING

At age twenty-one, after giving in to the pressures of others to be something I was not. I was sick of myself and asked God to change my life and forgive me of my sins by accepting Jesus' sacrifice for me. He answered that prayer overnight with a change in behavior, my speech, and in my thinking. I realized God's love for me once again. I did not understand what happened to me because I had never known of anyone's life being changed before. I had heard of someone being a sinner and changed when God

310

called them to be a minister or missionary, so I wondered if I was being called to be a minister. My dad was a minister but had no church, my uncle was a Bishop and my great grandfather, Rev. John Cressman, was a minister in a Lutheran Church. Was I now being called, I wondered? I was told by the minister at my mother's church that I would have to go to seminary after the Marine Corps. I wanted to be a missionary to Vietnam or Japan right away; I did not want to go to a seminary. I already knew repentance through Jesus. What else did I need to know? What a spoiled brat I was?

I started reading the Bible every day, for the first time in my life. As I read the gospels, I noticed I was wrong about Jesus' description. I saw Jesus was not this little baby, feminine looking, long-haired, weak hippie type man, but was a strong carpenter, and could walk long distances, endured a terrible beating, and survive. He was brave and determined as he chased crooks away from the temple. He was courageous, determined; he spoke the truth and called people as he saw them, liars, hypocrites, and vipers. I now found God to be a forgiving God that had the power to change people with His holy spirit. It did not go well for me to call religious people hypocrites, liars, and vipers. It may have been true, though.

I was so happy with my changes and thought all my Marine friends would be happy for me and would want to change as well. But, as I told my Marine friends about the change in my life, it was not always received well since they did not jump for joy, want to have a Bible study or go seeking the alter of repentance. They laughed, called me names, and argued about how they did not need changing. They claimed to be fine, the way they were. Their questions were the same ones I wondered myself and have heard all my life which are: Why should I believe what Christians says when they act like they don't believe it themselves and second, why would a loving God allow wars, sickness, pain and suffering? One more question they asked was, aren't all gods the same? Aren't all religions the same? Don't all religions teach to obey their god and then you will go to heaven, or the island in the sky, or the happy hunting grounds? Eventually, I would find the answers to those questions, but at the time I did not know how to answer them. Maybe seminary taught how to answer those questions? Wanting to be like Jesus, I would usually end up calling them hypocrites, liars, and vipers, which did not go over very well. It seemed to cause division at our mechanic shop where I worked on equipment. I knew I was causing division, and that does not go well with Marines. I expected to be buried in the sand at low tide, but they assigned me a truck and I became a mobile mechanic, like in Vietnam. I was to go out in the field where heavy equipment broke down or needed maintenance. It was an outstanding job, right up my alley, since with my knowledge of how things work, I could easily diagnose a problem. Also, when I did not have an assignment, I could sit in my truck and read the Bible. I still wanted to learn more about this God. I was like the Bereans who searched the scriptures to see if these things were true.

As I mentioned before, I was at some point transferred to an infantry training school and assigned to teach how to kill using various weapons. After seeing killing in war and the killing that took place in Hiroshima and Nagasaki, I did not feel comfortable teaching killing. My gunny sergeant put up posters of Vietnamese kids with the words KILL over them. Kids did sometimes cause harm to US Troops, but I lived with them and wanted to go back as a missionary to help them not kill them, so I tore the pictures down. That really made the gunny angry, so no promotions for me but possibly a swimming test in the alligator pond would be appropriate. I eventually asked to have a different subject to teach, and they transferred me to teaching escaping a POW camp, expose the recruits to some interrogation, torture, and how to handle it. I mentioned how the gunny and I came to agreement on my preaching while in the torture box. I saw many Marines had their ideas about God and they were not ready to change. I believe at some point they, like I did, will have their eyes opened and God will forgive them.

No longer using profanity, telling dirty jokes, getting drunk and other things I used to do before with the Marines, now made me one lonely guy. I prayed hard for a Christian friend I could hang out with and talk with.

GOD IS LOVE

I was now one lonely guy with all my Marine friends and my PA friends, not wanting anything to do with me. I prayed for a Christian friend and God gave me Diane. Now, I really saw God's love, and I loved God back. Another way I found God was to realize He first loved us and then He wants us to love Him back.

At that point, I thought I found everything I was looking for. God loves us, God answered prayers, God is the ruler, lawgiver, sustainer, and healer.

312

God wants us to tell others about what Jesus did for them so when God opens up their mind, they can come to Jesus. What else could I possibly learn about God?

During our honeymoon at the church camp, we told our story about what God had done for both of us and it went over very well. When we came back to Surf City, NC and got involved in church, we continued to read the Bible, ask questions and witness. My mistake was that as I read something in the Bible, I immediately told others where I thought they were wrong, including our families. Unfortunately, I only had limited knowledge of the Bible before I spoke. Either I was never taught a balanced approach to handle new knowledge or I was not listening. It did not take long to have our families not want to hear us preach to them, but on the same thinking, we did not want them preaching to us about their beliefs either. For some reason, we humans sure can get hardheaded even with God's spirit in us.

As I read the Bible, I read Mt. 24 and realized that Jesus said that the whole world would be deceived except for the elect. WOW. What did that mean? Was it possible to go through life thinking you are serving and loving God, the Father and Son, and be wrong? That caused me to study and seek if I was deceived or misled and to find out the truth.

Also, in Mt.24 I saw that before Jesus returns, there would be wars, earthquakes, famines and hatred would occur. I thought as a child that Jesus could return and just appear at any time in the clouds as a friendly, nice guy. I never heard anything about persecution, wars, earthquakes, diseases, etc. Some preachers I heard on the radio, offered a way to escape and I wanted that, but how would I get it? Would I sign up some place or would I have to qualify somehow?

Now is a good time for a question: I read in Lk. 21:36 in the KJV of the Bible, that we are to pray to be "worthy" to escape the things coming to the earth.

What could I do to make myself worthy enough to escape the end-time events?

A.   Be a church member

B.   Obey all God's laws

C.   Witness to others

D. Serve in the church and community

E. Give 10% of my income to the church

F. Just pray to be worthy

G. Do all the above

This is a question to make you think not for me to answer. It seemed, as I read Lk. 21:36 I my KJV Bible, that all I had to do was to pray to be worthy to escape. I found one church that said I had to be a member to escape the tribulation. Many Christians have the same concern as I did and believe the whole Christian church will escape the tribulation through the rapture. I do not think they are required to pray that they are worthy to escape. Most other translations of this verse add to watch, be prepared, and pray for strength instead of praying to be worthy. I am still working on trying to understand this verse. Is that strength to flee when the time comes, strength to endure the tribulation, strength to have the faith that God will protect me?

I kid around about a guardian angel, but I know God can protect us in various ways anywhere. I have seen God's protection during the danger. I have also seen protection by having circumstances changed or somehow, I was prevented from being exposed to the danger. Maybe strength or perseverance is illustrated by this tree. The flood came, it was hit by rocks, wind, logs and had its foundation washed away leaving just its roots which took years to grow.

I also learned during my entire life that God allows us to make mistakes and to learn. When I was teaching auto body repair and painting, I had students paint panels of a car, like a fender, door, etc. Some did very well, and some painted with little confidence and their painting showed it. They were afraid of failure or did not think they could do it. If I thought it would help them be a better painter, I would help them or possibly go into the paint booth after school and repaint the panel so it would look good. I had to be careful to not let someone think they could be sloppy and still end up with an excellent product. I had to know the student and make a judgement. I think God does the same with us. Many times, I did not experience the consequences of what I had done because I think God repainted the scene so I could learn something. But there have been many times I experienced the consequences of my work. I realized God is the best teacher. He arranges circumstances to teach us and shows compassion on us if we need to feel the pain of what we have done. I did not like the attitude that happened occasionally that the student started bragging about how good his painting was, and I am sure God does not like it either.

I did not have medical insurance the first ten years of our marriage, but I did buy an accident policy. I still have it today. When I file a claim, they must go to the archives to get information on the policy. I have gotten my money's worth from that policy for all the times I or my family have been injured. My doctor would often ask, what have you done this time? My body may pay the price today of all the injuries from wild, crazy shenanigans of my past.

GOD IS A SHEPHERD

In Ps. 23, in the NLT version, David claimed the Lord was his shepherd. He led David to rest in green pastures, which I am sure was a long, thick, plush, soft grass to lie down and meditate in. He led David by peaceful streams to get fresh water to quench his thirst, with the sound of a running stream so soothing to his soul. Maybe in that peaceful stream there were delicious trout to catch and eat to nourish his body. A peaceful stream is the best place to find peace. Maybe even getting in a pool of fresh, cool water flowing all over his body to invigorate him. He renewed David's strength through his holy spirit. He guided David along the right path to get David to the place he wanted him at and that was to be righteous in God's sight, unachievable on his own, regardless of how many laws he kept. David may not have known what God was doing in his life, but he had faith that God was directing his paths. When David walked through the darkness of night and saw shadows which appeared to be evil and there were terrifying noises all around, he knew God was there like a shepherd to protect him. It comforted David to know God was in charge as he felt the shepherd's rod correcting his path. God prepared a feast for David in the presence of his enemies. They honored David as God chose him to be anointed with oil. David was blessed so much that it overwhelmed him. David knew God's love and goodness were present in his life and always would be, despite what shenanigans he did. David knew when God comes to the new earth and has his home on earth that David would be on a throne over Israel forever. II Samuel 7:16 Psalms 89:35-37. David had faith God would do what He said. David's sons were all killed later so did God lie? Does He have power to do what He says? He does because David had daughters and kept up the family blood line. I enjoy reading about speculations. One is that Isaiah carried Jacob's stone pillow to eventually to be placed under the coronation throne in Westminster. Why would he do that, I had to wonder?

Looking back over the last 52 years, I can see that the Lord was and is my shepherd, even if I may not have realized it.

GOD HAS SECRETS AND MYSTERIES

Any time I hear the word secret, I want to investigate to see what the secret is and why it is a hidden. I remember as a kid, the other kids, mostly girls, would say, "I know something you do not know" and it would drive me crazy. Usually it was that some girl noticed my good looks, muscular body and superior intellect and was in love with me.

Hearing about God's secrets and trying to decode them was not new to me. Back in the fifty's when I was young, I was a member of the Secret Squadron of Captain Midnight. I qualified to be sent a secret decoder ring. All I had to do was to buy a jar of delicious chocolate Ovaltine, the secret drink for rocket power, send off the foil jar top. I then became a member with full privileges of being able to decode secrets. Without the ring, it would have been impossible.

When I repented of my past and invited Jesus to live his life in me, he put me into the special squadron. This special squadron is called the church, the saints, and the called-out ones and as you will see. I as well as all the other called out ones were given the code to understand God's secrets through His holy spirit. How exciting is that?

When I read in the Bible that there were secrets, knowledge being hidden on purpose and mysteries being revealed that were never known before, I wandered if the answers I was looking for were in the knowledge that was being revealed by Paul. It is exciting to know that mysteries that have been hidden for ages are now being reveled to the church, saints, and apostles about God's plan for us and all mankind.

Here are some of the mysteries I found:

1. The mystery of the kingdom of God. Jesus would someday set up God's kingdom on earth but was hiding the fact. Mark 4:11. Jesus used parables to hide the kingdom of God from everyone but his disciples. That is strange, I thought Jesus wanted to give people as much knowledge as possible so they could repent.

2. The mystery of blindness to Israel for a certain time. Rom11:25. I had to ponder on that for a while again that Jesus would blind or hide knowledge for what reason.

3. The mystery of Jesus Christ which was revealed to Paul. Romans 16:25. I Corinthians 15:1-27. Jesus revealed a gospel to Paul that was different than the kingdom of God gospel the disciples preached. By Paul's gospel we are saved. It was the gospel of Jesus death, burial, resurrection after three days, appeared to many people and then went back to heaven where "All things were put under his feet" and he became an adversary for us.

4. The mystery of we shall not all sleep. I Corinthians 15:50-58. I have heard many theories through the years about what happens to us when Jesus returns at the last trumpet. All the other trumpets before this one signal the return of Jesus Christ the Messiah to set up his kingdom on earth to end the rule of Satan as well as all the problems that he produced. It was hidden since the beginning that at the last trumpet, those Christians that are alive will be changed to immortal spirits and those that sleep will be resurrected to be an

immortal spirit body.

5. The mystery of Gentiles now being granted salvation. Ephesians 3:
2-8. Gentiles were now being called into the church, receiving the
holy spirit and becoming heirs to the promises.

6. The mystery of the church. Ephesians 5:28-32. This talks about the
relationship between the husband and wife. It also compares this
relationship to Jesus and the church. The church will become the
bride of Christ at his return.

7. The mystery of God's will. Colossians 1:26-29. Another mystery
hidden through the ages and now revealed to his saints. We are to
be presented to Christ as complete. I believe we must have the faith
that Jesus in us is working in our lives to make us complete.

8. The mystery of (guardian) angels. Revelation 1:20. Guardian angels
sure are a mystery to me but Revelation mentions that the seven
churches have sort of a guardian angel but nothing about individual
angels for us. I still like having fun thinking that I do.

9. The mystery of Babylon the great, mother of harlots and
abominations of the earth. Revelation 17:5-8. Now that is a real
mystery since I have heard that it is a false church deceiving people.
It could be since in Revelation 12:9 and in Matthew 24:24, it says
Satan and his false ministers are out to deceive the whole world
except for the elect. I would not want to be deceived but I have been
all ready in my life. How would I know if I was deceived or not? In
all my research, I have no answer, except that since I believe I have
God's holy spirit and am being led by Jesus, I must have faith that
he will see me through.

ON TOP OF A MOUNTAIN-I SEE THE ANSWER IN THE DISTANCE

I went to a cabin at World's End state park alone to devote more time
to study and prayer. I hoped to find many of the answers I was looking for. I
laid out all my notes of the last twenty-three years on top of two tables and
a bed. I hoped to leave there in a few days with everything tied together and
making sense.

For a long time, I knew that the true church of God was not a physical place, a building, a particular teaching, or denomination. Instead, it is the people with God's Holy Spirit placed in a spiritual church called the Body of Christ. I have found spirit-filled people in all churches we attended but is there a church with Bible truth being taught and the members are full of the holy spirit. When Jesus addressed the churches in Revelation, he found good in all of them. He had correction for all of them but two. I still wonder if there is a church that Jesus would say is his church.

As I read the letters from Jesus to the seven churches in Revelation 2, I realized that this the first time we heard from him, except for when he spoke to Paul, since he went back to heaven. When on earth, Jesus spoke to Israel, God's chosen nation. Now Jesus was speaking to churches that, I think, Paul started which were mainly gentile. I wondered if carefully examining these letters would give me understanding. Would he say anything different than what he said while he was on earth? Would he specify any changes to the way God instructed Israel? Would he mention the Sabbath, holy days, clean meats, tithing?

I read where Jesus in Mark 9:38-41 said about others casting out demons and that if they are not against us; they are for us. I also saw in Phil. 1:18, where Paul said if they preach Jesus, that is all that matters. I read in Deuteronomy 5:15, that the strict law of keeping the Sabbath was to cause Israel to remember that God brought them out of Egypt. I do not need a day to remember when Egypt came out of Israel. There is nothing wrong with using a day to remember important events. We observe the fourth of July, Memorial Day, Labor Day, Veterans Day to remember or honor people or events. I believe God allows us to make those decisions. I do not believe that man has the right to declare a day to be holy to God and we must obey.

As I read the letters to the churches, I was reminded me that each church has a guardian angel, but not sure if I have my own. I like to think so. Whether these churches are different ages of the church or not, does not change the fact of what Jesus said to them. All the letters went to the true churches of God. They were all part of the Body of Christ, but still had problems similar to what I see in Christian churches today. Jesus complimented them on things I see going on in Christian churches today, but he threatened some with removal if certain beliefs or deeds were not repented of.

Here are some things the churches were told to do or not to do.

1.   The church recognized that some men called themselves apostles but were not. Paul was the last apostle.

2.   Told to not grow weary. I find that is easy to grow weary.

3.   Told to keep their first love and zeal or return to it.

4.   The church hated the deeds of the Nicolaitans, which seems to be a mixing of pagan beliefs in with Christian. Some think they went to the pagan temples, ate sacrificed meats which implied they were part of it. This part concerned me. Is that still going on today?

5.   The church recognized some claiming to be Jewish, a called person, but were not. They were from Satan's church. Is there a Satan's church? What does it look like? How would I know it? Time for some more research.

6.   The church recognized the teachings of Balaam, which was to be misled or enticed away   from God by lusting after worldly pleasures. By the way, I did find a reason that I was told as a child that playing cards, dancing, drinking, going to movies and kissing were called sins. During the Christian revival in the 1800s, a person could leave church if a sermon was boring and go to the local saloon to drink, play cards, dance or kiss on the girls and later go to movies. Those took members away from the Christian church, so they made them sins. Of course, some of those behaviors can lead to addictions and ruining of lives so doing any of those should be done with caution.

7.   They were complimented on having love, faith, service, and perseverance and to "do greater deeds".

8.   Some churches were told they were wrong to tolerate the deeds of Jezebel which appears to be someone uses their looks or personality to gain a position in a church to teach their own thing.

9.   Hold fast to what you have.

10. Their deeds were not complete before God and they should wake up. Do deeds count and for what, I wondered?

11. If there were no changes, their name could be removed from the

Book of Life.

12. Do not let anyone take your crown, hold fast.

13. You may lose out if you have a lukewarm attitude.

14. Be careful to not think they were rich, have everything they needed, have it made because they were actually poor, naked, and blind. Maybe they believed they had the truth but did not but were blinded.

15. Told they needed eye salve to see. I wondered why eye salve? Were they blinded, was there vision foggy? I know that is true. God has the eye salve we need.

Here are the rewards Jesus offers to the churches:

1. They get to eat of the tree of life in the Paradise of God.

2. Our minds and hearts are searched, and we are rewarded according to our deeds. Deeds, I wondered again?

3. Given authority over the nations. Our job will be to rule over nations-what nations? Will there be nations? Maybe what we go through in this life will help us be better rulers. Maybe because there will be a variety of people in these nations, there needs to be variety of experience and backgrounds in Jesus's bride.

4. Walk with Jesus in white as a worthy overcomer.

5. They kept the word of perseverance, so they are spared from what is coming to the entire world to test those on earth. Is that the answer to Matthew 24? How to be worthy to escape, we must persevere.

6. Will be a pillar in God's temple. I am enclosing a deck to make a room. We had to install pillars 18" into the ground to hold everything that is built above it. We will be the base, the support of what God will be doing through eternity.

7. Have the name of God, name of the city of God, the new Jerusalem which comes out of   heaven. A bride does get the name of the groom.

8. Sit on thrones with Jesus. Jesus said the apostles would be ruling over the twelve tribes of Israel. We will also have thrones to rule from.

9. Receive crowns.

I concluded, like many other churches, that we must be careful of what pagan customs we adopt. There was no mention of keeping the Sabbath or Holy Days, eating only clean meats, paying three tithes, or they mentioned not even one tithe. Also not mentioned was a certain way of conducting a church service, how often and what day to go to church on. What does it mean to not have a day of the week commanded or even mentioned to worship on? Does that mean it does not matter to God? Many teachings I have been taught through the years are not mentioned whether to do them or not. Jesus also mentions what our reward will be as spirit beings. No mention of beautiful churches, choir gowns, color of carpets, what clothes to wear to church or dancing in churches. There are many things I was taught that are not mentioned. My next time alone will answer more of my questions. I was extremely happy with my conclusions for my sake. Once again, this book is written for my family to understand why we do or did the things we did and for my own peace. I am seeking a way of understanding the whole Bible not just what Jesus said or what Paul said or what Moses said. Since this book will also be published, it may help others with similar questions.

THREE WEEKS IN THE TAR HEEL STATE

Early in 2020, I went to our house in NC to get away for a while again to hopefully tie everything together. I wondered if I could get some of that NC Tar off my heel to glue together what I had been reading in the Bible. I was ready to bring this to a conclusion.

When not reading the Bible or praying, I was watching You tube videos on topics that I was studying. I watched one video that talked about how there were similarities between Genesis 1&2 and Revelation 21&22. That stirred up my curiosity.

When I read Genesis 1 and 2 and then Revelation 21 and 22, I found most of the answers to the questions I have had all my life. When I looked at Gen.1&2 which are two chapters in the Bible where there is no sin, it helped me understand God's plan from the beginning. These chapters show what God's intentions were at the time of creation.

Here are some things I found:

1. In the beginning, God created the heavens and the earth. Whenever that was, I have no problem with. If it was 6000 or 2 billion years ago, it does not matter to me. It is a non-issue. God is creator, not evolution, not love sick amoeba, not primordial soup, not molecules of life meeting in clay, not lightning creating life, not mineral catalyst for critical reactions in deep sea vents and not reactions under hundreds of feet of ice. Those theories take more faith than believing in a Creator. I used to think that the earth had to be as old as scientists claim until I was reading Jesus miracle of changing water into wine. The wine was reported as being excellent quality that would take years of fermentation but Jesus gave it an appearance of being an aged wine in just a few seconds. So now I believe Jesus could have given this earth an aged look at creation. Adam was created an adult man that had the appearance of an adult, maybe twenty to thirty years old. He created a full-grown tree that probably appeared to be about one hundred years old. I wonder if the tree rings would have indicated an older tree than it was.

2. God said, "Let us make man in OUR image". God is more than one person. We know Jesus is God's son. I am not convinced whether the holy spirit is a person or the power that God uses to do His work. Is it important one way or the other and why? It is a non-issue to me. Although, I recently heard a sermon that showed that when the Bible refers to the Holy Spirit, it gives it the attributes of a person. I am undecided because the pronoun he normally given to the holy spirit can also be the pronoun it. For some reason, some teachings seem to force a trinity on us. I wonder why. We are spoken of as children of God and brothers and sisters of Jesus, but we are to be the bride of Christ. I wonder if that union will produce children? Where would they come from and who would they be? Human or spirit? Is that what the universe is for, to hold God's family? If man is made in God's image, is God producing a family, all under His authority. I believe so. That is my conclusion from reading many scriptures, not just one scripture I could turn to.

3. God walked with man in the garden and had fellowship with him. God saw it was not good for man to be alone, so He made a woman, a help mate, a bride for Adam. He probably wanted Adam to see that he was not complete. Adam could not fulfil the purpose of filling the earth with more

humans, in God's image, without a bride. In managing the earth, he would need help with various differing opinions, a help mate, a bride.

4. Before sin, God was happy to dwell with Adam and Eve being naked. Once they had sinned, Adam and Eve made clothing to cover their sin, but God could not fellowship with manmade ways of covering sin. The Lord killed an animal and covered them with the skins which pointed to Jesus shedding his blood to cover our sins. The blood of the animal allowed God to have fellowship with man once again. So, I concluded that the more clothes a person wears to church, the more sins they must be covering. Ha ha. Not all my brat thinking is gone yet. God is happy with nakedness. It is the devil that makes us feel guilty. I reckon if I said that in church, they would accuse me of being two nuts short of a fruitcake and ask me to leave. We had a surfer missionary at Surf City, NC and went bare footed. Some people did not like that. One time he responded by saying God told Moses to remove his sandals at the burning bush because he was on holy ground. He felt he was on holy ground. What would you say? I might post a sign on the door, no shoes, no shirt, no service.

5. In Genesis. 2, it mentions a river of living water coming out of Eden. Is that the same living waters Jesus talked about and the same waters in Zechariah. 14 and Revelation 22? Is it the same rivers of living water that Jesus offered to the Samaritan woman at the well? John 4:4-15. Then the woman said they worship on one mountain and Jews on another mountain. Jesus said in vs. 22-25 that someday we will not need a place to go to worship God because the "true worshippers" will worship the Father in spirit and truth. That answered many of my questions. Things were coming together. I was so excited I stayed up into the night until I dropped over a sleep at my desk.

6. I have concluded for my own personal belief, which satisfies my curiosity, since I am the one that got confused by religion. I believe God created man to have fellowship with. Since the beginning, the Bible is a record of how He has been doing it. Our sin blocks fellowship with God, and He has been providing ways of covering our sins to help us look clean enough to have fellowship with Him over and over again. He used animal blood, washings, laws, rituals, traditions, eating certain foods and much more but it was all temporary. Jesus was the once and done forever sin covering and forgiveness, allowing us access to God forever. Once our sins are covered with Jesus' blood, they are gone forever. At the bottom of

the deep deep sea. The tearing of the curtain between the Holy of Holies and the people gives us an approach to God anytime and anywhere, naked or a three-piece suit, in a green pasture, a valley of death, on a speeding locomotive or lost in a deep cave.

I found more answers as I looked at Revelation 21&22 which are another two chapters in the Bible where there is no sin. I never thought of these two chapters as being without sin. These two chapters show what God ended up with. Are there any similarities to what he started doing in Genesis?

Here are some similar things I found when compared to Genesis 1&2:

1. Satan deceived Eve. That disrupted God's fellowship with mankind, brought sin into the world and caused mankind to experience the result of wanting the knowledge of good and evil. In Revelation, Satan and the demons are now locked up and will no longer deceive the nations and never again cause all the trouble man has known for thousands of years. Does that mean no more knowledge of the good and evil, and from now on it would be only good? I hope so.

2. There is a new heaven and earth. There is a ceremony with Jesus' bride, and God comes to earth to dwell with His family. He will be their God. There will be so much fellowship going on among members of God's family and God. Maybe God gave me a glimpse of family fellowship and what it can be like. My kids enjoy getting together and having fellowship with each other. My grandkids all enjoy being with each other. The aunts, uncles and cousins all enjoy each other. It is the kind of fun I remember from my family getting together when I was young. It is also like the fun we had at church picnics with the church people. The best memories of my life are the ones with my direct family and then the church family.

3. There is a river of living water that heals with fruit trees growing alongside the river. I wondered what will need healing?

4. I do not know when Satan first sinned, but God has been patiently waiting for this time, of locking Satan up, for a long time. That will be a day to celebrate.

Recently, I met a man from a church I used to attend, and we were discussing churches and why we chose to attend the church we were.

Through the years, I always thought I was heading in the right spiritual direction because my prayers were being answered. Suddenly, he spoke up and said, "I know I am in the "true church" because my prayers are answered." I was shocked and confused. His church was small, not growing, rented halls to meet in and has no outreach to the community. He felt it was the true church because they had the true teachings just like I used to believe. He kept the Sabbath, Holy days, paid three tithes, kept the food laws, etc. I no longer kept any of those except for some residual habits but nothing I thought was commanded. Somehow, we both felt God answered our prayers. I know there is a scripture that says, "God hears the prayers of the righteous". I was reminded that our righteousness comes from Jesus death, burial, resurrection and ascension to heaven to be an advocate for us and not from any laws we keep or physical things or works we do and having faith that God is going to do what He said He would. However, we cannot judge what is going on in another person's heart nor can we judge what God is doing in other people's lives. So, I learned that I cannot necessarily judge a church or a person by what they believe or teach. I can however decide if I want to be a part of that group.

MY "PERSONAL" CONCLUSION AND SPECULATION

I have had so many exciting adventures; it is hard to say which is the best. Helping to baptize my son and two grandchildren was certainly a high light. Also seeing my family including the grandkids volunteer at a church to help serve a community Thanksgiving meal was a high light also as the photos below show.

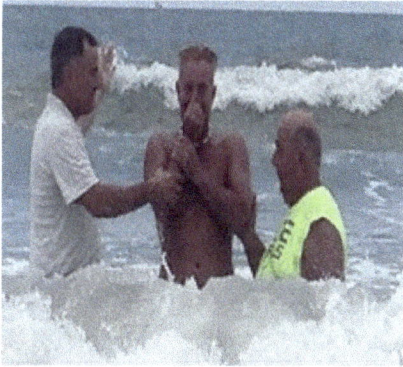

The many family activities are a real high light. I have always loved to learn, explore, research, and experience something exciting. I have really enjoyed being like that. I think God has allowed me to continue that desire even in my search to learn more about God. It is hard for me to accept the fact that not everyone wants the same thing as I do. I accept the fact that God made us all different, doing things differently and to believe differently. Maybe that is part of the curse, that truth is hidden from us and God reveals it when he is ready. The Bible says the Father and Jesus are one mind. If we have seen Jesus, we have seen the Father.

How then can Jesus' bride have so many differing ideas here on earth? Maybe that is why Jesus told us to pray that God's will be done on earth as it is heaven. As I look at creation, I see many varieties.

I sometimes wonder God made a duck billed platypus if not just for variety. Scientists thought it was a hoax but then said it is a hodgepodge of various animals. of As I look at my own kids, I see each one is different, but united on some ideas. Is variety wrong? I would say no, so do I find a church that believes like me or one that I can learn from and are willing to accept those that are not like them? I believe Jesus is looking for a bride that is creative. I love having a wife that is creative and different. I wonder when Jesus asks his bride where they want to go on the honeymoon, how many ideas will there be? Diane and I work well together. Just like Adam could not complete God's will alone, neither could I. Diane could not complete God's will without me, I hope. Without the two of us working together, there would only be two of us. I believe the pleasures of marriage help us overlook the differences in our personalities and ideas.

President Thomas Jefferson commissioned Lewis and Clark to explore west of the Mississippi after the purchase of the Louisiana Purchase. Upon their return, they had to give a report of their discoveries. As a side note: after Lewis and Clark returned from their adventure, William Clark became in charge of Indian Affairs and lived a good life. Meriwether Lewis became governor of the Louisiana Territory, but became bored and depressed. He eventually committed suicide. It seems to me that no matter what I did in the past, I better keep busy and keep on having adventures or I may get bored and depressed.

Here is my report of what I personally believe, for myself, to be true of my search for fifty-two years:

1. I believe there is a possibility that everything that happened to me since my return to the US after the Vietnam War may have a common cause. That would include my problems with the Marines, my problem with alcohol, my problem with churches, my desire to search for a church which was similar to the Marine Corps structure, how I responded to people that rejected me, how I may have even expected people to reject me and how anxiety and nightmares haunted me for many years until it appears as though God intervened. That common cause could be the possibility of PTSD which I later was diagnosed with.

Many Vietnam vets spend their lifetime wondering why their lives were different after Vietnam when they were not aware of any problems. The war had a way of forcing us to see the pain and suffering of war that would stick with us for a lifetime. The protestors added personal pain, shame, and humiliation to the equation. Then to add injury to insult, we wondered if the accusations that the government was not being truthful with us concerning our mission in the war. That thought in our minds destroyed our faith in our leaders and even our country. Many vets suffered divorces, employment problems, anger, drinking and drug problems and many just lived their lives alone unattached to the country and community.

I might add as well, maybe everything that happened to me was because of my '50s attitude of a spoiled brat, a little devil and a holy terror.

Did a loving God keep me busy for 40 years until I was ready to face the memories of war which disappeared, maybe hidden, at my conversion? I will let you judge the facts of this book. I know there are many hurting Vietnam vets out there that do not know why they do the things they do.

2. I believe God's plan is to have fellowship, a relationship with us as different individuals and to dwell in us, not a building or a man-made object. I Cor.6:19. I believe when I was told the church building was God's house for the reason of making me behave or to make me think I had to go there to earn points to please God was incorrect. To say we should be considerate and respectful of others when we meet in a building to honor, and praise God is correct. If a person believes that God is in a certain location, I will not judge them as long as they do not force me to accept their belief.

3. I believe what it says in Genesis 1 that God made us in His image. If God is making us in His image, then it sounds like God is reproducing Himself, in a less powerful version. I am sure it is for a spectacular reason. Regardless of our color, shape, height, personality, we are all reflections of a part of God. He likes bike riding, kayaking, and hiking as much he likes computers, reading and looking at his creation. I love to speculate on the reason God is reproducing Himself and am free to do so, but I will not teach it without proof.

4. I believe God is making a family. We are sons and daughters of God, brothers, and sisters of Jesus. God allows us to experience family to give us an idea of what He wants and feels. The way we feel about our children

is how God feels about us, except He has perfect wisdom and control of circumstances as we do not. As a child I remember all the fun things we did as a family. As a teenager I still remember family being there for me and we often had picnics and get togethers where the whole family gathered. It was always a fun experience.

As a Marine in NC, I drove 1000 miles a weekend to go home to family where I always felt loved and safe. Once married, we did many things with our new family and continued to do that as our family grew. Because our parents did not agree with the way we believed, we often missed out on activities with our parents or brothers and sisters. We did many things with our church family and enjoyed the love and support from them. Once grown, our children continued to do many fun things as a family. I believe all this is a shadow of what God is doing and wants. He wants a family to do things with and to share with. In the Old testament, God wanted Israel to represent him to the world. He wanted them to be kings and priests and set an example of show the blessings that come from obedience. His New Covenant puts God's laws in our hearts, gives us his Holy Spirit to allow Jesus to live in us and make us as his will is but basically is to be part of his family and a bride to Jesus. He will develop the fruits of the spirit in us as he exposes the works of the flesh or sin to us. It is like we are being trained to be part of a royal family.

Even in the Old Testament, God, as a father called Israel his son, his firstborn. Hosea 11:1-4, Exodus 4:22-23 and Deuteronomy 1:31.

Our family has a tradition of getting together for a Thanksgiving dinner and a Christmas dinner, even though not everyone observes Christmas. We try to practice being understanding and respectful of others that do not think like we do. Each family decides if participating in any traditions, helps their relationship with God or hurts it. We also get together many times during the year for birthdays, picnics and vacations in the mountains and beach. The whole family loves our favorite spots at Worlds End State park and Surf City, NC.

5. I believe God said it was not good for man to be alone, He made a bride. That is why he gave me Diane and other men their wives. The group of called out ones, the church, is also Jesus' bride. There will be an outstanding wedding ceremony at Jesus' return to earth. I have an invitation to be there and better yet, an invitation to be part of the bride. This ceremony to come is mentioned in Revelation 21&22. It sure would be cool if that union produces children. Would they explore and populate the universe? As I look up in the sky, I still ask what is the universe for anyway? Will there be a need for explorers?

6. I believe when Jesus died, it tore the curtain between the Holy of Holies and the outer court. I believe it now makes God available to everyone. We can now just walk into God's presence through prayer in the name of Jesus Christ. No longer do we have to wait until the day of Atonement, when a priest would go to God with blood to cover our sins. Jesus is our high priest now. Man has devised many a way to cover his sins and seek a relationship with God, they may even call some religions. I believe Paul taught that everything that limits our access to God to certain days, certain places, certain times or certain types of clothes to wear was all done away at Jesus' death, burial, resurrection and ascension because we can now pray to God in Jesus name anytime, anywhere, whether naked or clothed, without even a human priest to intervene for us. I believe this is the key as to what God's will is. He wants to dwell in us as his house and all we must do is keep it clean. Paul talks quite a bit about what the fruits of the flesh are and what the fruits of the holy spirit are in Galatians 5:19-26. The holy spirit will reveal to us the fruits of the flesh and help us to develop the fruits of the spirit. Then Paul said concerning the Feast of Unleavened Bread in I Corinthians 5:8, Let us therefore celebrate the festival, not with

the old leaven, the leaven of malice and evil, but with the unleavened bread of sincerity and truth. I believe I should be putting out the works of the flesh, the leavening of malice and evil and let God's holy spirit build me sincerity and truth. Truth and sincerity are all I ever wanted from my parents, my teachers, businesses, pastors, politicians, and everyone on this planet. This would be a pleasant place to live in. Of course, I must be that way to others also. If I do that, I have also fulfilled the purpose of all the laws of God.

7. I believe Genesis 1&2 are two chapters before sin occurred. God walked with Adam and Eve, taught them, and provided for them. There was a tree of life and a stream of living waters. There were fruit trees growing along the river in Revelation 22, were they also in Gen 1&2? I might could speculate on what that was, but I am sure it was something good. Did you ever walk through the forest or some beautiful spot with a friend to share with? That is the way the Lord walked with Adam. I have always enjoyed sharing my special spots with other people. especially Diane. When we first got married, I got up early to pray as the sun rose over the water. I soon found myself thinking that God was in the sunrise and I had to be there to talk to him or I would miss him. It is so easy to relate to God in an object but that is not correct. When I built the chapel, I felt like I had to go there to talk to God. Again, it is easy to start thinking of God as the object. That is why God warned us to not use images to worship him in the law. What I really need is a place that is quiet and as I look around; I see God's handiwork and can meditate on what an awesome creator he is. Then as I pray and talk to God as if he were standing there, I feel a peace and may have scriptures come to my thoughts that makes me feel like I am communicating with God. Sometimes when I leave, I feel like I only talked to God about things on my mind and do not feel like I received an answer. Sometimes it took many years to see an answer to that prayer one way or another.

8. I believe the shape of the crucifixion device is a non-issue for me. Some say the cross was a capital T shape, some say it was a small t shape and some say it was a vertical pole. All three will cause a person extreme pain and death by exhaustion and asphyxiation. The cause of death for Jesus had to be the sword the soldier thrust into his side to cause him to bleed to death. I am sure the beating and nails helped drain much of his blood. If a person must believe in a certain shape of a cross, I might ask why is it important?

9. I believe everything in between Genesis 1 & 2 and then Revelation 21 & 22 is man's way of seeking a relationship with God through such things as a man-made religion. During that same time period, I believe the Bible shows various people being used by God through the years to establish a relationship between God and men. Man's sins had to be covered up to allow that fellowship. The covering of sin was temporary until Jesus died to give us a permanent covering and deleting. If I look at every scripture or every question with that in mind, I can make sense of the plan in the Bible, even though I do not have an answer for all my questions.

10. I believe the Sabbath, Holy days, clean meats, the Ten Commandments, sacrifices and many other traditions and commandments given during the Old Testament time were commanded by a nation that God called out to be His own people. They were a sinful people, and he told them in order to have fellowship with him they would have to appear clean enough to do so. Except for a few people, Israel did not have God's Holy Spirit to lead them to fellowship with God, so God gave them ways of cleaning up so they could. Once again, it was temporary and not complete. Some got so involved with the cleaning process that they missed the purpose of having fellowship with God. I always wondered if the Sabbath and Holy Days were so important to God and the Israelites should have been aware of that, how comes there are no instances of a captive Israelite refusing to work on those days. There are cases of Daniel continuing to pray when ordered not to and the three Israelites refusing to bow down to an idol. Daniel also refused food from the king's table. Some say it was because the food violated the food laws mentioned in Leviticus 11 and others say it was just something like rich pasties. No mention of anyone refusing to work on the Sabbath or Holy Days. Why? I thought possibly it may be because the Sabbath was a national worship day which also required a holy convocation (meeting) at the temple. God was king of the nation so to have a day of rest is fine. In the book of Ezra, God works his will through a pagan king by having him give favor to and allow Israel captives to go rebuild Jerusalem. God wanted Israel back so he could have them as a nation again and fellowship with his people. God kept the sabbath but there was no command for us to keep it. He rested after a week of work and looked back and said it is good. I think I should do the same, rest and look back at my work and ask if it is good or should I make changes? In Zechariah 14:16-19, nations will go up to Jerusalem to keep the Feast of Tabernacles. It also appears people will keep the Sabbath in a

future time to come. Isaiah 66:22-23.

11. I believe that anyone that wants to keep anything in the old testament is not wrong BUT ONLY if it is not done to be righteous in God's eyes, to earn salvation or do it because it is commanded today. During disease epidemics like the Corona Virus, we were told to quarantine just like they quarantined sick people of Israel to keep from spreading the disease. Resting farmland every seven years or rotating crops is a proven valuable tool in raising healthy crops. Resting one day out of seven is a healthy physically, brain wise and spiritually. Judging condemnation for keeping or not keeping them, I believe is wrong. Paul seems to indicate that if you are NOT in Christ's body then you are under the law and would worship God appropriately. People with God's holy spirit worship God in spirit and truth.

12. I believe when I have a question about something in the Bible, I ask how it fits into God's plan of wanting to have a family and fellowship with us. Is it man's way of seeking Him or God's way of seeking us? When we take time to rest and focus on God or his creation, it seems he reaches out to draw us to him. I believe if we respond to him, he will respond to us even more.

13. I believe that I and many Christians have had our share of rejections but is that so we would understand what God goes through. At creation, Adam and Eve rejected God. All mankind rejected God by Noah's time. They rejected God as ruler of Israel because Israel wanted a king and an army like other nations. God warned the people that their children would die or be wounded in war, but they wanted it anyway. As a vet and cyclist who rode a bike with wounded warriors, I have seen the evil of war and not much good comes from it. I look forward to the time when there will be no more wars. It is staggering what war costs in pain, suffering and loss of life. The latest war cost figure I found is 100 million dollars an hour for soldiers, ammo, and war machines worldwide. I always pray for protection of my family but would defend the ones I love if I had to. I believe God is very capable of protecting us. In Matthew 26:53, it says Jesus could have asked the father to send twelve legions of angels. In II Kings 6:17 Elisha was protected by many horses and chariots on a mountain.

14. I believe the twelve apostles taught Jesus was the Messiah, the son of God that the Jews crucified. It appears as though all you had to do was believe Jesus was the Son of God and the Messiah. They had the old

testament scriptures saying a messiah would come. Paul, once he was converted, went away to be taught by Jesus. He did not come back with a scroll of the new testament church constitution, nor a cloud and fireball to lead the church, nor tablets, written by the finger of God, to be the laws of the New Testament Church. He taught to follow him as he follows Christ. He also taught that we are saved by his gospel. His gospel was one of grace by the death, burial, resurrection, and ascension of Jesus. That was more than just believing Jesus was the son of God as taught before. God loved his son so much for suffering and died for mankind that he puts our sins away and sees us without sin. Nothing we can do can get that, only believing and having faith that Christ has done it for us. That was hard thing for me to grasp for a long time.

15. I believe that when Jacob had a dream about a ladder with angels going back and forth to heaven, he called the spot God's house and built a memorial there. He is not condemned anywhere for saying that. I am sure God just used the spot to reveal God's plan to Jacob, not that Jacob had accidently slept in God's house. To Jacob, it was a special spot. I believe God allows us to keep a special spot where God reacted with us, even though that is not His permanent dwelling place. One of mine was the chapel I built while in the Marines. Another was a rock overlooking a spring. I have no problem now hearing people say "God's house" because maybe to them, it is a special place where God reacted with them. I would not use it to force others to observe my spot. I may ask them to be respectful of my belief if they come to visit my spot.

16. I believe when I accepted God's salvation, with limited knowledge and truth, I did not understand that there was so much to learn about God. After many years of study, I understand that plan better but am still learning. There are many theories out there of what God's plan is and what the Bible says about it. I believe God put in us a desire to seek God and believe in Him, but Satan has put obstacles in front of that desire to hide, confuse and frustrate us in that search. I believe God reaches out to us, like it was for me by seeing creation. We must be ready to respond when he does. That is where Satan tries to keep us distracted or so busy that we do not see God calling us. I believe I have found answers that help me personally in understanding God and his plan. However, like the Japanese man told me to not be content with what I have but to keep searching, learning and changing as I learn more. As I learn about other beliefs, I am concerned that some of the beliefs have been unchanged since the 1800s.

With the new translations and better research tools available, should not some doctrines be changing? If we have the truth, we do not want to change it, regardless of society. Did they have the truth back in the 1800s or did it come from traditions of other churches? Since the time of Christ, has truth been lost or watered down? I have it almost impossible to know for sure but I believe God wants us to keep searching and trusting him that the holy spirit will lead us to know what we need to know.

17. I believe I must be careful whom I trust to explain an individual scripture meaning or the overall meaning of the Bible. I noticed some people will use certain phrases to push their interpretation on others. It could be the phrase "this scripture makes it so clear that we are to" do something. Unless I see it and understand it, I will not go along with it. I guess that is part of the '50s attitude or possibly a spoiled brat attitude. I am not sure if it is a '50s attitude or an attitude of someone who trusted the people who taught me and I was hurt to find out their teachings were wrong. To be fair, I taught my kids for twenty-five years what I thought was true only to find out I was wrong. I did not do it intentionally just as I am sure my parents and pastors taught me what they thought was true but they believed the people that taught them were teaching truth. Peter said in Acts 3:21 that Jesus would not return until there is a restoration of all things. Could one of those be a restoration to knowing and telling the truth. I know someone is going to say, what is truth? There is something I also wonder about. During my 60 years of learning auto technology and collision repair technology, I have never seen any changes as to how an internal combustion engine works or how the techniques of straightening dented metal has changed or been untrue or of personal opinion. I recently watched how Apollo 8 orbited the moon in 1968, totally successful with the technology of the day. Tonight, they will launch Space X and we have a space station orbiting the earth with people living on it all made possible by building on truth learned in 1968 and the years before. Astronauts depend on that knowledge and depend on it being true. There may be different designs of rockets being built but they all will all depend on a common thread of the same truth.

I am still searching for the common thread of Christianity that will give us success at accomplishing what we and God want. I would say we what all want is to have eternal life with God the father, Jesus and all the other believers. Is that common thread, to make it simple for my brain, what Paul and Jesus taught. Is it the belief that Jesus is the Son of God,

336

the Messiah and that he died, was buried, was resurrected by the Father and then ascended to heaven where he intercedes for our sins? As far as other ideas go, would we say what Jesus said in Luke 9:50, that if they are not against us, they are for us. Also, Paul said in Philippians 1:15-18, [15] It is true that some preach Christ out of envy and rivalry, but others out of goodwill. [16] The latter do so out of love, knowing that I am put here for the defense of the gospel. [17] The former preach Christ out of selfish ambition, not sincerely, supposing that they can stir up trouble for me while I am in chains. [18] But what does it matter? The important thing is that in every way, whether from false motives or true, Christ is preached. And because of this I rejoice. I should also be putting out the desires of the flesh and put on the fruits of the spirit

18. I believe I should be like the Bereans mentioned in Acts 17:11. They received the word with all eagerness, examining the scriptures daily to see whether these things were so. I believe we should also be like that to search for more truth.

19. I believe I can keep any traditions I want if it does not interfere with my fellowship with God. If a custom, symbol, tradition that takes my mind away from that fellowship, I would try to avoid. If we get together as a family to eat and enjoy each other at any time of year, I have no problem with. If I am going to observe a day to remember Jesus' birthday, then I should be sure and use that day to honor him. Any traditions I do should add to how I look at God. I prefer traditions based in the Bible with meaning. I would have no problem sitting down and eating a Passover meal with some Messianic Jewish friends. I ate a four-hour Passover Seder meal with some orthodox Messianic Jews one time and I thought it was too long to be meaningful. When we kept the Holy Days, it was great to think about what the days meant to Israel. They also had a new meaning in the New Testament, like the Passover pictures Jesus' death as a Passover lamb without blemish. I Corinthians 5:7. It says we should celebrate the Feast of Unleavened Bread with the bread of sincerity and truth. Growing up we had a tradition of doing what my mother called spring cleaning. She hired a cleaning woman to thoroughly clean our house every spring. Where did the idea of spring cleaning come from? Did it somehow come from the northern ten tribes of Israelites as they moved through Europe after being captured and taken away? The tribe of Benjamin and Judah stayed around Jerusalem. Just some interesting concepts to think about.

Our family thoroughly cleaned out all leavening products from our house and cars. The children were involved, and we all enjoyed it. It was not made to be a burden but fun to search out those crumbs the kids dropped or the snacks that were hidden. Leavening pictured sin, and sin would always show up after you thought you were free of it. The vacuum cleaner bag and trash all had to be emptied off our property. Months later, we would find a dozen donuts someone hid under a bed and realize we just never knew when sin would be revealed.

Pentecost was the feast of first fruits from the farm. The main harvest was at the feast of tabernacles in the fall. The church is the first fruit of called out ones because the holy spirit was given to them. Will there be a time of a bigger harvest of people to be in God's family pictured by the fall feast days? I believe so. Pentecost was always on a Sunday and some called it the beginning of the church. Was that a signal for a new day to worship on? Not sure, no mention of that. It does not matter; we can worship anywhere and anytime.

Some people believe Jesus will return on the Feast of Trumpets, or at least it reminds us of the time of trumpets, Jesus returns to the earth and the end of Satan's rule on earth. In Israel, it was a day of repentance and redemption.

The Day of Atonement pictures, some believe, the time when man will be "at one" with God with Satan locked up. In Israel, the priest went into the holy of holies to make a sacrifice for all of Israel to bring them back into fellowship with God. Jesus blood forgives our sins now. It is a much better sacrifice.

The Feast of Tabernacles was when we and Israel stayed in temporary dwellings for a week and celebrated a fall harvest. It was a feast unto the Lord for a week. We believed that great fall harvest would be people born in the 1000-year period and would have it much easier to accept salvation with Satan locked up. Our church made the judgement that our temporary dwellings would be a motel room or condo at a resort. We often met in a convention center or stadium. The Bible commanded Israel to save ten percent of their income to spend at these holy days and for no other purposes. We may have several thousand dollars to spend in one week. It was like a super church convention vacation. We paid three tithes. One was for the church; one was for the holy days and one every three years to help widows and orphans. We could help Diane's mother since she was a widow.

The tithes showed God's priorities, support the church, save money to go fellowship with Him and help the widows and orphans.

The Last Great Day or the eight day, of the feast, was a separate feast or holy day. I never saw much proof, but it pictured something taking place after the millennium, possibly the second resurrection and the white throne judgement. Church leaders speculated it was a time when people who never heard the true gospel of salvation that they would be resurrected and given their first chance at it. It is also a time when Satan is released for a time. It was nice to hear these things, but the scriptures are not there yet to back it up. Many people including well known evangelists have the question of what happens to people that never heard the true gospel, so to me, it gives hope that God has a plan. I think everyone has speculated about the so-called lost people so nothing wrong with speculation unless preaching it as proven truth. I recently read that many evangelists are going to a belief that we are judged by what we do with what we know, including those that never heard about Jesus. I do not see that in the Bible.

20. I believe God gently, lovingly corrected me about my belief in the cross. It is easy to put too much emphasis on an object and miss out on the purpose. If Jesus were shot with a handgun, would we argue if it was a 45 caliber, a 9mm or a 22 caliber? That sounds ridiculous to me. For Jesus to be our savior, he had to bleed to death like the Passover lamb, and nails and a sword caused that. I do not think of Jesus when I see a nail or sword. The important part is that is the love of the Father to allow it and willingness of Jesus to do it. Because of that death, we receive a salvation; we do not deserve. As mentioned before, it is a non-issue.

21. I believe I should not allow myself to get caught up in myths, paganism, history or genealogies that I miss out on what is important and that fellowship with the father God and His son Jesus Christ who have a magnificent plan for mankind and this universe as it says in I Timothy 1:3.

22. I believe the Bible tells us what he hates listed in Proverbs 6:6-19. There are six things that the Lord hates, seven that are an abomination to him: haughty eyes, a lying tongue, and hands that shed innocent blood, a heart that devises wicked plans, feet that make haste to run to evil, a false witness who breathes out lies, and one who sows discord among brothers. The Sabbath, Holy Days, clean meats are not mentioned.

23. I believe God is working with us as individuals. I enjoy listening to

how God is working with different people. I especially hearing a person's testimony and what God has accomplished in their life. It is inspiring how God tested them and how taught them. Sometimes as I read the new testament, I get the impression that when people got together, they shared their stories of what God was doing in their lives, sang songs and prayed. They probably needed someone to keep control of the gathering. I have been saying that I have been examining everything in church to not take it for granted. An interesting fact is that it appears in the Jewish synagogues, early churches and some apostles speaking in public did so in what we call today a teaching, interactive lecturing or a dialogue sermon. In other words, after a person spoke for a short while like Jesus read the scroll about himself and then sat down but others may have had questions or interactive discussion about the subject. In I Corinthians 14:29, we find non clergy members taking turns in standing and speaking. Today in church, it is mostly a monologue sermon for 30-90 minutes with no public question and discussion.

I read an article about how the typical monologue sermon started in the first few hundred years in the church from the Greeks. The Greeks had a group of teachers, called the sophists, going around teaching the art of persuasive speaking, they were experts in debating, using emotional appeals, physical appearance, and clever language to sell their arguments. Those Greeks must have gone to the Marine Corps Instructional Training School where I was taught. That is the exact way they taught us to teach. Anyway, eventually that idea of teaching found its way into the church as a sermon instead of a discussion. Just an interesting concept. I imagine that would be impossible in the mega churches of today. Some people like the idea of dressing up, sitting through a sermon, singing a few songs of praise and then going home. It would not work for everyone. It is just interesting to me knowing how we got to where we are. The local church would decide its own of teaching.

24. I believe a healthy family is pleasing to God. It gives everyone involved an idea of what God is doing in his build of a family for himself. I believe it is quite apparent that Satan is trying hard to destroy the family. Family must be important to God since we see Satan working so hard to destroy it. Satan is trying to destroy what God designed in sex, both the act and whether a person is male or female. Satan is also trying to destroy the family structure that God started in Genesis 1, of a husband, wife and children. Is it possible that Satan found out about God's plan to create a

family and got jealous? Since Satan was so powerful and beautiful, did he think he deserved a family?

25. I believe, after years of searching, I have a personal understanding of God's plan for mankind. That understanding gives me a great deal of peace, compared to the confusion and lack of certainty the last twenty-five years. I think that understanding is the common thread that runs through Christianity. I would say the common thread is that God offers us, as a gift, eternal life to be with the Father, Jesus and all the other members of the Body of Christ, the church. We cannot accept eternal life as we are because our human nature sins and rejects God. The Father made it possible for us to accept eternal life by forgiving our sins through what the Bible calls justification. That justification is possible because of the love of the Father and Jesus who was willing to come to earth, be tortured and die on the cross, like the Passover lamb. His blood makes us look clean to God and he grants us eternal life. All we must do is ask for that sacrifice to cover our sins. We also must believe that Jesus is the Son of God, the Messiah and that he died, was buried, was resurrected by the Father, and then ascended to heaven where he intercedes for our sins. I still believe that common thread is mentioned in John 3:16, For God so loved the world, that he gave his only Son, that whoever believes in him should not perish but have eternal life. [17] For God did not send his Son into the world to condemn the world, but in order that the world might be saved through him. [18] Whoever believes in him is not condemned, but whoever does not believe is condemned already, because he has not believed in the name of the only Son of God. It helps me to know the Father said whoever does not accept his gift of eternal life will perish.

I know the other problems I face are seeking the truth about what is required after we believe and are put into the Body of Christ. I believe repentance comes with believing but is there anything else? Baptism was certainly done a lot in the new testament church by looking for water for immersion. The other part of God's plan is Sanctification which is defined as: the action of making or declaring something holy, the action or process of being freed from sin or purified, setting aside for God's purpose and the action of causing something to be or seem morally right or acceptable. We cannot sanctify ourselves, God does it.

I believe once we receive God's holy spirit, we will have God's law in us to give us thoughts as to what we should do or not do. I would say reading the Bible, fellowship and prayer help those thoughts come to us. We can expect the spirit to work in us to produce fruits of love like God has for man. Galatians 5:13-26, For you were called to freedom, brothers. Only do not use your freedom as an opportunity for the flesh, but through love serve one another. [14] For the whole law is fulfilled in one word: You shall love your neighbor as yourself." [15] But if you bite and devour one another, watch out that you are not consumed by one another. [16] But I say, walk by the Spirit, and you will not gratify the desires of the flesh. [17] For the desires of the flesh are against the Spirit, and the desires of the Spirit are against the flesh, for these are opposed to each other, to keep you from doing the things you want to do. [18] But if you are led by the Spirit, you are not under the law. [19] Now the works of the flesh are evident: sexual immorality, impurity, sensuality, [20] idolatry, sorcery, enmity, strife, jealousy, fits of anger, rivalries, dissensions, divisions, [21] envy, drunkenness, orgies, and things like these. I warn you, as I warned you before, that those who do[5] such things will not inherit the kingdom of God. [22] But the fruit of the Spirit is love, joy, peace, patience, kindness, goodness, faithfulness, [23] gentleness, self-control; against such things there is no law. [24] And those who belong to Christ Jesus have crucified the flesh with its passions and desires.

[25] If we live by the Spirit, let us also keep in step with the Spirit. [26] Let us not become conceited, provoking one another, envying one another.

As far as other ideas go, would we say what Jesus said in Luke 9:50, that if they are not against us, they are for us. Also, Paul said in Philippians 1:15-18, [15] It is true that some preach Christ out of envy and rivalry, but others out of goodwill. [16] The latter do so out of love, knowing that I am put here for the defense of the gospel. [17] The former preach Christ out of selfish ambition, not sincerely, supposing that they can stir up trouble for me while I am in chains. [18] But what does it matter? The important thing is that in every way, whether from false motives or true, Christ is preached. And because of this I rejoice. I should also be putting out the desires of the flesh and put on the fruits of the spirit.

26. I believe all good gifts come from God. If I experience a blessing, as it is called, or see something good in my life, can I say I earned it or I built that. Every Thanksgiving as we all get together as a family, I give thanks that for 52 years of our marriage, we have never had a death in our family, no serious sickness, or major tragedies. Is that due to anything we

have done? There was a time when I believed we were healthy because we drank raw milk, ate clean meats, home grown organic foods, exercised regularly, and tried to stay away from doctors. I must admit I was wrong. I believe it was a gift, expressed in the love of God for whatever reason. I believe we have the perfect house for my disabilities. I can ride my bike out of my garage and ride ten to 20 miles in my area without lifting or transporting a bike somewhere.

I can go out my basement to our lake and jump in a kayak or canoe and paddle around the lake, go fishing or just observe the wildlife. I can also go out the basement door and cross-country ski, if there is snow, around the lake or ski on the many trails near the lake in the forests. I could also walk the trails through the forest land around us. Diane and I can sit on our deck and observe the deer, turkey, bear, fox, coyotes, hawks, or eagles swoop down and grab a fish. Did we get this by my wife's constant searching listings or was it because of God's grace and him knowing exactly what we needed. We prayed for a house with what we thought we needed but God knew exactly what we needed. As I look back on my seventy four plus years of life, I see God's hand in my life, Diane and my life and my family's lives that I had no idea at the time he was involved. I just wanted to give credit where credit is due. It reminds me of the movie "The Ten Commandments" when Moses at the Red Sea said, "The Lord of hosts will do battle for us, behold his mighty hand."

ONE LAST QUESTION:

In my wild imagination, if someday I could create a planet the way I want, what would I create?

A. A wilderness planet that would allow others to come and explore it much like the early American pioneers explored the west.

B. A planet where people would leave civilization behind to follow mighty rivers, cross amber waves of grain, explore unchartered wooded wilderness timbers, scale the purple mountain majesty, see the fruited plains just like the early explorers and pioneers did.

C. A planet where people would have to use primitive methods of survival, live off the land and enjoy God's creation at its fullest.

D. A planet where I could call on Sam's Squadron of Rescue Girl Scouts to go rescue people scared to death on cliffs, hanging on trains for dear life, people trapped in elevators or sewer pipes, people lost in the wilderness, or people unable to move in freezing water.

E. All the above

Do I need to give you an answer? It was E.

Also, when not busy, I would go visit my guardian angel in the nursing home on Venus or wherever guardian angels retire at. Just kidding.

A photo of Sam and I still loving the outdoors. Also, a photo of his wife Cindy, his gift from God. We get together several times a year.

The photo was taken at our 50th wedding anniversary at Surf City, NC. It has our six kids, their mates and our 16 grand kids.